Abraham Bisno, Union Pioneer

An autobiographical account of Bisno's
early life and the beginnings of unionism
in the women's garment industry

Abraham Bisno
Union Pioneer

with a foreword by Joel Seidman

THE UNIVERSITY OF WISCONSIN PRESS
Madison, Milwaukee, and London, 1967

153497

Published by
The University of Wisconsin Press
Madison, Milwaukee, and London
U.S.A.: Box 1379
Madison, Wisconsin 53701
U.K.: 26–28 Hallam Street
London W. 1

Printed in
The United States of America
by the George Banta Company, Inc.
Menasha, Wisconsin

Library of Congress Catalog
Card Number 67–20752

Publisher's Note

Abraham Bisno was, at the beginning of this century, one of the best-known labor leaders among the Jewish garment workers in Chicago and New York. Born in Russia in 1866, the son and grandson of tailors, he was apprenticed to the trade as a boy, and when his family migrated to the United States in 1881, he went to work at once: for a short time in Atlanta, where the family first lived, then in Chattanooga, and finally in Chicago, where the family settled in 1882. It was there that his interest in improving conditions for workers developed, and for more than thirty years he took a leading part in union activity in the garment industry, serving in 1890 as the first president of the Chicago Cloak Makers' Union, one of the forerunners of the International Ladies' Garment Workers'

Union, and later as chief clerk of the Joint Board of the ILGWU in New York City. Although after 1917 he devoted most of his time to the real estate business, he never lost his interest in union affairs. He died in Chicago in 1929.

Sometime during the years 1924–1926, Bisno dictated to three typists his account of his early life and the beginning of unionism in the women's garment industry, as he had known it. He read the typescript, made a few corrections, and indicated his intention of adding more material, but nothing further was done. Forgotten after Bisno's death, the manuscript was found in 1944 among the possessions of his wife, who died that year. A nephew of Bisno's, Julius Bisno, became interested in the manuscript and persuaded the family, in 1963, to have it retyped. Six copies were made for the members of the Bisno family; another copy is in the archives at the headquarters of the International Ladies' Garment Workers' Union in New York. Later, Bisno's grandson Sidney used the manuscript as the basis for a thesis for the degree of Master of Arts at the University of California, Los Angeles. Professor Jack Barbash, of the University of Wisconsin, learned from Sidney Bisno of the existence of the manuscript, and brought it to the attention of the Press.

The manuscript as Bisno left it was clearly unfinished, and the marks of its origin as dictated copy are evident. In preparing the manuscript to be retyped in 1963, Julius Bisno arranged the pages, some of which were unnumbered, in what seemed to be the most logical order, provided a number of paragraph divisions, and broke up some of the long, rambling sentences. These changes have been incorporated into the present version, which reproduces the original manuscript, with such routine editing as the standardization of spelling and punctuation and the silent correction of occasional minor grammatical errors. Substantive editorial emendations have been enclosed in brackets. The text has been divided into chapters, and a few footnotes, based on information provided by Sidney Bisno, have been added. No rewriting has been undertaken, and no deletions have been made.

Foreword

During the last two decades of the past century and the opening decade of this one, the women's garment industry was a
jungle of miserably low wages, oppressively long hours, unsanitary conditions, and ruthless competition. Manned largely by immigrant workers, most of them Jews from eastern
Europe, the industry expanded rapidly, providing American
women with stylish ready-made garments at moderate prices,
and permitting its more fortunate businessmen to climb the
American economic success ladder, while subjecting its
human resources to pitiless exploitation. Working in tenement homes up to sixteen or more hours daily during the
busy season, the employees were nevertheless unable to put
aside enough money to provide the necessities of life during
the months when the highly seasonal industry had no use for
their services.

The resentment that workers inevitably felt against such
conditions was tempered by the helplessness of impoverished

immigrants, accustomed to grinding poverty and insecurity in eastern Europe, unfamiliar with the language or customs of their new country, possessing few other industrial skills, and striving for an economic foothold amid strange surroundings. Bad as conditions were, at least the immigrant Jews were physically safe here from the pogroms that swept periodically over Russia. Evil as the sweatshop was, it was but a temporary prison to those who could hope, after saving or borrowing a little money, to open small businesses of their own. Indeed, the volatile garment industry offered such opportunity to those who were a little more enterprising—and perhaps a little less scrupulous—than their neighbors, since the prevalent system of contracting and home work made it possible for one to go into business with a minimum of capital.

Under the prevailing system in the industry, the manufacturer had the option of carrying on production in his own factory with his own employees—an "inside" shop—or of producing only samples, giving out the cloth to those who agreed for a specified price to produce matching garments. The contractor who received this work, who needed only a small investment in sewing machines, carried on production in his home, using members of his family along with other employees if he had room for and could furnish work to them. The work went to the contractor who would accept the lowest price, in competition with other contractors eager for the work; since he had little expense, except for labor, this competition was necessarily in terms of the lowest amount that the workers would accept for their services. Thus shops bid against each other for the available work, driving wages to the lowest possible point, while a steady influx of immigrants provided a seemingly inexhaustible supply of cheap labor.

Union agitators, some of whom had become socialists or anarchists in the old country, were not lacking among the Jewish garment workers, and unions and strikes made their appearance in the 1880's in both New York City and Chicago. The contractors, however, were powerless to raise wage levels unless the manufacturers increased payments to them, while the manufacturers took the view that wages and hours in outside shops were matters for contractors and their employees to settle. Let wage rates rise and hours be reduced in some of the outside shops, as a result of union influence there, and work would flow to non-union shops, where people would work longer hours for less. The unions found that partial control of a market was ineffective, as they also found that union sympathizers saw no reason to pay dues during the slack season, when there was no work in the shops. It took three decades of effort before seasonal unionism gave way to permanent unionism, and before the union was able to control the flow of work from manufacturers to contract shops.

Among the union pioneers who struggled with these problems and who built the union in the face of all these obstacles, Abraham Bisno occupied a leading position. The acknowledged leader of unionism in the women's garment industry of Chicago, he was called several times to the much larger center of New York City to take a prominent part in the affairs of the garment union there. His career spanned the entire period of seasonal unionism, from the mid-1880's to the formation of permanent stable unionism in the years just before World War I. For brief periods he occupied the leading posts in each of the two major centers, New York City and Chicago, where much of his energy went into plans to reform the industry in order to provide security for union workers. His basic ideas, then considered visionary and impractical by many, have long since been incorporated into reform plans formulated by the union and accepted by the employers.

Often the pioneering agitator lacks the temperament necessary for successful administration, or irritates or antagonizes those with whom he must work over a period of time, and so is less suited to the union in its period of success than in its earlier uphill struggles. Certainly it took one with more tact and patience than Bisno possessed to keep the loyalty of radical workers, win the support of more conservative national union officers, and obtain from the manufacturers with whom he dealt the grudging co-operation necessary to sustain himself in office. Whatever his personal shortcomings, however, it is indisputable that Bisno made a major contribution to unionism in the women's garment industry and to reform in the industry's conduct of its affairs.

Born into a poverty-stricken family in Russia in 1866, Abraham Bisno followed his father and grandfather in the trade of tailoring, becoming an apprentice at the age of eleven and earning his own living from that time on. His descriptions of social conditions among the Jews of Russia of that period, and his contrasting of their way of life with that of the Russian peasantry, are fascinating indeed, whether he is discussing poverty, religion, family relations, customs, sex behavior, or attitudes toward life. His account of the pogrom that resulted in his family's emigration to America is vivid. Despite his lack of formal education, Bisno shows himself a shrewd observer of industry, customs, and people in Russia as later in this country, where he was concerned with differences between Jews and other immigrant groups and with the impact of American conditions on Jewish attitudes and behavior.

Though not equipped by nature to become a skilled hand tailor, Bisno proved adept as a sewing-machine operator. More important, he learned the language and customs of his adopted country more quickly than other members of his family, so that, beginning at the age of fifteen, he was the one who went downtown to the manufacturers to obtain work for his family, to consult with the designer when the work required it, to buy sewing machines when necessary; he also hired additional employees as they were needed, and organized the work for them and for members of the family. At the age of sixteen he was a successful contractor in this highly competitive industry. That he could have had a successful business career, had he not developed an overriding interest in unionism, seems beyond question.

Serious efforts at organization among the Chicago cloak-makers began in 1886, when Jewish strikers marched downtown to close "inside" shops, only to be clubbed by the police before they reached their destination. Ignorant of the English language and without Yiddish newspapers, the strikers did not know that a bomb had exploded at the Haymarket the day before, with a loss of life among the police. Two years later Bisno, now twenty-two years of age and an American citizen for a year, was one of the moving spirits in the formation of the Workingman's Educational Society, which sponsored lectures by trade unionists, socialists, and anarchists. Shortly after that the Society formed a union of cloak-makers with Bisno as president. When the union decided that contractors were ineligible for membership, Bisno gave up his contracting business to become a wage-earner, despite the opposition of his family.

By this time Bisno, who had begun to read widely in the area of social problems, had embraced the socialist philosophy, though in his view political action of any sort, along with proposals for the fundamental restructuring of society, was secondary in importance to trade unionism. As the years went by, his interest in changing the economic system diminished, while his concern with the practical and immediate problems of trade unionism remained as strong as ever. Bisno found himself in the interesting position, in the earlier period of his career, of being considered a visionary by practical men, because of his plans for reforming the garment industry, while the radicals of the time denounced him for his willingness to compromise. Some people who met him in his later period, however, could describe him as a pure-and-simple trade unionist of the Gompers type.

During his early years of activity in the labor movement, Bisno suffered periods of unemployment and blacklisting when strikes were lost and the union was too weak to support its leader. His family lived in poverty for years while his earnings as a union officer were less than he could have earned as a worker in the trade—and far less, needless to say, than he could have made as a contractor. Even worse were the periods when he was unable to work in the garment industry because of his reputation as a union leader, and when he had to take any job he could get in order to support his family. Thus for a time he did heavy, unskilled factory labor, for which he was completely unsuited, as he also worked on the elevated lines as a ticket collector, seven days a week and twelve hours a shift, for a weekly wage of $10.50.

An early participant in educational activities at Hull House, Bisno formed close associations with that group of public-spirited reformers, taking an active part in the campaign for legislation to abolish sweatshops in Illinois. This agitation led the state legislature to appoint an investigating commission, for which Bisno and Florence Kelley collected information. Finally a bill prepared by the Hull House group to regulate home workshops, limit the hours of women workers, and prohibit child labor under the age of fourteen, was adopted by the legislature, and upon its enactment Governor Altgeld appointed Mrs. Kelley as chief factory inspector. Bisno thereupon resigned his union presidency to become one of her deputy inspectors, a post that he occupied for four years until a Republican administration took office in the state. In the meantime a key portion of the law, limiting the hours of labor of women, had been held unconstitutional. Nevertheless Bisno's experience as inspector was a valuable one, since it familiarized him with industrial conditions in a broad range of industries in the state.

It was following this experience, and while he was employed as a fare collector on the elevated lines, that he testified before the Industrial Commission authorized by Congress to investigate the Chicago labor disputes of 1900. This was the second time he testified before a Congressional body: in 1892 he had appeared before a subcommittee of the

House Committee on Manufactures investigating the sweating system, to explain the operations of the system and to urge passage of legislation to prohibit the manufacture of clothing in tenement houses.

In 1900 Professor John R. Commons of the University of Wisconsin was engaged in an investigation of immigration for the federal government, with attention to conditions in American industry. At Commons' invitation Bisno joined him in this study, spending six months accumulating information on wages, hours, and production methods in industries in which large numbers of immigrants were employed. The manuscript of his autobiography ends during this period, when Bisno was only about thirty-four years old, before the unions in the garment trades had established themselves as permanent institutions in their industries, and before Bisno occupied his posts of greatest union influence and power.

In the meantime, however, Bisno had again begun to enjoy some degree of business success. Unwilling to become a contractor in the cloak industry, because of the low wages and long hours which the contractors had to impose on their employees, he became a partner in a ladies' tailoring business, which proved moderately successful. He was always ready to leave business for union work, however, as when the International Ladies' Garment Workers' Union invited him to visit a number of cities in order to popularize the union label on women's garments. Later he joined a real estate firm, working in a garment factory during busy seasons and earning his living as a real estate agent during the dull seasons in the garment trades.

Although the women's garment industry in Chicago was quite small, compared with the size of the market that developed in New York City, Bisno's reputation was such that he was called to the major center several times to take a leading part in union affairs in the industry there. In part this was a tribute to the qualities of the man, and in part it was a recognition that the Chicago union movement, though much smaller in size, had early achieved a degree of influence in the trade that came to the New York City organization somewhat later. Invitations from New York found Bisno responsive, in part because of his realization that Chicago conditions could not greatly improve so long as manufacturers there were exposed to competition from New York City, or had the option of producing their garments at lower cost in the eastern metropolis.

Bisno's first invitation to New York City came about 1892, when the socialist faction in the cloakmakers' union there invited him to run for the office of president against Joseph Barondess, who had the support of the anarchists. Seeking to center attention on a program to reform the industry, Bisno found his group of supporters much more interested instead in personal attacks on the established leader, and he thereupon left for Chicago. During a later stay in New York as manager of the United Brotherhood of Cloak Makers, Bisno found that the manufacturers would sign an agreement with the union, only to send most of their work to non-union outside shops. In Bisno's view the key to the situation was "control of the bundle," to assure that the work would go to contract shops operating under union conditions. Finding too little response to his program, he again returned to Chicago.

Bisno's opportunities to put his ideas into effect came after stable, powerful unionism was finally established in the two markets, in New York City with the successful 1910 strike of the cloakmakers and in Chicago several years later. The 1910 strike in New York, in which over 45,000 workers were engaged, ended with a "Protocol of Peace" that was intended to bring permanent industrial peace to the industry. A permanent Board of Arbitration, consisting of employer, union, and public representatives, was to hand down binding decisions on important issues, while minor disputes were to be decided by a Committee on Grievances. Wages were to be raised, sanitary conditions established, and a preferential union shop put into effect.

In 1911 Bisno, then manager of the Chicago Cloak Makers' Union, was invited to come to New York City to become chief clerk of the Joint Board, the key union office in the administration of the protocol. His successful experience as a union leader in Chicago, his work as a deputy factory inspector in Illinois, his reputation as an honest and aggressive unionist, and his fluent knowledge of English all helped to make him a logical candidate for the position.

Among Bisno's main objectives were to reform the industry, to eliminate competition between the inside and outside shops, and to control the bundles, to make sure that they went to union shops. He insisted upon the registration of contractors, so that the flow of work could be controlled, and upon other structural reforms. Impatient with conciliation, he urged appointment of an impartial chairman whose decisions would be binding; at the same time, he called strikes to enforce protocol conditions, despite the provision in the agreement barring strikes. Besides antagonizing the employers, he led a running battle of the militant leaders of the Joint Board with the more conciliatory officers of the International Union. As a result Bisno was replaced as chief clerk in 1912, though he continued for a time as general manager of the Joint Board.

Two years after Bisno's office in the New York City union ended, he was called to a comparable post in Chicago. Seasonal unionism in Chicago ended at last in 1915 with an arbitration award which raised wages, standardized hours, prohibited home work, regulated contracting, and established the preferential union shop. Bisno had been one of the two union spokesmen before the arbitration board, as he had also figured prominently in the strike agitation which led to its appointment. As in New York City, Bisno was appointed the Joint Board's chief clerk—in reality its manager—to deal with the employers' organizations. Again the relationship proved a stormy one, in part because of Bisno's readiness to call a strike whenever he believed that the agreement was being violated, despite the availability of arbitration machinery.

His period of union officership ended when his term as chief clerk expired in 1917. Thereafter he became a full-time realtor, engaging in this type of work until his death in 1929. He retained his interest in unionism, however, writing and speaking for labor groups as opportunities were available.

Despite his many years of experience as a union officer and his prominence in the period of agitation that preceded stable unionism, Bisno was less than a full success as a union officer when the trade was organized and a collective agreement required administration. In part this was due to his aggressive tactics, to his readiness to call strikes even though the agreement prohibited them; in part the cause lay in his inability to work successfully with other union leaders, to his lack of the gifts of the successful politician; and in part it was his search for ways to reform industrial practices in the interests of the workers, a trait that led to his being considered visionary and impractical by the hard-headed realists of the day. Yet the practices that disturbed him, that led to the breakdown of union conditions and insecurity of employment, have since been reformed, often by the very type of controls that he advocated.

Central to Bisno's thinking was the belief that the worker was entitled to economic security, to continued employment, to treatment with dignity on the job, to satisfactory working conditions, and to an acceptable living standard. Where he found industrial practices in conflict with these objectives, he urged reform, whether by legislative enactment or by union action in collective bargaining. Thus he agitated for legislation to establish the eight-hour day, protect women workers, prohibit child labor, and outlaw manufacture of clothing in home sweatshops. He sought to end the competition of shop against shop and of worker against worker, and to establish the principle that the manufacturer was responsible for the distribution of his work to contractors who maintained union standards in their shops. He urged the adoption of an arbitration system headed by an impartial chairman, whose decisions were binding upon all parties; yet, somewhat paradoxically, he insisted upon the right to strike whenever he believed that the provisions of a collective bargaining agreement were not being observed.

In part Bisno was the agitator and strike leader, as in part he was also the teacher of the immigrant garment workers, educating them to the importance of joint action and permanent unionism. In part he was the student of sweatshop conditions, gathering information on the basis of which legislative bodies might act to eliminate evils. In part he was the practical industrial reformer, using the union's power before arbitration boards or directly at the bargaining table to regulate the use of contractors and establish comparable standards of wages and conditions in inside and outside shops. In part he was the industrial philosopher, seeking to replace strife with an arbitration board headed by an impartial chairman, and looking forward to an era of co-operation between union and management.

In the volatile women's garment industry the union has become the chief stabilizing influence, ending the home sweatshop, eliminating unsanitary conditions, raising the level of earnings, and bringing job and income security to the union member. All of these objectives, commonplace today, were preceded by years of effort on the part of the union's pioneers; and among these pioneers one of the foremost names is that of Abraham Bisno.

JOEL SEIDMAN

University of Chicago
December, 1966

Abraham Bisno, Union Pioneer

1

The family on my father's side originally came from Litaw.*
In the latter part of the eighteenth century, there was a famine and plague in Litaw. A great portion of the population
died of the plague or starved to death. Amongst those who
died were my great-grandfather and his wife, who left my
grandfather, Chatzkel, an orphan at the age of seven with no
one to care for him.

One of the neighbors in Litaw, a tailor by trade, made up
his mind to leave the country for a better and more prosperous land. The Ukraine was his destination, a country where
the soil is fertile and where there are no famines. So he pro-
ceeded to travel south. It was this tailor who took pity on the
seven-year-old orphan and adopted him. He had a trade, was
able to earn his living in the numerous communities along
the road southward, and so it took him seven years until he

* The Litau district of Lithuania.

3

finally reached the province of Kiev. By that time he had taught my grandfather the trade of tailoring, so that when they reached Kiev, Grandfather was fourteen years old and a full-fledged tailor. In Kiev, his benefactor died.

In those years, Jews were not permitted to live in the city proper, so Grandfather moved to a village about twenty miles away from Kiev, called Wasilkow. While living in Kiev, he had ingratiated himself into the interest of a rich landowner, so Grandfather made the clothes for this nobleman's family all week, and every Friday returned to Wasilkow. In Wasilkow, lived Razel the bagel baker, and her very homely daughter. This daughter was not only exceedingly hard to look upon, but had no dowry, moreover. The matchmaker of the town suggested a match between Grandfather and Razel's daughter. He was an orphan and glad to come into her family, so they were married. Goldie, his wife, in the course of time, gave birth to thirteen children, of whom only four survived, two boys and two girls.

I was told that one of his sons, Herschel, had fallen off a table at the age of four. After three years of suffering, he was taken to Kiev and there operated upon by a famous surgeon. This operation left him a hunchback and cripple for life. It was Herschel who, at nineteen, married Malke, the fisherwoman's daughter. Rochel had been left a widow at thirty with five children to care for, so she was glad to marry her daughter Malke to Herschel the hunchback, my father.

Grandfather died when I was seven years old but I have few memories of him. He had a very hard life. Grandmother was bad-tempered. She was continually cursing, scolding, or bossing him. Grandfather in turn was very kindly, very religious, very hard-working, and exceedingly humble in spirit. In those years, the Jewish population was composed of traders and storekeepers in the upper strata, and of laboring men in the lower. Tailors, shoemakers, blacksmiths, and bakers were looked down upon by the brokers and shopkeepers. Of these, Grandfather was of the humblest. His earnings were very small, and so he never managed to own his own home but rented a room or part of a room of some poor family. During his entire lifetime, he never knew peace. Children were born, children were sick, children died. Life was one stretch of sickness, great poverty, and hard labor.

It will be hard to describe fully the nature of the poverty of those days, but one little story may throw some light upon it. Mother told me that immediately upon her marriage, her husband and herself lived with the old people. Once Mother brought some butter from her own mother's home back with her, and Father's sisters bitterly complained that now she had butter, she would eat too much bread, since it would slide down so much more easily. Another illustration—the coat which Grandfather had at seventy was the same in which he had been married and the bed, made of a board placed on four wooden legs, had seventy years of service behind it.

Grandfather was a very honest man. Stories are told of him that when cloth was brought to be made up into clothes by a specified time, he would always refuse the order, since "I do not know whether I shall live until tomorrow. How then can I make you any promises?" Of his work, still another story is told. Once, the Czar passed through his village with a great show of officers, regiments on parade, musical instruments blowing, in fact, a great occasion. They passed down the very street on which Grandfather lived, but he refused even to look out of the window on the parade. He believed in sticking to his work while at it.

A great proportion of the poor peasants were then serfs, and while amongst the Jews working people were not serfs, as amongst the peasants, in the estimate of the storekeepers and traders they were little better. They would, for instance, not be allowed to occupy the front pews of the synagogue nor were they given the honor of reading the scroll. Grandfather was especially humble since he did not even have a shop of his own. He had worked on the estate of this rich landowner and had no independent commercial station in

5

life. As wages he received a barrel of flour, or one of potatoes from time to time, which he carried on his back for twenty miles from Kiev to Wasilkow. Sometimes, before holidays, he would receive gifts of cloth from which he made clothes for his family. His rent he managed to pay by converting some of his gifts of food into money. Grandmother told me that the great family ambition was to own a pew in the synagogue. But this entailed the saving of ten rubles, or about five dollars, and during their entire lifetimes they never managed to attain their ambition.

My father learned tailoring from Grandfather and led about the same kind of life. They were extremely poor: children were born, were sick, and died. Only the hardiest survived in that awful struggle to exist. My father was perhaps a little more fortunate, since Mother had learned the trade of making peasants' bonnets. She would embroider lengths of cloth, make them up into women's bonnets and sell them in the open market. They, too, were very ignorant, very religious, very superstitious, and also had thirteen children, of whom only four survived.

Some years after Father's marriage, a friend of his became the cutter and manager of a small tailor shop in the town of Belayacerkow, about fourteen miles away from Wasilkow, and he agreed to employ Father. Thereupon we moved to Belayacerkow, and settled there.

The town of Belayacerkow in 1870 had a population of about 8,000, consisting mainly of Jews. In the center of the town a few houses were shingled, but most of the dwelling places were peasant huts thatched with straw. In the heart of the town was a block of one-story stores arranged in a ring and the mile of space in that ring was used as the community market-place by the neighboring peasants. The town was situated on low land along the bank of the river Rosch, and since there were no pavements, in times of melting snow or rainy weather it became one big mudhole. There were a few Gentiles on the outskirts of the city who had small vegetable farms and supported themselves by the sale of these vegetables in the market-place. Peasants from outside villages would bring wheat, potatoes, rye, or buckwheat to the market and the Jews would trade them back salt, kerosene, oil, tools, or hardware. Belayacerkow was also divided into two sections: that of the traders and storekeepers, and that of the humble furriers, teamsters, mechanics, shoemakers, and blacksmiths.

I was born* in a one-room peasant's hut right by the village well in the poorest part of the city. Father, by working very hard, earned weekly about three rubles, and Mother the same amount. My memory goes back to the age of three. At that time, Grandfather was seventy-five years old. Both he and Grandmother had come to live with us when they had grown too old to work any longer. In that one-room hut, then, lived grandfather, grandmother, mother, father, children, and occasionally relatives who, through misfortune, were cast out with no other place to go to. Once, I recall, Mother's sister and her children stayed with us—her husband had driven her out of the home—and again—a younger brother of Mother's sought refuge with us.

My memory recalls playing with Grandfather. He was a very kindly old man. I would take the ends of his coattails, while he played horse around the house to my shouts of *"Beyo! Beyo!"* There was a cooper nearby, and I would pretend Grandfather was a barrel, and put hoops all around him. Along with Grandfather, I would pretend to be a tailor. It was he who taught me the letters of the Jewish alphabet, and my prayers. As I recall it, our house was anything but peaceful. Grandmother was always shouting about something. Children were sick. Father would arise before light, and work until after dark. When he left the house, the children were sleeping, and when he returned, again they were sleeping. All we saw of him was the short period on Friday

* In 1866.

and Saturday when he was not at the synagogue, and Saturday night he would go back to work. We lived in constant want and filth. My most significant memories of my childhood are constant vermin, and the lack of food. We were always covered with lice, the bedclothes were always bug-ridden, and our constant worry was how to get rid of vermin. That, the lack of food, and constant sickness in the house, were our continual worries. Since out of thirteen children, nine had died in childhood, and the remaining four always caught the germ diseases then current, there was always sickness in the house.

Father and Mother were very ignorant and superstitious. They were taught to pray in the Hebrew tongue but had never learned the meaning of the words they were mumbling. The spoken language used in our house was Yiddish, a composite of words picked up in the travels of the race—mainly a German dialect with Hebrew, Russian, Polish, Lithuanian, Spanish, and English words intermixed. Some were even of Asiatic nations amongst whom the Jews had lived centuries ago. But the prayer-books were in pure Hebrew and few understood that Hebrew. They merely muttered words without meaning. Hebrew religion imposed prayers before meals, at sunset, at night, on washing the hands—it imposed eating food prepared in certain fashion, and the wearing of clothes in which linen and wool did not mix, and numerous other stringent laws which kept one alert religiously in century-old precedent.

I cannot recall a single instance of joy at our home. It is true Mother sang at her work, but only songs that told of the persecution of the Jews, the complaint of the deserted woman, the complaint of the maiden on her lack of dowry, that of the young man about to be recruited into the army, that of relatives separated from their kin. The folklore was teeming with the hardships of life arising from want.

Father and Mother were not very happy together. While Mother was a dutiful wife and religiously devoted to Father, she did not care for him. He was hunched in form, had little earning capacity, and less capacity to satisfy her most cherished ideals. Father was an ignorant tailor and Mother had come from a family of traders.

As I said before, the neighborhood I lived in was not the only one in the town. On the other side of the public square lived the richer portion of the population—this section was called the New Town. The culture among these people was much higher than that of the poor. They were better dressed, had better houses, most of the homes had house-servants and their male-folk had a great deal more of Hebrew learning. The history of the Jew, the Bible, the Talmud, and other Hebrew books were to be found in these houses. In the synagogue one found two institutions: one devoted to religious services and one making the *shul* a social club. Just as the Gentile of the town had his inn in which to make acquaintances, to talk over the day's events, so did the Jew, after evening services, or perhaps on a Saturday afternoon, discuss various current topics, sometimes actually transact business, analyze the nature of various charity enterprises, and discuss the politics of the village and neighboring country.

Although there was quite a difference in the culture of the members of the Old Town shul and the New Town shul, there was not as much as could be found between the peasant of the Old Town, and the wealthy Gentile of the New Town. The social position of the peasant was fixed. His pedigree came with the land he tilled, and since land seldom changed hands, he remained neither richer nor poorer through the years. The Jew, being a trader, might make a lucky stroke and add materially to his wealth and social position. The culture of the Jew, too, was more evenly diffused through all classes. The shoemaker's son might be educated to be a rabbi, a cultured man who could interpret Jewish law. The rabbi might have a son who might turn shoemaker but the peasant would never become a teacher at a *gymnasium*; the cultured man would certainly never become a peasant. Jewish culture

9

was the link between all classes. The Jew delighted in theoretic discussion of all the conditions of life. His Talmud itself is a series of dissertations on modes of conduct. While the Jew kept his eyes fixed on the heavens, questioning them with regard to the why of life, the peasant was concerned only with the earth, its fertility, its very material values with regard to himself. The Jew questioned life; the peasant accepted it, worked with it. In myself, all through life, I have felt the imprint of those two forces; the theoretic Jew in me has made me stop to understand the movements of life and the example of the doing peasant has made me demand action in all my dealings with life.

It would be difficult to describe the attitude of mind the Jews had towards their Gentile neighbors and to social life in general. The government of Russia was then Czaristic—the Czar had despotic powers. The police, the courts, the legislative bodies were all appointed by the central government. The people, even the Gentiles, had nothing to say about it. But the central government was Russian, and the Jews were not permitted by law to participate in government affairs. So the Jews found themselves aliens in Russia. The fact that they had a religion different from the Gentiles', an especially strict religion which forbade them to intermarry with the Gentiles, to eat at Gentile houses, formed a condition of alien relationship even with their neighbors. They were a very small minority as compared with the Gentile population in Russia. The ordinary Russian considered Russia as his home and his country and even in his mind did not consider that the Jews had any rights there.

The government passed certain laws against the Jews. They had no right to buy and own land; no right to live in the greatest part of Russia—and similar oppressive laws showing a sense of animus towards the Jew. Under these circumstances, an atmosphere was created making the feeling of the average Gentile one which held that the Jew had no rights and no protection. It would be difficult to describe the state of mind of the Jew under those circumstances. In the first place, the Jew formed a sense of clannishness—that in reality he, as a Jew, was all-important; that the Gentiles had no souls, no spiritual life. Even when permitted [to do otherwise], the Jew would freely choose to live only with Jews in preference to Gentiles. This condition existed as a spiritual situation. As a practical, everyday proposition, the Jews were afraid of the Gentiles. They constantly felt a sense of violence hovering in the atmosphere. They were afraid of being beaten up, of losing their property, of having their women raped by the Gentiles—a mother, wife, or daughter. They were constantly being subjected to numerous indignities.

In this atmosphere, the division between the two races was complete. They could not have been more different than if they had lived a thousand miles apart. In their ordinary conduct, in their religious and ethical conceptions, in their sense of loyalty to the state and in their general attitude towards life, they were most different. They, the Jews, spoke about themselves in their relation to Russia as if they were in hated exile (*Golus*). The word "exile" does not really define the meaning of *Golus*. Every sense of insecurity, of protest against indignities, the feeling that the Gentile could not mentally comprehend the logic of having one God, one central, universal authority, or even see the contradiction of three divinities making one, all combined to make the Jew feel absolutely unable to appeal to the intelligence of the Gentile.

The Jew considered himself far superior in understanding and culture to the Gentile. Therefore he felt it to be a hopeless matter to appeal to people for mercy who had a pagan religion and could not at all comprehend the Jewish religion or processes of Jewish thought. The Jews were absolutely at the mercy of the Gentiles. They had no legal status; whole communities could be driven out at the will of the authorities; they were subject to tax with no government of the tax possible to them; they had little recourse when physically assaulted.

Under these conditions the ordinary Jew worked out a psychology that was purely Jewish in numerous relations to life. There was almost a complete absence of patriotism for Russia. Most Jews would try very vigorously to evade drafting into the Russian army, and many would run away to escape it. The feeling of contempt for the religion of the Gentiles; a very weak sense of moral obligation to his Gentile neighbor (cheating a Gentile was an answer to violence by the Gentile toward the Jew [and] was not considered a serious moral offense). Honesty in business with relation to the Gentile was only a mode of conduct because of necessity and not inspired by any real sense of moral obligation. All [this] arose from their subjection to the Gentile rule. Gentiles knew of the readiness of the Jew to cheat them and responded to their attitude by a complete absence of confidence in the Jew.

As I have said before, the city was divided into two sections; [on] one side of the market-place lived the poor. They too were divided into the [less poor and the] very poor, such as beggars, common laborers, widows who had no male support, families composed of shiftless never-do-wells. That district was called "Grass" because there were practically no houses; the people lived in dug-outs where the roofs of the hovels were almost on a level with the surface of the earth, and grass grew on the roofs. Next in the social order were families like our own who lived in peasant huts, but they were above earth level. These huts usually consisted of one large room with an enormous oven at one end which was used for baking and cooking by the family. In winter the surface of these ovens, once the fire had died down, was used to sleep on. Beds were mostly four wooden posts on which a plank was laid, on top of which were hay mattresses in the very poor houses, and feather mattresses in the somewhat better-off homes. Removing quills from feathers was quite an occupation for most poor families in their spare time. Mothers would carefully prepare bedclothes for their daughters when they had little else in the house. It was a cold country and warm coats and feather-beds were a necessity. They might have been handed down for long years, it is true, but most families had them.

On the other side of the town were the stores and not far off lived the more prosperous traders. There the houses consisted of two and sometimes three rooms, and were thatched with shingles, or even roofed with sheet iron. All houses stood in mud. There was no drainage. No separate toilet-rooms. Water was to be had only if brought to the houses by water-carriers who carried water in buckets from the river, or town well, on their shoulders and sold it to different families at a cost of twenty to thirty kopeks weekly.

There were two playgrounds for the children in the city. The playground for the poor was a little outside the village, a big stretch of desert land where the dirt and filth of ages could be found. The burying ground of the city was there, as was the local slaughter-house. This slaughter-house attracted innumerable dogs who lived on the refuse lying about, so the playground was filled with stray, dirty curs, the odors of the slaughter-house, and the accumulated rubbish of centuries. That was where, after school, gangs of boys would come to play, run around, fight, and have a good time.

On the west side of the city, there was a large strip of ground that belonged to the nobility who owned the town. This land adjoined the palatial buildings of the nobles. On the ground was a high school attended by Gentiles almost exclusively. At the time, Jews could not send their children to such schools. That strip of ground was clean, a great deal of it covered with grass in summer. It was used as a playground by the children of the well-to-do.

As I recall, I was quite a personality at the age of seven in the Talmud Torah I attended. The children of my age looked to me for leadership in games. One of these games called for fights with the children of the more prosperous section. We never did dare to cross the border and go into their ground, but we did allow some of those children to come into our fields and play. Occasionally a squabble arose whereby war was aroused between the two factions. There was a class feeling amongst us with regard to the children of the other side. We felt them to be snobs who looked down on us. They were better dressed. [They] had more and better food, and some even had some money occasionally, and in our judgment that was no reason for their looking down upon us. So, when a fight did arise we were always ready to fight. I led a group of boys who expected me, on such occasions, to lead the way.

There was a regiment of soldiers in town who used to drill a great deal of the time. We boys would imitate those soldiers. We formed ourselves into companies, would march to the tune of two sticks playing on a sheet of tin, and imitate the drum of the soldiers. We would imitate the maneuvres of the soldiers and decide who was to be victorious by dividing into groups and actually fighting our way to victory. My gang was composed of the poorest because they were recruited from the charity school. Roughnecks, the others would call us, and I suppose we were.

One of my chief lieutenants was a boy called Vove. He and I met at school first. He was about seven then. I first noticed him especially because he never would take along any food to school. When some of the children had bread, baked potato or a piece of cheese, perhaps some fruit, which was nibbled at when Teacher was out, Vove would sit around, his face plainly showing hunger as he watched us. I made friends with Vove and offered and finally induced him to eat some of my lunch.

One day, after school was out, I followed him to his home. Vove lived in the *Hegdisch*. This was a sort of pest-house for the town. People who had no place to be or who were left ill with no one to care for them, old people too feeble to beg, those chronically ill, widows with children who could not leave them in order to earn a living, the refuge of the diseased, old, and helpless, this was the Hegdisch. It was an old, dilapidated building covered with straw. It was divided into two compartments; one very large room was the home of all the women, old, young, sick and healthy, and their children. The other room was kept for all the males, old, young, sick and healthy as they might be.

The institution was maintained by the Jewish community out of a charity fund which came from a tax on kosher meat; but the income was very small and the food furnished by the institution was not quite enough to maintain life, so that a good many of the residents used to add to their food by begging, or going out to do odd jobs, or thieving. It was a nest of everything low, and the community looked upon the inmates of the Hegdisch as those lowest in the scale of humanity.

That was the home to which Vove took me. He introduced me to his mother and told her that I was his playmate Avremel, of whom he was very proud. His mother was a woman about thirty, very sickly, with an emaciated face. She put her arms about me, and said, "Avremel, do you play with my boy? Did you know he lived in Hegdisch? Did you tell your mother that you are playing with a boy who lives here?" Then, Vove told her that he knew my mother too; that he had been over to our house, that Mother gave him food, fine-combed his head, washed him when she washed me, which made Vove's mother cry with joy. In her extreme sense of gratitude to our family because her orphan boy had found friends, she cried to God to reward us.

A great many years have since passed; I have married, raised a family, have children of my own, and still have to recall anyone who might be devoted to me with such loyalty as was Vove in my younger days. In our scraps with other boys, Vove would make it his business to receive most of the blows intended for me, and while he had nothing to share with me, he had a kind of devotion and appreciation of my heroics that has never been effaced from my memory even after the lapse of a great many years.

During that period of my life,* our family sold our little hut, and bought another one which had three rooms: a great

* In 1873.

kitchen with the oven in it, a large living room, and a bedroom. As I recall, the bedroom was always rented out to another family, who shared the kitchen with us. In the front room lived Father, Mother, Grandfather and Grandmother, and when my older brother Sholem was married, he was given a corner of the living room too, and Grandfather and Grandmother had their bed put in the kitchen. Our family was always in debt, especially since we had bought a larger house.

By the time I was nine years old, work in my father's shop was very scarce and the family indebtedness increased materially. Therefore, a relative of ours advised us to move out into a farming village about twenty miles from the city and open up a general store for peasants. As Mother figured it out, Father could sew for the peasants, she would embroider their caps, we could raise gardening stuff in the strip of land back of the hut, and we could also keep a goat, as well as have an additional income for the family from our merchandising. She also figured on the trade she might get in selling the peasants caps, receiving in return food which she would again sell in the open market. Father was paid for his labor, too, not in money but in peasants' food. For a week's work he would get a sack of potatoes, or one or two bushels of rye, or a few chickens, or a basketful of eggs. The house we lived in after we had moved to this rural community was a peasant's hut, about the same as our city hut—a one-room house with a great oven. In that one room were all our household utensils, beds, tables, groceries, dry-goods, and whatever possessions we had. Our merchandise did not amount to more than thirty rubles in all.

The first shock in our new quarters was when the Oorodnik [police officer] discovered we sold tobacco without a license. They caught us red-handed in the act of selling a package of tobacco for three kopeks to a peasant. The license for selling tobacco would have been five rubles, which Mother figured she would try to avoid buying until she had sold some merchandise. The Oorodnik threatened to report both Father and Mother and file a complaint against us to the higher authorities in the County Office. I remember the scene very vividly. Both Father and Mother on their knees kissing the boots of that very tall officer, and he, half-drunk, shouting at the top of his voice that Jews never would obey laws and that Jews ought to be driven out of the village. But he meant really to be merciful with us. Therefore, he tried to find out how much money there was in the house. I remember Grandmother taking out all her savings from her stocking, about 1 ruble, 80 kopeks. There was all told about four rubles to be gathered up, and after he got this amount he promised not to write out a report against us, which would have laid Father and Mother open to a three-month jail sentence.

I recall another special occasion in that same community. One of the peasants became drunk and came in to buy something. He ended by beating up Father so that he was sick for several weeks, and generally wrecked our hut so that it took over a year for us to save enough to repair the damage. Life was not very much different there than it was in the town. Labor from early morning to late at night with only bare subsistence as a reward. Buckwheat soup, potatoes, bread, garden vegetables, and occasionally meat prepared according to Jewish ritual and brought from town, were on our table. For six months or so, I was sent to town to the Talmud Torah because my teaching in Jewish prayer had not been completed. Otherwise, life went on monotonously.

I suspect very much that in those years I was puzzled and formed some real opinions on the subject of religion. I was a religious child in a way. Religion with me was not a conviction but a condition. Simply, I had to pray every day, and did, in the Hebrew language, of which I did not understand a word. But I knew there was a Jewish God, that this God was different from the God of the Gentiles, but up to the time we moved into a Gentile village community, the subject of religion had never disturbed me very much.

It was when we moved into the Gentile community and I

had acclimatized myself there, that I discovered that there were really two Gods, a Gentile God, Gentile church, Gentile prayers, separate from a Jewish God, Jewish church, and Jewish prayers. Both Father and Mother used to tell me that there was really only one God, and the claim of the Gentiles that they had a God of their own was not true. They, it seemed, had no God at all. While Jews were to be rewarded in the next world for their good deeds here, and punished for their evil-doings here, Gentiles had only punishment in store for them because they did not believe in our God. Our Gentile neighbors whom I would visit while playing with their children would tell me the same story except that it was their God that was real, and ours who was no God at all, and had no power. As evidence of their claim, they submitted the fact they they were the real power in Russia and the Jews were strangers and outcasts with no authority or rights. This left quite an impression on my mind.

I remember once asking Mother this question pointblank, "Ma, you say we are a Chosen People and that ours is the only God, almighty and powerful. How is it that these Gentiles treat us so badly then? Why doesn't our God protect us against our enemies?" To this Mother would say that ages back our people failed to live up to the commandments of God, and that now we were being punished by having the Gentiles drive us out of our homes and scatter us amongst the nations of the world. We were in Golus, or exile, she said. This did not seem to me reasonable. Why my father and mother and my brothers should be punished because our forefathers sinned did not seem fair to ourselves. We hadn't sinned, so why should we be punished?

Life in the peasant village was from the social point of view very different from that of the city that I was raised in. There was only one other Jewish family in the village—all the others were Gentiles and peasants and their lives were completely different from that of our own. Both men and women in those communities worked very hard in the fields; there was a great deal of liquor-drinking on the part of the men and many of the women partook of the same. Both men and women were very strong, and very hardy, nothing like the Jews: big men, raw and bony, coarse hands, coarse faces, coarse characters. There was a great deal of violence there; almost every man beat his wife and both men and women beat their children. Fights amongst the men were the order of the day beginning from their youth, all through life. On every possible occasion the men used to come together in the village inn, drink themselves to bestiality, and fight.

The religious morality which permeated the life of the Jewish community was in its reality almost absent in the village community; violent and reckless in thought, violent and reckless in conduct. There was almost no real respect for human dignity; the sense of human dignity was almost completely absent. The normal curse word was, "I fuck your mother ten times," or "Ten devils into your mother." And when a little under the weather because of whiskey, a poke in the rib, a stab in the face, a blow between the eyes was a quite common occurrence. The physically weak man in the community had almost no rights and the woman had no rights except as she could physically assert them.

The sex morality only had a meaning amongst the people in so far as it could be enforced by violence. A woman was afraid to sleep with her neighbor because if her husband knew it he would give her a beating. Very seldom have I heard that a girl would receive a beating from her father because she allowed boys to have sex relations, I take it because the offense was not considered serious except as it touched the husband by way of taking something from him because it belonged to him.

While amongst the Jews the boys and girls did not mix at all, in this village community they mixed very much. Boys and girls, men and women, worked side by side in the fields. The males would be reaping the harvest and the women would be binding up the straw; the males would be cutting the hay and the women would put it in piles. In potato fields the males would be digging out the potatoes, the women would be picking them out and putting them in sacks. Truck gardening was done almost completely by women except where the ground was plowed up; plowing was done mostly by men. There was some sort of separation because I remember as they were coming from fields the girls used to go together separate from the men and sing village songs. And the men used to come together too in bunches, but even at that they weren't completely separate; from time to time a few boys would get in amongst the girls, especially those who had sweethearts, and partake together of some of the songs.

It didn't take me very long as a kid to learn the Ukrainian language. I used to love to spend time with our peasant neighbors. That was especially true in the barn. I used to love to hang around the horses, be of some help bringing hay or oats, or would even clean the horses, and, when I was per-mitted, I enjoyed getting a big man's fork and digging into and cleaning the manure or helping in my small way to load wagons when they had to go to market. I even learned how to use the flail during thrashing times and help thrash.

Even in those days [when] I was no more than nine years old I couldn't help but notice the difference between the sex conduct of the Jews in town and that of the Gentile peasants in the village. Over and over again boys and girls used to come into our little hut to buy small trinkets or some flowers and while there would openly caress each other.

I remember on one occasion our neighbor's daughter, a strong, healthy peasant girl about sixteen or seventeen years old, was chewing on a sunflower in our house. A neighbor's peasant boy came in, a big, strong, healthy fellow about twen-ty years old. "Let me feel you around, Parasky." "Why? Thirty devils into your mother," she replied. "I'll buy you sunflowers," he said, "that's why." At that the girl thought it was a good bargain. He bought a sunflower for a kopek, took her on his lap, put his hand in her naked bosom, and played with her breasts. She kissed him and was very happy, but when he picked up her skirt she resisted. "You ought to be ashamed of yourself," she said to him, "before all these people. Time enough to do that when we are by ourselves."

On another occasion Mother was invited to a wedding. And when she came there at sunset, the time set for the wedding, everybody was there, bridegroom, his parents, the bride's parents and relations, except the bride. Everybody was waiting for the bride. They waited there for about two hours and then the bride's mother came in, took hold of the bridegroom, pulled him into the center of the house, and began to dance. The bride just had a baby, and according to her [Mother's] version, the family would save money since they could have the wedding and the christening party for the same expense.

A soldier came back from the army. He was away from his home for four years. When he came back he found that his wife had a baby only a few months old. That angered him very much and he beat up his wife with a horsewhip until she was writhing in pain on the ground. But he didn't divorce her. There were no divorces under the Russian law. Once married, married forever. He had a right to beat his wife; he had a right to work her to death; he had every right over her life and possessions except the right to get rid of her. He could drive her out but that did not mean that he could remarry again or that she could remarry again. People were married for life in those days.

Violence had a great deal to do with the relations of male and female. Women used to say that if a man did not beat his wife, he evidently did not love her. On one occasion I overheard a conversation between two girls in our little hut who came there to buy some house necessities. The subject of the conversation was last night's experience in the Dusweetky. The Dusweetky was an institution arranged among the peasants which meant this: that for wooing purposes boys and girls used to come together to work and play at one of the houses in the village. The girls used to spin linen thread, and the boys used to hang around the house, sing songs and feel the girls around and play.

One of the girls said that a certain boy succeeded in getting on top of her and very nearly committed rape on her but she was so strong that she threw him off and beat hell out of him, while the other girl spoke of the experience she had with another boy who she said had hands like iron, and his feet were like wooden pillows, and that she was helpless while he committed rape on her. She comforted herself with the threat that [her] father and relatives would make him marry her for that. The subject matter was discussed without any sense of bashfulness or any sense of surprise.

Even in those years I felt that these peasants had a saner view on sex relationship in their lives' experience. It must have influenced my own attitude of mind and vigor of emotions. I think I must have been about eleven years old when I was bathing early in the morning in the village brook that Gypsy was bathing in too. Gypsy was a kid about the same age or a year older but she was much bigger than I was, much more developed, and when we went out both of us naked, it was she that opened the conversation. "You're a Jew," she said. "Nobody here likes you." "And you're a gypsy, and everybody says your mother is a whore," I said in retaliation. "But that isn't as bad as being a Jew," she said.

But that evidently was only a beginning. Before long the conversation drifted in other channels. I imparted the information that the cow of Ivan, a neighbor of ours, gave birth to a calf last night, and she in turn related the fact that her mother left the village to go into town early that morning, and while I was talking I went nearer to her and began to play with her breasts. She had no objections evidently to letting me do as I pleased for a little while. Then she turned to me and asked me whether I had five kopeks and I told her, which was true, that I never did have a sum of money equal to that amount. Upon hearing that, she got very mad, said to me, "Thirty devils into your mother," raised a handful of mud from the brook and threw it on me with all the violence she could. Not only that, she very quickly filled her two hands with mud and began to throw it at me with all the might that she had. I was half scared to death, got ahold of my cotton breeches, and ran for my dear life.

A great many years have passed since. Many members of the gentler sex have crossed my path, and the question, "Have you got five cents," has come up over and over again in my experience when I made the approach.

The mother of this gypsy girl was an orphan peasant girl and was impregnated by a gypsy out of a band that passed through the village. Since she was very poor and had no dowry, with, moreover, a baby on her hands, there was no one in the village that would marry her. Therefore she lived by herself in a peasant hut and raised her baby, and went out to work, either on the rich man's estate, or doing day labor for the peasants.

She thus earned her living for herself and her child, and remained unmarried, the only unmarried woman in the village. She earned money also as the whore of the community. It was known in the community that she would occasionally get a sack of potatoes or bushel of wheat from the unmarried men working on this nobleman's estate. In spite of all her industry, she was very poor. I take it the reason her daughter asked for five kopeks was because she had learned that trick from her mother.

While this was my first actual experience in touching a girl's breasts, I was not altogether ignorant, even at that age, of sex passion. When I saw the peasant boys playing with the girls, I remember that even at eight I would flame up with a warm sensation running through my body. And even before I understood what was what, I had a yearning and a striving that made my senses very keen on the subject of sex. When I used to hang around the village barns or haylofts or granaries, the men always talked of their sex experiences, of what they did with their girls at Dusweetky. So, even at eight, I knew all about sex, and learned to masturbate, especially when the boys used to talk about it and fired my imagination. The impression the men left on my mind in talking about sex was that there was a union of sentiment between the girls and the boys both in playing and in sex intercourse.

So, when this peasant girl threw mud at me in such a rage, I was very much puzzled. I could not quite understand the offense I committed. I knew that if Father learned of what I had done, I would be punished, but that was because Father and Mother were religious Jews. But this girl seemed to have no scruples on religious grounds, and I could not quite make out the reason why she was so mad. Even at this age, I don't remember having a sex morality. There was no taboo in me whatsoever. The way the peasants spoke and in the main the way they actually conducted themselves held a perfect sense of moral sanction both in their sex approach and conduct.

Boys and girls kissed each other often, embraced each other, the boys held the girls on their laps, played with their breasts, and were only held off when the boys tried to raise the peasant girls' skirts in the presence of others. It was my understanding that the boys had no trouble on that score when they were by themselves. I think, in those years, I looked on sex play almost in the same way as if the boys and girls were singing together, or walking together, or working side by side in the fields. The thing that interfered with my doing the same as the other boys was my extreme youth and that I had no girl friends. I was a Jew, they were Gentiles, and their opportunity of meeting me on any kind of common business was almost zero. I did think about it very much because the men I associated with talked about it so much.

While the peasants conducted themselves very much as savages do normally, they had some very noble traits in their characters. The principle of hospitality was lived up to by the peasantry quite generally. A strange peasant passing through the village during mealtime would find practically every door open for him for food and lodging. If there was no room in the house, he could sleep in the hayloft just as any member of the family might do. I suppose that the reason for this compliance with the sense of hospitality was because all the peasants were very poor and were obliged during some period of the year to leave home looking for work with no money on hand. So, whereas the peasant would entertain a stranger in his own home at times, during other seasons he might expect to be likewise entertained. Hospitality was naturally reciprocated and was the very life of the community.

They also had very strongly developed a social sense of relationship. A peasant seldom hired labor. If he needed help he would simply call on his neighbor, and his neighbor would respond as naturally as he would perform his own work. When a young man got married and needed to build himself a hut, his neighbors came together and helped him to build his home. When a man died, his neighbors plowed his fields for his widow, and the village women helped to spin her thread, weave her cloth, or sew clothes for her children and help her maintain the family. All this was true in the fields. When a man was through with his field and his neighbor still had to work, he normally helped him to finish his field, with plowing, harvesting, or what not. There was a sense of co-operation, a mutual-help desire practised by the entire population, not as a special virtue, not even as a duty, but simply as a condition which prevailed, the same as a condition of labor for oneself and one's family.

There was not very much respect in the community for the village "pope" (the village priest). The men-folk, sometimes even the women-folk, would crack jokes at the expense of the priest's reputation. They would say that the priest was a grafter, that he took too much money for marriage ceremonies or the baptism of children or during confession, or during burial ceremonies. At heart, the peasants were religious, but had no respect for the priest and other Church functionaries.

The difference between one peasant and the other, in the main, was only a difference in the amount of money they spent for whiskey. The peasants were more or less drunk most of the time. Some were very heavy drinkers and would sell their last bushel of wheat or their last sack of potatoes to buy whiskey. Then they would be forced, in winter, to go about looking for work. Drunkenness and sobriety were the main differences between one peasant and another. The size of a peasant's family, also, determined its prosperity in a measure. Peasant families having more children working for them were normally better off because the children helped them to raise both fowl and cattle, and feed for them.

In the discussions relating to marriage, the subjects always brought up were—is the girl healthy or sick, willing to work or lazy? Health and willingness to work were of the first importance in the matrimonial bargains. The same was true of the estimates of the young man. Was he willing and able to work—or was he lazy or sickly? The question of dowry was also of prime importance. There was a love song of those days, and its refrain went—"Where will you take me if you have no house?" As to differences in social status between the peasants, those were very slight. One could distinguish between the wealthiest peasant, and the drunken, destitute family, it is true, but in the main, social distinctions were lacking, and of no meaning in the life of the peasants.

There was absolutely no sex morality among men there. If a man had a chance and failed to take it, he was labeled a fool. But very few men failed to take those chances. Women on the other hand had a very definite sex morality. The motif for this morality was self-protection. Protection against conception, for instance; a sort of dread that women might lose caste in the eyes of the community by being promiscuous. Men would naturally go to the woman to whom other men had found access; the woman would be considered more or less public property, and much lowered in the estimate of the village-folk. There was quite a difference in public estimation between the woman who stayed with other men when her husband beat her or was drunk or the woman who had a lover, as opposed to the woman who was really promiscuous. Morality among the women was forced on them by their male relatives—husbands or fathers. The latter feared they [the women] would lose caste by being considered whores who might come to anybody for a consideration. In civilized society, there is a taboo existing with regard to intercourse outside the marriage relation. Women claim they cannot consider such relationship to other men. It is a matter of emotion, of feeling, with them. But in this peasant community no such taboo existed. The only considerations were practical ones.

It is difficult to tell the mode of life and culture of the two peoples, the peasantry in the village and the Jewish trader and handicraft men in the small town, but they are very different. The peasant seems to draw his cultural sense from the soil. He stands with both feet on the earth. He is sure of everything, is simple, feels himself safe, works hard, is very poor, but he has a complete sense of security and in a certain sense is master of his destiny. The soil is fertile and he is always sure of support. A great deal of his life is spent in the open air; he is very ignorant but at the same time on his own husbandry, in his own village community, in his relations with his neighbor, he is quite intelligent—the intelligence acquired from generation through generation gives him a stable level of culture. The peasant may lie sometimes on items that are not germane to his life, a sort of smart-aleck lying, but on anything germane he is normally truthful, he doesn't cheat, has no occasion to cheat—to be honest is normal with him. He doesn't trade much, he produces almost everything he needs to live on, his shelter, his food, and a great part of his clothes. All members of the family work and there is a homogeneity in the attitude of mind of men, women, and children which is both savage to a certain extent, and honest.

It is quite different in the Jewish community. Most of the population live by trading and business enterprise. There is no such sense of security amongst the Jews in the town. The element of chance and speculation is quite a part of the so-called normal life of the population. The Jews haven't the same rights as the Gentile population. The government constantly is issuing new orders against the Jews. Their earnings are almost never safe; their property is not safe; sometimes even their very lives are not safe. They live amongst a population that is hostile to them, and their enemies are almost a hundred to one.

The Jews have a much older heritage of civilization, mainly a city culture. To the Jew the Talmud is much more real as law-giver than is any of the religions of the Gentiles. The Jew's religion keeps him busy morning, noon, and night. He prays Saturdays and Holidays, and the constant interpretation of religious law is a live item in his daily life. The Jew's prophets and his hopes and aspirations are a real item of his life. The Gentile is secure with his day while the Jew speculates and hopes as to what is going to be tomorrow. The Jew's mind has developed to be a great deal more fertile, flexible, learned, tricky, and uncertain. It is amongst both of those peoples that I have acquired the fundamentals of my being at (the early age) up to about eleven years of age.

I do not think that I have ever had real religious convictions. Father and Mother had no opportunity to take care of me and while the atmosphere in the house, as all over, was very religious, I have personally not received religious instructions in a way to make them take hold of me. When we moved into the village community and I associated with the Gentiles and found that the Gentiles had denied completely the authority of the Jew's God, and I knew that the Jews had denied the authority of the Gentile God, so that between and betwixt, I have formed an opinion that heeded no religious convictions. I would quietly eat pig meat in a Gentile house

28

without the least scruple though I knew that if my father and mother knew it they would consider me lost both in this world and the next.

Amongst the peasants I acquired a larger sense of veracity —not that I had any theories about it; I simply got it because I have inhaled it from the village grass, so to say, and yet I have not acquired fully that matter-of-fact simplicity which was natural to the peasants, because economically, my life and that of our family was not as secure as that of the peasants. We always had to rack our brains where our next day's meal would come from, and the question, What's next? was always on our mind.

In those years my oldest brother got married to a girl that turned out to be a shrew. He didn't earn a living and they had to live with our family and his wife made life miserable for all of us, her husband, my father and mother, and all concerned. She was always complaining, cursing a good deal of the time; nothing that we had or did seemed to be suited to her needs, so with all the poverty and want and suffering in the house, along with that, we have had the misery of quarreling and fighting; the very atmosphere was charged with spiritual poison which made us all suffer intensely. This woman seemed to have a great deal of influence on me and on my future life; I became in those years very sensitive to quarreling; a complaint or a sense of dissatisfaction will go all through me; I actually felt a physical pain and my mind was constantly on the alert on this subject as to when is the next blow coming.

I used to envy our neighbors, the peasants, that in their quarrels at least violence was the relationship, and I considered violence much the lesser evil of the two. Part of that sense was developed in my early years from my grandmother —she, too, was always complaining and quarreling. Physical, matter-of-fact relationship formed a preferred sense in my make-up. I liked the way those peasants went about their lives. They ate and drank and worked and played with their women-folk somehow more naturally, more directly, than our people. They had less taboo, less things that were forbiden, less speculation, and less worries in their daily lives, and I loved that.

Especially I have acquired a great liking for their attitude on the subject of women and sex. They talked and conducted themselves so simply and so honestly that the sex situation was almost no problem to them at all, while amongst the Jews the taboos on that subject were so rigidly enforced in opinion and conduct that it was criminal to even think of it.

I think it was from the Gentiles I learned both to talk and feel like them on the sex subject and would constantly wish and hope to be like them. Yet our family were so different, and, while I preferred the Gentile attitude of mind, I had none of the Gentile opportunities in the life of sex and began to be envious of the Gentile mode of living at quite an early age, I should say, when I was eight years old.

Occasionally I had opportunities to see their free relationships; I always heard them talk about it, mostly men, and sometimes women too, and sometimes, men and women. While their talk amongst themselves was so natural, open and direct, translating conduct into thought and thought into conduct, I couldn't talk about it at all nor did I have opportunities in the field of conduct, so that I began to be hungry that way from the time I was a kid.

By the time I was eleven and a half years old, Father and Mother began to worry as to what would become of me. There was nothing they could do for me except either Father should teach me the trade of a tailor or hire me out as an apprentice to some tailor in town. Father worked for the peasants, mending their clothes and occasionally making a new garment, either of sheepskin or a top-coat of coarse, heavy woolen cloth that was both spun and woven in the village community. That kind of tailoring required very little skill and Father and Mother thought that if I was apprenticed out

30

to a tailor in the city it would be better for me, because I would have an opportunity to learn the scale of the tailoring trade, and so Mother took me to town and apprenticed me to a relative of hers, a journeyman tailor who worked at a ready-made shop, the same man Father worked for before we left for the village community.

Mayre used to work about the same number of hours my father worked. He used to get up early in the morning—in fact, before daylight—and worked until late at night on about the same ration, bread, potatoes and herring—occasionally, buckwheat soup, fruit, vegetables, and sometimes meat. No cooked food in the morning or at noon, no supper on time, only when we came back late at night, we ate whatever we found in the oven, normally a plate of either buckwheat or cabbage soup, bread, potatoes, and sometimes meat.

It seems that nature has failed to give me the proper in-gredients to become a skillful tailor. My fingers used to sweat; my needle, being wet, entered into cloth with great difficulty and screamed in the process. Normally it takes only two or three months until an apprentice gets over that difficulty. As for myself, I think I never got over that difficulty. If I should begin to sew today by hand I think my fingers would sweat and my needle would scream with every stitch.

The men in the shop used to have a great deal of fun with my work on that account. "Where did you wet your hands," they used to ask me, "did you put them where it was warm or hot?"—and other such remarks. With this fault, I could not learn to sew properly. It took me much longer to learn to do anything and even when I learned it I never learned to do it quite right. The normal treatment an apprentice received in those years, if he didn't do his work right, was to receive a beating for each offense. Mayre was not stingy on that; I used to be beaten several times a day for my failure to sew seams right or to learn the intricacies of the trade. I took it as a matter of fact that it was perfectly proper for Mayre to beat me, a slap in the face, a poke in the leg, a kick in the foot, or even sometimes put me across his knee and give me several smacks where it was soft. I tried my level best to learn the trade but compared to others, I was not very efficient.

There was another problem that I had while learning the trade and that was, I thought too much. I could never quite understand or acquiesce to the beating. Why should he beat me, I thought. It doesn't help any. I am attentive enough. If anything, when I am beaten, I am so wrought up that I don't know what I am doing, and so do even worse than I did before I was beaten. Occasionally I used to talk back, try to explain it wasn't my fault, that I can't help if my fingers were sweating and the needle was wet and screamed with every stitch, that under those circumstances, no one could do very fine work; but that used to get him very sore; he used to say, on the gab I was all right, I could talk much, but when it came to doing the work, I was impossible—which was true; however, there was no remedy for it.

As time went on, my relation with Mayre became even more strained. The beating was more severe, my sense of resentment and talking back more vigorous, so that at one time when he threw me on the floor, stepped on me with both of his feet, kicked me with his boots, I could stand for it no longer, and I went away to my aunt, my mother's sister, crying that he was going to kill me if they didn't take me away from him. Aunt took me by the hand and led me back to the shop and began to curse Mayre for his troubles.

I remember the argument between my aunt and Mayre— "If you beat him that way you'll kill him," Aunt said to him. "If he won't receive a beating, he'll never learn the trade," Mayre answered. Nobody learns the trade without being beaten. I was beaten by my journeyman tailor, was his argument. All of us are. Whoever heard of learning a trade without being beaten. It can't be done. And my aunt left me at Mayre's, tacitly agreeing that beating me was part of the training necessary for my becoming a tailor.

I remember once we took work at home for a Saturday night. Mayre and I were working until late at night. Some pair of sleeves that I made didn't suit him as to workmanship and he beat me, beat me hard. Goldie, his wife, was present. She couldn't stand to see him beat me so hard so she took me away from him, put her arms around me, shielded me, and somehow my sentiments responded to hers; I felt a great sense of gratitude and friendship for Goldie and before I fell asleep that night I was thinking of Goldie, and was very envious of Mayre that he was sleeping with her. I imagined myself in his place, had a feeling that she would have responded to me. The sex urge occurred over and over again, went all through me, and subsequently, when Goldie and I looked at each other, I was under the impression that we had a union of thought and that according to the Mosaic law I had then and there violated the commandment, Thou shalt not covet thy neighbor's wife.

I remember in those years and even before, my sense of sympathy and pity were very much on the alert. When one of our peasant neighbors used to beat his wife, or a big boy beat up a smaller one, or a little girl was beaten up by her father or mother, and I happened to be present, every blow was registered on me the same as on the victim and my sense of resentment was at white heat, only I felt myself helpless to do anything about it. In the case of females, when they were beaten, my sense of resentment always associated itself in the way that I would like to take them away from the brute, caress their wounds, and somehow or other, the sex sense always came uppermost in my mind and translated itself in terms of abandoning myself sexually to them. Sex relationships formulated themselves in my mind as something I would give because I would need to give to those beaten and ill-treated.

The sense of resentment was growing on me. Mayre became more and more convinced that the only hope there was for my learning the trade was to get me to pay more attention to my work and since I was absentminded, and thought of other things besides my work, as he suspected I was thinking how to use my gab, so the only hope for me was more and more beatings, until one day he beat me so much that I made up my mind, I'll leave him. It was no good to go to Aunt again; I tried that and it didn't do any good, so I thought I would go back home to the village. There wasn't much hope for me to learn the trade with Mayre anyway. All that suffering was to no purpose. He didn't teach me much and he only beat me. So on a certain morning when it must have been several degrees below zero, I ran away home.

The distance between the town and village was about twenty miles. I had no overcoat, my shoes were torn, the cotton jacket I had on me gave me very little protection from the frost and wind. But I felt that it was all right; I would rather be frozen to death than killed by Mayre. After I was running for about six or seven miles in one breath, as they say, I was exhausted and began to slow up my speed. For the next two miles I was walking slower, the chill went all through me, my ears, nose, and face were quite frozen, ears red and swollen, nose, and cheeks red and swollen, and my feet smarted painfully while freezing, my wind gone considerably, my strength ebbed and gone down to zero.

It was then that a peasant with a pair of horses came along. He didn't belong to our village but to a village next to ours some two and a half miles distance. "Jew," he said to me, "you're going to be frozen on the way." "I suppose I will be," I told him. He took pity on me, took me up on the wagon, and sat down on me to cover me with his big fur coat. He says he is sitting on me in order that I may warm up under the weight of it, first on my feet, then on my back, but I was so cold and frozen that I didn't come to quick enough to suit him. "Get down and run," he said to me, "run with all your might because you'll be frozen if you don't."

So in between running after the wagon, having him sit on me with his fur coat in the wagon, and after an all-day's traveling, he brought me to a Jewish family, in the village of

Bloschintz, who knew my people. It is my understanding that I was brought there unconscious. Rivike was the name of the Jewish woman there. She and my mother were great friends; she was very poor. Her husband had one foot and one arm paralyzed. They lived nearly on charity, on what members of the noble family donated to them for service by way of trading for the nobility.

When the peasant brought me in to Laib's house, Rivike felt for me just as much as my mother would have. She rubbed my hands and feet with snow; she then covered me up with every bit of warm clothing there was in the house, warmed up milk and gave it to me, and washed me and worked around me all night through. She cried all night. The way she expressed it, it wasn't me she was crying after, but Malke's son; that Malke's son should come to such a pass was the constant refrain of her sympathy and suffering.

In the morning she hired a peasant who took me home wrapped up in quilts and clothes of all kinds. I was sick in bed for about two months. After this experience the entire family agreed that while Mayre was a brute I wasn't altogether innocent and that I must have been very stubborn to cause Mayre to beat me the way he did, and I suppose I was.

The family fortunes in those years—I must have been then about twelve or twelve and a half—were very low indeed. There was very little work for Father to do; we had very little merchandise in the store to sell and what little we had our neighbors, the peasants, seemed to have no use for.

There were additional misfortunes befalling our family. The wife of my oldest brother, who had been married only a year and a half or so, had a baby. They lived with us. My brother was recruited in the army and ran away, was caught, and there was a serious threat that he would go to the punitive regiment, where he was almost sure to be killed because of the very severe treatment by way of incarceration and physical punishment that the soldiers were subjected to in that regiment. In order to save Brother from what my poor father and mother considered almost a death sentence, it was necessary to have a couple of hundred rubles to bribe the authorities and get him out, as they called it.

The family had a little interest in the town house, we had hypothecated it with a loan shark, we sold the merchandise from the store for half its value, got loans from all our friends and relatives, and succeeded in bribing the officials so that my brother would not be sent to the punitive regiment, but in doing all that we so stripped our home that there remained nothing to live on and we were obliged to go back to the city and have Father and myself go back to work for the firm where my father worked before we left for the village.

All things considered, I was better off in the village than in town. I couldn't become a fine tailor; my needle was still screaming, my fingers were sweating, and the very fine work it was necessary to do in the city was beyond my possible capacities. The extreme religious discipline and atmosphere of the city were not to my liking, and besides, we were extremely poor. We shared a room with another family that was very crowded, almost no place to sleep.

By that time I was already twelve and a half years old and considered myself a burden on the shoulders of the family, for whom life was hard enough without me. I will go away and leave the family, I thought; I know something of tailoring and what I don't know, I will still learn; I will try and get work in shops that make cheap merchandise where they will not exact such fine sewing; even if I am not able to make a living, I haven't any right to impose myself on my sick father and my overworked mother, especially in such times of stress and distress.

I had a cousin in Fastov, a ladies' tailor, and it was to that cousin I made up my mind to go. He may be able to employ me, and if not, he'll probably find something for me. I had no money for railroad fare; shoes were torn, practically no laundry and no clothes other than those on my back. But I thought, I'll go anyway; I was told that a kid like myself could hide under the benches in Pullman cars, [that] normally the people in the railway car would sympathize with a kid and would cover him up with some clothes or put bags around him so that they would hide him from the conductor, which was true. The people in the car, mostly Jews, going to Kiev, which lay along the same route, beyond Fastov, did advise me to get under a bench and put a lot of handbags and stuff all around me so that I thought I was safe. One of the passengers was a Gentile who evidently thought that I ought to pay my fare and he informed the conductor that I was hiding under a bench. The conductor pulled me out, asked me whether I had any money, and when I told him I didn't, he wouldn't believe me, searched me carefully, both through my pockets and on the body, and when he found that I had no money he promised to have me locked up in Fastov but evidently didn't want to bother with me, for when we came to Fastov, he gave me a kick and threw me off.

My cousin David would have kept me and employed me, though I must confess that I wasn't of very much help to him in the shop. My fingers sweated, my needle screamed, and the people in the shop had a great deal of fun. But David's wife, who was not related to me except by marriage, saw no reason why his relatives should be helped, since her relatives did not get a share of the same kind of bounty. And so I was obliged to leave.

Kiev, the capital of the province, was my next destination, a city of some 200,000 population, but Kiev was a city where Jews were not allowed, especially a Jew that had no passport. But I took a chance. Nothing was worse than to go back home, so I came to Kiev in the same way as I did to Fastov, under a bench, covered up by the passengers, with their clothes and handbags and what not. There were two cousins living in Kiev, both of whom I had never seen. Neither of them knew of my existence; both of them sympathized with me but could give me very little help, since under the law it wasn't legal for a family to furnish shelter to anybody illegally residing in Kiev.

Under the laws of Russia, no man could leave his birthplace without taking with him a birth certificate which served as a passport in travel. So, when I finally came to Kiev it was necessary for me to first register myself by showing my passport. I had no passport. Government documents could only be secured by paying for them, and one had to spend much time in getting them. Since I had no money, I could not make application for a certificate, and so took no passport along on leaving home. All my relatives could not very well shelter me without endangering their freedom and right to live in Kiev at all. There was one way out of my difficulty. One might bribe the local officials, but that sort of bribery required more money than I could raise. I was, in fact, penniless, and so found myself in a big city among strangers, with a constant feeling of Golus hovering over my head, surrounded by strangers and enemies with no place to be. I could get food from my relatives—perhaps they would have permitted me to sleep with them—but I was afraid to subject them to such a risk and refused to stay with them.

My first night in Kiev was spent at my cousin's blacksmith shop without his knowledge of my being there. His shop was simply a shed outside in a yard; while some of the tools were locked away, the shed itself had even no door, and its boards were mostly rotted away, or knocked out of the walls. I came in late at night, after walking through the city for a long time, and fell asleep in a corner there. Even before lodging there, I looked a sight, and the dirt and soot there finished my unrespectable appearance. So, dirty, unwashed, I went out to look for a job in the morning. I was then little over twelve, dressed very raggedly and of an extreme thinness, encrusted with dirt, and haunted by fear of any passers-by, especially of policemen who might ask me for my passport. It was, therefore, not surprising that most tailor shops turned me down, but after a long day's search I was finally hired.

I was told by this particular tailor that I wasn't greatly needed, but he had five small children, his wife was kept busy with a stand on the market-place selling cooked beans, and the children had to be taken care of in her absence. He thought I might make a nurse to these children and also carry the pails of beans to and from the market-place. He promised to teach me tailoring while I was employed with these other jobs of freight carrier and nurse. I was to have no money for my work, but I was promised free making of my clothes if my parents would send cloth to me. However, on inquiry, he discovered I had no passport and promptly said he could not keep me at all without it.

For two weeks, I stayed, jobless, in Kiev. I slept wherever I could. Sometimes a poor tailor would let me sleep in his shop; sometimes I would wander around all night and sleep during the day at my cousin's; sometimes I had to beg for food where I looked for work. By that time I was covered with vermin, completely exhausted, and in despair left Kiev for Wasilkow in order to visit an uncle of mine, my mother's brother, who was fairly well-to-do, in the hope that he might place me somewhere.

My uncle received me very generously; made me some clothes, cleaned me up, and kept me there for two weeks—but no tailor could be found who wanted an apprentice and I had to go home to Belayacerkow. At home, conditions were somewhat bettered. Father had gotten work, and took me as a helper. Not long afterwards, things again became very difficult for us. Both myself and Father could only get partial employment and did not earn enough to live on. We then planned that the whole family go to Kiev, which we did.

In Kiev, Father did find work for my brother, himself, and myself, but after living in Kiev for half a year, there was a pogrom, or riot against the Jews by the Gentiles.* Times were then very bad. The poor population was suffering great

* In the spring of 1881.

hardship and there were a great many unemployed. Wages were very low; even when there was employment they were very low. Unrest and dissatisfaction were general, and in order to allay this unrest, the Gentile government found it politic to blame the Jews for the general poverty—the Jews, they said, were aliens taking work away from the Gentiles, by cheating and thievery. Fanatical priests aided this feeling against the Jews—the Jews were heathens and Christ-killers, they cried—Russia was a holy land, Kiev was a holy city, the Jews contaminated the country, contaminated the city. "Drive them out," these priests cried, "get rid of them."

While the wealthier Gentiles did not want to do this themselves, the more ignorant and poor were only too ready to riot against the Jews. Bands of Russians assaulted the Jewish quarters, broke out doors and windows, destroyed all the furnishings, and stole whatever could be of any use to them. Not all the Russians participated in these pogroms. Some even sympathized with the Jews and sheltered and fed them—but comparatively, these were only a few. In those days it was not safe for a Gentile family to so befriend a Jew, accursed as they were. There were cases where Gentile homes were fired because the owners had sheltered Jews.

Those who participated in the pogroms were mostly drunk, since the first buildings to be wrecked were saloons owned by Jews. The vodka found there was speedily consumed, so that before the pogrom was a day old, most of the rioters were drunk, and completely unresponsible for their conduct. A number of Jews were killed, there were innumerable cases of rape, property was either stolen or destroyed, and the Jewish population was completely terrorized. The building we lived in and the place we worked in were assaulted at the same time. Mother ran for her life while we struggled for ours; we were all separated by the mob—the shop was destroyed, the goods carried away, and we all looked to find shelter with a Gentile family.

I hid myself in a clay hole in an old brickyard on a hillside. Below, in the valley, was a large Jewish population. On the hill lived those whom we had lived among, and while in the clay hole, I witnessed the mob coming down the hill to assault the Jewish settlement. I saw children and old people beaten—buildings burned—I heard women screaming—it was an experience that one never can forget. After [I had been] four hours in that clay hole, the mob returned up the hill. One of the drunkards pulled me out of my hole. I pleaded for life and was finally thrown to the ground and released. My impression is that I ran continuously for at least five hours on the highway until exhaustion. I stopped at the house of a peasant Gentile family along the road. The women in the house had heard of the pogrom, took pity on me, gave me cabbage soup and bread, and put me to sleep in the attic.

The old peasant was very religious, and considered it a great sin to do violence to the Jews, and said he would stay up all night to watch so that no rioters could snatch me away. Over and over again, during the night, I heard people pass asking in loud voices whether Jews did not live here. Always the old man, with a great many oaths, declared there were no Jews at his house. When they persisted, the peasant woman came to her husband's aid, crossing herself again and again, swearing there were no Jews at her home. At two in the morning, I heard someone climb the ladder to the attic, and was almost certain there was someone after me. Every sense and conception of pain and torture at the hands of drunken Gentiles formed in my mind until these climbers started to prowl around in the darkness and to talk among themselves. Then I knew they were Jews like myself.

These people had been permitted to come in by the Gentile peasant, also. After considerable consultation on the part of the family and myself, we all agreed that we Jews must leave before sunrise since we had already troubled the farmer enough, and it would be dangerous to leave in broad daylight. So in the early morning, before light, we went out. One of the men told us that the governor of the state had assigned a powder cellar on the church hill to the refugee Jews, and that if we circled around the town carefully avoiding the roads on which the peasants usually traveled, we might evade the drunken populace and safely get to this underground cellar. This family of Jews had little ones with them who could travel only slowly and I made up my mind to run ahead of them.

I finally caught up with a group of pilgrims who were traveling on the road towards the church mecca—Kiev was considered a holy city. One of its large churches, called Lavra, contained some holy relics from the original crucifix, and so was considered by the populace a sacred place. People would come to this church on foot for hundreds and thousands of miles, and this group of peasants which I had caught up with were pilgrims traveling from a distant estate some thousands of miles away. I told them my story and asked them for protection and food, which I was given. I remember an interesting discussion I had with these people in reference to myself. "You son of a Christ-killer," one of them said, "God forgive us—" But they did have sympathy with me, and permitted me to travel along. Along the road, we passed a brickyard where there were several of the *pogrom-schikies* (rioters), all drunk, but all let us alone save for one man who recognized me as a Jew, cursed tremendously, and followed our train, but was too drunk to keep up with us, and so did no harm.

The powder cellar was a cave probably a thousand feet long and about three hundred feet wide. There were three or four of these cellars wherein were crowded the refugee Jews of Kiev, about ten thousand souls and more. The government had assigned a regiment of soldiers to guard these people against assault on the part of the rioters. Army kettles were put up in the open air on short notice and army food was hurriedly cooked—army bread supplied—and we all lived there until the heat of the riotous populace had subsided. We stayed there for about ten days and then returned to our destroyed homes. There was famine, after these riots, among the Jews. No work, no food, and very poor shelter. We lay around on dirt floors with not even necessities available.

The riots took place in May and during the next six months there was a great deal of suffering until word was received that a commission had been formed in Paris called "Alliance of Israel," which had collected enough money from the Jews of Europe, and other parts of the world, to transport large numbers—thousands of families—from pogrom-infested districts to America. This commission had established headquarters in the city of Brod [Brody] in Galicia, just across the Russian border in Austrian Poland. It was said that Jews coming there would be supplied with money with which to come to America, as well as their most immediate needs.

Some forty rubles was needed for railway fare from Kiev to Brod. Our family sold a sewing machine which had not been destroyed in the pogrom for twelve rubles, sold whatever clothing could be spared—even some from our very backs—relatives were taxed to capacity, and the forty rubles was collected. We came to Brod without an extra kopek, with little personal effects, I barefooted even. In Brod we found a mob of thousands of people. It took us six weeks before we succeeded in registering for the committee. These six weeks were weeks of starvation.

The people of Brod were extremely poor; labor was almost of no value, and Father and I worked for mere life, and only occasionally would we find a day's work. Mother offered to help in kitchens, wash clothes, anything for bread and lodging, but work was very scarce. My oldest brother could hardly find work. The most helpless were the two youngsters, my brother's nine-year-old son, and my youngest brother, only two years old. I was standing on street corners begging for a kreutzer. Some days I did get enough to buy bread for the young ones. Some days Mother would bring some home. We slept with a poor family, paying very little for our shelter. While our experience with poverty was nothing new, the six weeks in Brod were probably the most horrible, up to that time, we had yet experienced. The entire population was hungry, as well as all the emigrant mob.

For a few days we had work gathering potatoes. For this, we received as wages twelve kreutzer for the young ones and eighteen for the adults. A kreutzer was worth two-fifths of a cent. These were golden days for us there in Brod. Bread was not high and we lived on that alone. The rest of our pennies went for shelter. But we felt few of these lucky days.

Dr. Saffir, who had charge of the commission, took notice of my father in the crowd. Father was a hunchback. His clothes were very shabby and torn; his appearance was the last word in human misery; and so the doctor stopped to talk with him. He inquired as to his needs and found that he was stranded with a family, wanting to go to America, with his needle as his trade. He said Mother was a hatmaker, the boys tailors, that if we got to America we could all earn a living, that we had nothing to live on in Brod.

Dr. Saffir gave Father fifteen gulden at once and an order on the commission to be taken to America with his family with the first transport to leave. Ours was about the third transport leaving the city of Brod, and our starvation was ended right then and there. Donations were given us all along the road. The Jewish communities we passed were generous. Lembrich,* Breslau, Berlin, Hamburg, and Liverpool all helped. The city of Liverpool furnished food and clothing for the entire transport.

* Possibly Lemberg (Lvov).

2

Finally we landed in New York, and were stationed in a boarding house that gave us so much meat to eat that I was sick for three days. It was the first meal there. I remember that I could not then conceive of how anyone could actually get more meat than he could eat. After we cleaned up one serving, we would get another and another until I had eaten myself sick. It was the first time that the cloud that was hanging on my mind about food all through my life—what would I get in my next meal?—had somewhat cleared away. I cannot say that I have ever lost that feeling about food, but it did somewhat lessen right then on first coming to New York. America was to me a land where there was no czar and, therefore, no restriction by punishment on fighting and murder amongst people—a land where people stood on their heads—was it not on the opposite side of the globe?

The American committee then formed to take care of the

emigrants had distributed the families all over the United States where there were Jews to be found in October, 1881. Our family along with four other families, all tailors by trade, were sent to Atlanta, Georgia, and were there provided for with rooms, furniture, house utensils, and such other things as we needed—besides money enough to live on until we found work. We found work practically within the first week there.

Father and I were given work with a Jewish tailor; my oldest brother was employed in a bottle shop where he filled bottles with some sort of soft drink. Mother took care of the children at home. Father was paid $10.00 a week, I, still an apprentice, got only $1.00 a week, Brother got $3.50 in the bottle shop—so together we brought $14.50 home every week.

From this amount, we paid $2.25 for rent, for rooms in the barracks. There was in Atlanta an entire section of the city where a great many barracks had been built during the Civil War, about three miles from the City Hall, at the extreme end of the city. It was here that we had rented three rooms. Our neighbors were Negroes and poor white trash. Our employer was very pleased with Father's work, but Brother and myself did not fare so well. My hand still sweated, the needle screamed, and my attention to my work was very lax. I was not able to concentrate on my tailoring.

My workmanship was poor and I was finally fired after a three months' trial. While working with Father, I had no opportunity to learn English at all, since our employer was a Jew and we talked Jewish both in the shop and at home. But when I lost my job, the deacon of the Jewish synagogue advised me to go to Chattanooga, Tennessee, a city about a hundred miles from Atlanta, where his brother was a chief of police, and he promised this brother would find me a job. He then gave me a letter to his brother. Mother, who had saved some money, gave me railroad fare and five dollars besides, along with some clothes, and I left for Chattanooga.

I was very well received by Mr. Schwartz, a Hungarian

Jew, who was the chief of police of Chattanooga, and he found a job for me with an English tailor, to whom I was apprenticed out for a dollar a week and my board. I worked for this tailor five months and during that time learned to speak English. I had practically no one in town to speak Jewish to and I learned English quickly because of that.

I had also improved greatly in workmanship as a tailor, nothing to brag of, but very much better than I had been. My employer treated me kindly. His wife, who used to work along with him, and her sister took a great interest in me, teaching me the trade and the manners and behavior of the Americans as well as their language. I cannot recall that period without a sense of appreciation of the kindness of those people.

As I recall, I was quite a raw youngster. There was a Negro hired girl working for the tailor and since the atmosphere was antagonistic to Negroes, I think I excelled more than any other member of the family with meanness and contempt. A great many years have since passed and I have not yet lost my sense of regret for my treatment of that poor girl—it stands out as almost the only case of regret I have had in life.

Mother was very much dissatisfied in Atlanta. There was no place where she could buy kosher meat, nor was there any Orthodox synagogue in town where Father could pray, and so it was her ambition to move to a city where a larger Jewish community could be found, so she might be able to practise her religion thoroughly.

So after nine months in Atlanta, [when] Mother had saved about a hundred dollars, [she] wrote me to return so we could all go to Chicago, and I returned. We got to Chicago in about July, 1882, and rented three rooms over at Canal and Twelfth streets. There were then cloak factories in Chicago who sent work out to tailors to be made up at home. They furnished the cloth, cut and trimmed, and the samples to be copied, and we would carry the cloth home to make up there. These were the first sweatshops established by the Jew-

47

ish immigrants in Chicago. I was to do the machine sewing, Father the hand sewing, with Mother's help, and Brother, who was very incompetent in tailoring, was doing odd jobs such as pressing and a little sewing.

As time went on, we engaged helpers so that we employed six or seven people all told. The mode of getting the work was something in this fashion: a number of people would come to the factory to get work to take home. The superintendent of the factory would put a sample on a figure and would consult everybody as to what should be paid for making it. Normally there was not enough work to go round, so each of the tailors would bid rock-bottom in order to get the work at all. In a number of cases, the bidding was done away with. The employer simply offered bundles and paid for them after they were completed, just as little as he saw fit. We would be obliged to wait for hours at the factory before the employer would notice us at all.

The employers were very particular and it was very difficult to satisfy them as to workmanship. Over and over again we would get the work back for resewing to suit the whim of the boss, or [the] examiners. Ladies' garments was a seasonal trade and during the busy season we worked day and night with very little let-up for sleep. Again in slack seasons, we had nothing to do and no income. Our earnings were very small. The whole family could only earn in those early years twelve or fifteen dollars a week in season about six months of the year.

We lived in a building in the rear of a lot, above a stable. The building in front contained a store downstairs, where there was a rag shop. The owners lived upstairs. Both front and rear buildings and the yard were full of rags, junk, rats, and vermin, besides manure from the horses. It was an old frame shack, dilapidated beyond belief. Our first years of immigrant life were not happy for us.

Since I was better acquainted with English than the rest of the family and since I was now a good machine operator,

48

which is the major portion of the work to be done on ladies' garments, I became the most important member of the family. I went downtown to get the work, to speak to the designer, I went to buy machines, organized the shop, assigned the work, and so early, before I was fifteen, had the whole family under my direction, as well as the shop. Everybody looked up to me because I was so easily able to get work and speak English, to manage the shop, and to bring home money enough to live on. I worked very hard, occasionally up to the point of exhaustion. Sewing machines were then driven by foot-power, and it was only after the machine sewing was done that the others could work. So I had to supply everybody with work and I worked very hard.

At fifteen I first began to learn to read. Both in Jewish and English. I learned English from signs and from advertisements I looked at during the slack period of the trade. Jewish I learned when there was no work and a man who peddled Jewish stories loaned them out weekly to me for five cents a week. He persuaded me to learn to read these stories because they were great romances. An agent of a Jewish newspaper got me to subscribe to a weekly paper. In those years I was very ignorant. I practically knew nothing of what was happening in the United States, and outside of my work and family experiences, knew very little. The Jewish stories I read opened my eyes to new worlds. A man named Shomer wrote a great many Jewish romances copied from the French with a change only of names and habits from the French to the Jewish. He wrote a great many of them and I would read three or four a week, absorb their contents enthusiastically and eagerly.

The stories went like this: a poor girl, but very beautiful, talented, fell in love with a rich young man, whose parents would not permit a marriage. Tragedy would follow. The boy would talk of suicide, the girl was miserable, until something happened where the girl was found to really be an heiress, the family smiled on her, they married and lived happily ever after. In a great many of them, there was an intriguing character who would cause either the boy or girl to distrust the other by false tale-bearing. He would be found out in his lies, and the differences were patched up again. Some tales of adventure and enterprise, but most of them about romantic love, the difficulties besetting the path of love, the difficulties ensuing, marriage, and everlasting happiness. But for me these were great finds. When there was no work I read them day and night and would tell about them to any who would listen.

A boy friend of mine took me to Halsted and Harrison streets, where a company of actors played stock drama. Here, for ten cents, on a Saturday afternoon, our one day of rest, I would enter a new world. I waited all week for Saturday to come around. I knew how to read English only slightly. I learned it very slowly. Occasionally I would decipher advertisements distributed on bills in our neighborhood. On these ads there were pictures of the wares to be sold and so I was able to associate the English word with the picture next to it.

These were the years when I first got personal possession of money. When I went to the factory to get my pay for the week, Mother would never know just how much I would get, so I was able to hold out fifty cents or a dollar without anyone knowing the difference. A friend of mine, a carpenter's son, a boy of about sixteen, first suggested that we visit a whore house. I had [had] a sex urge for years before, but was never able to buy satisfaction before. Now, with money, I was able to have my first experience in a whore house. This first experience left such a mark on my mind that I visited those places regularly once or twice a week after. My attitude of mind in connection with that experience, even in those early years, was different from the attitude of most men to whom I have spoken about it.

As I have noted in relating my story, I have formed no sense of sex morality. Even when I was only nine or ten years old, I used to hear the peasants, particularly the men and sometimes the women, speak about their sex relationships with no sense of taboo, a matter-of-fact daily experience of life. The same was true when I worked in a shop and the young men, who were unmarried, used to relate their experiences in whore houses. They described the processes to each other; the fever, the nature of approach and conduct on the part of themselves and the whores they were with, without any compunction. So I had acquired a morality similar to theirs. The problem with me was not whether I ought to do it at all, but the opportunity to get a chance at it was my difficulty.

Amongst Jews, it was absolutely impossible for a young kid like myself to have an opportunity to play, even, with girls; not to speak of staying with them, and it was only after I had money of mine that I could think of attempting some such experience at all. But I did have very strongly developed a sense of human morality, not a sex morality, but a human relation morality.

I, for instance, felt a very strong sense of friendship to the prostitute I first had my experience with. I remember I asked her whether or not she liked me to play with her, and she said, "You are a nice boy—you are nice to me," and I felt a sense of relief. The fact that I was paying her for it did not seem to interfere at all with my sense of intimate friendship and gratitude, nor did it interfere with my desire to make her reciprocate in that friendship. I even remember that she had noticed that attitude and she laughed a little and said, "You are a queer boy. You seem to like me. Will you come again?" I thought—naturally I'll come again—and at the same time I thought that on her part the invitation might have been inspired by the thought of the money she might get rather than by her desire to have me. I asked her about it— again she laughed and said, "You are friendly to me. You seem to be interested in my well-being. Why would I not enjoy our friendship?"

When, afterwards, I told my friends of my experience, they

laughed and said to me, "She's a prostitute. Don't believe her. She's a liar. She doesn't care for you. You're simply a customer to her." And that doubt worried me considerably. There was another doubt, too, that worried me, and that was that my friendship and my passion were not naturally and intimately related. Next week when I went again, another girl attracted my attention, and the opportunity to have a new experience was for the purpose of sex relationships stronger than my desire to meet the same girl for whom I had had that feeling of friendship. That girl had said, "No, you won't come again. You'll want some other girl." At that time, I had not understood the meaning of her remark. She associated human interests and friendship with sex passion, and in her mind my desire for her was the only reason for any human interest, while I thought, in turn, in a completely different fashion. I saw no reason why either sex relations or friendship was limited to one person; that while as a matter of fact when I went to another girl I was not then keeping my promise to come to her again, I wasn't violating my own convictions on the nature of my attitude to do both to the satisfaction of passion and friendship.

In those years I was highly sexed. I think I almost constantly thought about it. Every experience stood out vividly in my mind; the problem and mystery of life where life and life meet on such intimate terms, the nature of the response to the approach, the actual mechanics of the situation, constantly charged my thoughts and were always accompanied with a sense of friendship, of admiration, and of yearning. I was interested in different nationalities, in differently aged women, and always really anxious to reciprocate and give them pleasure and satisfaction to the same degree I was pleased and satisfied. There was in me a complete absence of a sense of taboo as regards the sex act itself, and a very strong charge with regard to my spiritual relationships, along with my fever and passion.

I remember once I found myself in this discordant situation. I had made friendly approaches to a Jewish prostitute who was quite young, not more than seventeen, who liked me very much, and whom I liked very much. I told her so. She then naturally asked me the same question that most of the girls asked, "Will you come again?" I said, "I might, and might not. Some other girl might attract me. But you don't care," I said to her, "you are only interested in money."

The girl got quite angry and wanted to slap me and then began to cry. "Don't you think I need any friends? Don't you think you've made me like you by your behavior? Besides you're a nice clean fellow. I love to stay with you. Honestly I don't mind the money so much. I'd love to have you as my steady and my friend. Sometimes I get into trouble and I need a friend very badly. That's why us girls take pimps. We know that they don't care for us, but in return for money, they at least pretend to be our friends. They do take an interest in us and when we are in trouble, they come to our help. They don't lose any money on us but money don't count. We need someone to take an interest in us and here you come to me, say you like me, enjoy staying with me, try to evoke a feeling of friendship on my part to you—pretend to be a friend of mine, and then say you don't care if you cut if off— go to someone else. You're queer. You're either crazy or a damned liar."

And I must confess that this sermon worried me a great deal. Either human nature was discordant or something was definitely wrong; since my real nature and my best intentions were messed up so woefully, with no opening by which to reach out for the truth. I finally formed the resolution to be loyal and to visit the same girl regularly. For several months I did until I found in the same house some girl that attracted me from the point of view of desire very strongly and I broke my resolutions. I was very much worried and felt a great sense of contempt for myself.

As we developed efficiency in the shop, we increased our

earning capacities, moved into larger quarters, bought more sewing machines and press-irons, taught more of our immigrant neighbors the trade, until we had a shop employing ten or twelve people. In those years, our earning capacity increased materially. At sixteeen, I was quite a contractor, making women's clothes. With money saved, we sent for my oldest brother and his family, also for some of our relatives, cousins, etc. We also acquired quite a reputation for efficiency with both the manufacturers and our immigrant neighbors. Our chief concern was to make money. If any of the shops introduced any innovation in production, to make the work better or faster, information about it was distributed among the workers very rapidly. If any of the shops produced more than others, those which failed to keep up with it were very jealous. Competition among the small shop-keepers was very severe.

Immigrants came in almost daily and were mainly Russian Jews. While most of us were very ignorant about the United States and its people, yet some light did penetrate our lives. Peddlers used to come in from the country and tell us how prosperous the American farmer was; junk and rag peddlers spoke of the fine streets at some distance from our neighborhood. The nature of the population was described by those peddlers. They were Irish, German, French, English, and a sprinkling of Bohemian; men who bought old junk in factories used to speak of the big shops where hundreds of people were working, both on wood and on metal. Someone related in the neighborhood that there was a big store over on State and Adams called the Fair Store, where merchandise was sold much cheaper than in our neighboring stores, and so we dared to go as far as State Street to shop.

At that time, the entire neighborhood seldom went three or four blocks out of their familiar ways. We were not surrounded by neighbors any too friendly. In our immediate neighborhood, the population was Irish. There were a number of Irish saloons, and most of the time a great many men hung around saloons. Parents would not allow their children out of sight. Occasionally children were beaten up by children of our neighbors. Jews with whiskers were continuously assaulted as they went along. They were stoned; in winter snowballs were thrown at them; and some of the street bums would run by, pull their beards, and beat them. When a Jew moved a block or two away from the immediate congested neighborhood, his neighbors considered it an innovation, and the youngsters would stone the windows of his home, beat up his children, and sometimes even make their lives unsafe. Almost every move that our people made west or south, the people among whom we moved would resent it vigorously.

As I remembered, our Irish neighbors were not much richer than ourselves. They were mostly laborers; the only point to their advantage was that they were older immigrants and knew more about America. There was practically no sense of hospitality towards the Jews, and the opinion was common among the Jews that here too they were in Golus. Our neighbors hated us, and as we say, our lives and property were not safe. It was only after some years that our people learned the nature and significance of American institutions. We found that, at least under the law, we had equal rights, and that our neighbors were not all hostile. Some did not hate us at all. We could find justice with nearly all the police and in the courts, so as time went on, and our population increased, we found courage enough to resent the abuses we were subjected to. We would get together a number of the younger men and show fight when sneered at, or called Sheeney, or assaulted.

I remember innumerable fights in the ghetto streets between Irish rowdies and our own rowdies and more respectable members. When the Irish won, it wasn't safe to show your face on the street for almost a week, but their victory would last only a short time. Our resentment grew. We would talk of it in the shops, in the synagogues, and on every possible occasion of assembly, as at parties, marriages, etc. I remember at one time our group was very large and we were quite determined, so we beat hell out of them, and then it was these fellows who did not feel safe on the ghetto street. After a few such lessons, the atmosphere was greatly cleared. It is true that here and there a Jew was beaten up when found alone; in one case a Jewish watchman was murdered by hoodlums, but these cases were rare. Life in glass windows was a great deal safer. The opinion of our people as to being in Golus was greatly modified.

In those early days most of our people were as religious as when they were in Russia. Houses were fixed up with synagogue paraphernalia; the day of rest was observed each week on the Sabbath, as in Russia. We would pray at the synagogue faithfully, and lived very much a secluded life. But the influence of American civilization did penetrate somewhat, especially where Jews had to make a living outside our immediate group.

As to myself, I acclimatized myself soon. My five months in Chattanooga had made quite a Yankee out of me. They almost completely wiped out every sense of affiliation with my people from the point of view of religion and other Orthodox habits. My outlook was American in spirit and I was hungry to find out more and more what America might mean to me. I spoke to as many country peddlers as I could find. They would tell me about the people in the farms and villages they peddled with, or would tell about the people in the factories or shops outside of the ghetto district.

I even dared on a certain Saturday to go along with a Jewish woodworker into the lumber and woodworking district and was astonished at the kind of machinery they used in the lumber yards. One day I traveled all through the stockyards along with a man who used to work there. The firm of Nelson and Morris offered to employ a great many immigrant Jews, so many of us worked in the yards. Some of our next-door neighbors worked in the stockyards. They would come home reeking fearfully, but we did not consider this too bad.

The significant thing was to have a job at all. A steady job was a man's index to social position. A man who found a job didn't only find a job for himself, but he found an opening for other Jews, and the subject of industry and jobs was a great item of conversation among all families.

Business was even a larger item of conversation. Earning capacities were daily estimated. It was said in the neighborhood that a certain peddler had earned six dollars in one day, and everybody talked of it. A certain grocer made lots of money and we all wanted to go into the grocery business. Some of our people even dared to open shops of their own. One made a mattress factory, another a cap shop, a number of our girls went downtown to work on making neckties. Earnings were constantly being figured. Each increase was talked over and over.

All information was common property and everybody was hungry for information about this country and its people, especially about business and labor and making money. Almost none of the American culture penetrated into our ghetto settlement; no one was able to read English, so there were no American newspapers in our neighborhood. Our immediate neighbors, the Irish, did not mix with us much, so what we acquired by way of culture was almost completely that of our own, except that some of us received some of it when we went out from the ghetto district.

The relation between Mother and me was very strained. Already way back at the age of eleven, when we lived in the peasant community in Russia, Mother found me to be anything but regular. You may recall the experience I had with the Gypsy girl. The kid told that story to her mother and her mother in turn told it to other peasantry in the community, and the women had a great laugh on Malke and her kid. When they came in to shop in our little store they couldn't miss the fun and told that story to Mother.

After they left, Mother took me to task. "You know it is

forbidden," she said, "and that you are so young and she is both Gentile and a Gypsy. Why did you do it?" I knew it was forbidden, but I didn't understand the reason why it was forbidden and the sense of taboo controlled neither my action nor my thought, so that I told her frankly that I didn't know why I did except that I wanted to do it very much. And she wanted to know whether I thought I ought to do everything I wanted to. And when I told her yes, since I saw no reason why I shouldn't, she looked at me and I noticed a great deal of pain and suffering. Tears came into her eyes. "God punishes me for my sins," she said. "I'm raising a Goy and a good-for-nothing."

She then tried to explain to me that it was written in the Holy Scroll that Jews and Gentiles should not mix and that boys are not allowed to play with girls, or girls with boys; that it was very vicious for a boy to do that; that I was particularly so young that she never heard a kid of my age who would dare to do that thing, especially a Jewish boy; that a thing like that may take place amongst the Goys because they had no religion, no morality, lived like beasts, but that I was born a Jewish child of Jewish parents; that God gave us the Scroll to guide our conduct into righteousness; that I disgraced myself, disgraced the family, and that God was going to punish me both in this world and in the next forever after.

She did that with a great deal of energy and a great deal of pathos; she was crying while she was speaking, spoke about my grandfather who was such a holy Jew, spoke about the fine behavior of all our relatives, made comparisons between the conduct of the Jews and that of the Gentiles—"You're going to grow up a drunkard, a thief, a good-for-nothing; I have raised you, I have worked for you and you are going to poison not only your own life but mine and your father's also." She bemoaned her fate over and over again to have had such a child. I sympathized with her but constantly wanted to understand the reason for my behavior.

Even in those years, young as I was, I couldn't find in my

own heart any cause for blaming myself. Ma says, I thought, that I was created by God. If that is so, I didn't create myself then. Why did he create me so that I wanted so intensely? What harm would it do anybody? The only trouble was that I didn't have the five kopeks, but if I did, I would have enjoyed myself, had a wonderful time with the girl. Ma was evidently not able to convince me that I had done something wrong. The fact that she was very much troubled, that she cried and suffered, didn't seem to me to be any reason why I should not have done it, since it wouldn't have hurt her or anyone else.

The argument that I owed it to her because she had raised me did not influence me at all. What did she raise me for, I thought, [if] not to get what I want? Only for trouble, and no enjoyment? To my notion, under those circumstances it would have been better if she hadn't raised me at all, and I wasn't sorry for what I did, and said so to Mother too, and that event left a strong impression both on me and Mother. Our relations were strained.

I loved her, it is true, loved her very much. Appreciated her kindness and devotion, was impressed by that, tried my best to emulate that, but in this item, she and I simply couldn't understand each other and we both felt a sense of strangeness. I was not the proper shape of the family block. Not necessarily vicious, because in other items Ma would understand and appreciate me. I was always very much worried for the family well-being; I wasn't lazy, helped Mother to work on the garden, or other housework, but in this one item, Mother thought, and I knew she was right, I was very much different than other children amongst the Jews.

On another occasion I ate a meal in our Gentile neighbor's house, which under the Jewish rule was *trafe*. Mother found out about that and was very much upset. She talked to me about that too. In her opinion, this was about the same kind of an offense as playing with the Gentile girl. "We're raising a Goy," she said to my father at mealtime; "we will never be forgiven by our Maker." And she cried very much. I couldn't say that I was not worried because Mother and Father were troubled on account of me, but since I couldn't understand the reason why I shouldn't partake of food that the peasants ate and lived on, I wasn't willing to give in, and told her so. It wouldn't have hurt her so much if I said that I'll not do it again, but the fact that I reasoned about it, explained to her that since God made me the way I was, that I wanted to eat and wanted to play that way. That sort of reasoning, in her judgment, was sinful, and I was a great tragedy in her life.

I, too, was troubled about myself. Why couldn't I be like other people? But I couldn't. Unless an argument appealed to me, I couldn't abide by it. All along through these years things happened which more and more strained the relationship between myself and my parents. My religion was not their religion, my morals were not their morals, but we did have a union of opinion on a great many other items, and naturally, I was their child, so that while I loved Mother very much and she loved me, we rubbed against each other's grains almost constantly. She was assertive in character; she was very kind; was always willing to go out of her way to do somebody a favor. Our neighbors, especially the Jews, looked up to her as a guide in life, paid much attention to what she said, consulted with her on very intimate items of life, and she had the habit and sense of authority so that these relations with her own child were, therefore, so much more painful. I was very much willing, and even anxious to please her, and did please her on a great many occasions, but when it came to an item of conscience, I always thought that she cannot be an authority for conduct where my own conscience tells me differently.

I think one reason was my sense of rebellion against the situation of Golus life. Why shouldn't we be like the Gentiles, I thought. Why should we be prosecuted, persecuted, and hunted all through life? No real reason for it even if we were better than they were. That was no reason why we should be different; we weren't essentially different. And therefore, I didn't give in to Mother's request. Here in America when I was even more independent than I was in Russia and smoked on Saturday, occasionally ate *trafe*, the wall between myself and my mother grew even taller than what it was when I was younger. The relations were more strained, we suffered more from each other, made each other's lives miserable. Father, too, didn't approve of my conduct, but he was much less assertive, much more tolerant, and occasionally we did have an opportunity to enjoy each other's company, in conversation and conduct, but everytime Mother and I talked, the rift between us was made wider.

On the day Mother discovered I was visiting houses of prostitution there was quite a tragedy in the house. Mother was actually laid up sick from the blow. She overheard young men in the shop talk about me. They said that I was too young to do such a thing, liable to get myself infected with disease. Along with the other items, that I wasn't religiously praying to God every day, that I was smoking on Saturday, and this, she thought, was the last thing that would lead me straight to hell. "And so young," she repeated, over and over again, "no one else's children are like that." "Explain him everything," she used to say, "isn't that an explanation—God doesn't want you to do it, and that's all. It's part of our commandments, it is the tradition of our people; isn't that enough explanation for you?" she asked with a sense of conviction and finality of which there was no appeal, and I couldn't say anything, I couldn't talk about it, I only knew she was wrong and I was right.

As our earnings increased, we began to live a little better than the way we formerly lived. We rented a bigger flat and while we still had a tailor shop in all the rooms, we weren't quite as crowded as formerly and we had enough room to enjoy some social life. The younger folks used to come together in our house, the boys would crack jokes, tell stories, and have social visits, and the girls used to sing Jewish songs and we used to have quite a nice time. Occasionally we used to do what we called square dancing, quadrilles, schottishes, and what was called the shears. I used to behave differently at those dances with the girls than the other boys. I was more forward with the girls, kissed them often, kissed them in the presence of others, and occasionally would be what the girls called rough, embraced them, squeezed them, felt their breasts, made them blush.

The girls used to slap me, call me a ruffian, said they hated me for my behavior, but I felt it wasn't so. Almost in every case when we were by ourselves, the attitude of the girls toward me was different from that of their attitude toward me in public. That used to make me very sore, gave me a great deal to think about. I used to call them hypocrites, liars, etc. I couldn't understand why if a girl would let me kiss her when we were by ourselves and even let me embrace her, feel her breasts without much protest, why, when I did that in the presence of other people they were so terribly provoked and hated me so much.

Mother would never argue that with me; with her I had no business anyway, by myself or in public, and I was a ruffian no matter under what circumstances I did it, but once an older girl did have an argument with me. "It would hurt my reputation," she said. "Men don't want girls loose, men want girls to behave themselves and keep themselves with dignity." When I crowded her over and over again in argument, "Why, why, why?" she said, "Men want girls to be virgins for marriage and a girl that allows a boy to feel her around, kiss her and play with her, would not be believed of her virginity. She would lose her chance to be properly married and any assault on your part on her sex dignity is mean and vicious. You provoke us; we're human, too. We may have the same passion you have, but we may not and dare not allow ourselves the same conduct because while it does not hurt you, it will hurt us. You're mean and brutal, you have not normal considerations for others. You are selfish and while you are a very nice boy in other ways, you seem to be very stupid in this."

That gave me the first inkling of what this whole thing is about and I tried to modify my conduct and what I then called behave myself. But then I noticed something else, too. I was good-looking, of a jolly disposition, was well thought of by my neighbors since I was the whole thing in our shop, earned well, dressed decently, was able to speak English. The girls thought well of me, and while I made up my mind that I would not molest the girls any more by too close approaches, the girls themselves did not behave as though they really wanted me to be a good boy. They would tease me, provoke my passion, comb their hair, dress, laugh, touch me in our plays, which would make me feel very passionately toward them. In my thought it was natural for me to reciprocate that by conduct on my part suited to my feverish feeling. And so occasionally I did, even while I restrained myself very much, but very seldom, and suffered because of it.

When I had a girl, though, by herself, I almost invariably made approaches and on these occasions different girls responded to the same in different ways; some girls got mad and reprimanded me very vigorously; others didn't get mad at all but would reciprocate my embraces, would allow me to open their waists and play with their breasts; in a very few cases I was even permitted to raise up their dress and play with their sex. I did not make any attempt at all in those days of sex relationship; I knew it would be a disaster for the girl if I destroyed her virginity, and if conception took place, it would also be a disaster for myself, but I suffered very much for that restraint and occasionally I was sick as an aftereffect, balls and penis were swollen and I felt quite miserable. In those days prevention for conception was not known as yet.

As I form an estimate today of my life in those years, I can find very little of modern culture in me. I knew absolutely nothing of modern sciences; I knew nothing of politics; nothing of daily news or events; had almost no sense of patriotism except a strong sense of sympathy with our Jews when they were persecuted by the Gentiles. In suffering want, I formed one great urge to make money. And for that I was willing, and did work very hard, seventeen or eighteen hours a day during the busy season and thought of very little else besides money-making even during slack season.

Suffering because of want and sickness I had plenty. We had sent after the oldest brother, who came here and had three small children; two children were sick, his wife was a shrew, she made the house constantly on fire with numerous complaints and quarrels; she was cursing constantly her children and her husband, and occasionally us. In slack season, when our money was all gone, we used to get ourselves in debt with the grocer and landlord and other storekeepers for the merest necessities of life. We were in debt also a great deal for transportation tickets, having sent for my brother, his wife and children, and other relatives of the family, so that want regularly stared us in the face, especially during slack season.

It was in those years that my oldest brother, who was working with us very hard as a sewing-machine operator, contracted tubercular lungs and after suffering for some three years, he finally died, [and] left his wife and five children to be taken care of by our family, which increased very much the misery of our house. We could neither live with his wife nor separate, and suffered very much. The next oldest brother to myself happened to be very incompetent as a tailor. His mind wasn't so very much different from other people's minds, but it seemed that his hands did not follow his mind and, while he was willing to work, he would spoil whatever work he did and it took him about five times as long as it took anybody else, so that he was almost useless in the shop.

As I think back on these years, I was not completely devoid of a moral sense. There were two young girls, sisters, working for me; one was about eighteen and the other was about six-

64

teen. The girl of eighteen was rather different from most of the girls I have known; she seemed to feel nothing on the subject of sex, no sense of bashfulness or resentment nor any sense of passion. I used to think she was made of clay; she had no objection for me to play with her but she never responded; if I kissed her, all right; if I asked her to kiss me, all right, too; she had no objection to do it for me but would never do it on her own volition, nor did she have any objection for me to play with her body; if I asked her to unbutton her waist she did; she wouldn't do it if I didn't ask her to, had no objection for me to play with her breasts; the same was true with her skirt. If I asked her to she would herself raise her skirt, let me play with her sex, but evidenced herself no feeling in connection with it.

It seems that she told her younger sister the way I behaved towards her; this younger sister was altogether different in character from the oldest; she was a very live kid, charged with a world of passion, used to make approaches to me, used to watch our house when all the other members of the family left and I remained at home; that was the time she used to visit with me and made personally very vigorous approaches until at one time she laid down on the bed with her skirt and knees up, all aflame, ready for sex relationship on her own motion. The feeling not to do that because of the damage I might do her in depriving her of her virginity, and the fear of conception, and my passion, had a battle royal and my moral sense won out. But in that case, too, I was sick for a week.

3

The year of 1886 was a year of great activity in the labor movement. The Knights of Labor had had a previous convention and resolved to engage in an effort to establish the eight-hour day. In May, 1886, and some months before, they had entered into an agitation to accomplish their purpose. There was no knowledge of that movement in our group at all; information about it was distributed through the American and German press, but since we could read neither German nor English, since we did not, as a matter of fact, read any newspapers at all, we knew nothing of that movement; but it was in the atmosphere and it seemed to have crossed the border of our settlement, because in the months of February and March there was quite a lot of dissatisfaction among our people about the prices paid for work. The earnings were very small, but that was true at the beginning of any season, but we seemed to feel it much more during that year than during previous years. Whenever we got together we talked about it, cursed at the bosses, but in a very impotent way. We knew that we were helpless but there wasn't even a suggestion of rebellion nor was there a suggestion of anything that we might do.

One fine day—it must have been in the month of April—Mother came from the butcher shop and informed us all at the shop that there was going to be a meeting in De Koven Street Hall. I asked her what the meeting was and she said she didn't know but it was her understanding that everybody would come together in that hall on Saturday afternoon. I asked her who told her and she said she didn't know except the women in the butcher shop spoke about it.

On the next Saturday afternoon I went over along with other people from our shop and a few other shops to that meeting. When I came there I found that there were a great many people assembled around the hall, that the hall was closed and the Bohemian who owned the saloon and the hall was at the door explaining to everybody that nobody rented a hall and that he knew nothing about the meeting. Some of us assembled thought that we had better make up a purse of a few dollars to rent the hall. He said he wouldn't open the door for less than three dollars, that that was cheap but that he figured that we were going to patronize the saloon downstairs in addition to that. We chipped in a nickel apiece and had three dollars and even more on short notice. The man opened the hall and within fifteen or twenty minutes we packed the hall to capacity, standing room, mainly. The hall was ordinarily used for a Bohemian dance-hall so there was only standing room.

There was a great tumult; everybody was talking and nobody knew quite what this whole thing was about until one of our men asked everybody to be quiet and began to speak. He thought that the price for labor was very low; that the treatment we were receiving in the shops was very undignified; that the examiners were exacting very fine work and were sending the work back over and over again; and that the operators wanted too much money for their work and since he was a contractor, he couldn't pay it because the employers downtown wouldn't pay him enough to pay it; that he didn't know who called this meeting together and intimated that even if he did know, he wouldn't say, because he believed that somebody would carry the message to the employers. But anyway he didn't know, but no matter who called it, it is good that we are here to jointly talk matters over and see if we can't find any way to remedy conditions as they are.

Next to him another man got up, said that he was a sewing-machine operator, that all he was able to earn was seven dollars a week, that it was hard to support his family on that income, that he didn't have steady work, that in between seasons there was a great deal of slack, that he hardly earned enough in busy seasons to be able to live during the slack seasons. He assaulted vigorously the conduct of the contractors. "Who tells you to bring work home when it don't pay enough?" he asked. "Why do you bring work home without knowing how much you are going to be paid for it; don't take that kind of work; never mind about the independence of the employers; if they don't need you, they'll give you no work anyway. Since they are giving you work, they evidently need that work and if they need it, you can be independent too. Tell them just how much you want for the work, don't take it unless you get your price; then you will not kick if we want a decent wage for our work."

An old presser got up to talk. He described how hard he worked; he made motions with his hands showing how hard it was to work with a twenty-two-pound iron, that he was all in after a day's work, that the hours were too long, that those operators wanted to eat up everything, that nothing was enough for them, and that unless they worked for less there wouldn't be enough left for the presser, and that he was afraid he was going to contract consumption like other people that he knew from the charcoal gas in the burner and from too hard work.

To make a long story short, we continued that meeting all along until very late at night. I remember I got up, too, to say something, but when I noticed everybody looking at me my knees began to bend, blood rushed into my head and I would have collapsed right then and there if it wasn't for a friend of mine who evidently sensed my predicament and got ahold of me, led me to a chair, and sat me down. One of the men, an operator, finally took the floor. He was a very healthy-looking chap, rather raw and rough in appearance, and in a loud voice shouted something to this effect, that tomorrow nobody goes to work and that Monday we will select a committee to visit the manufacturers and tell them that we will not work until they raise the price for work and that the foremen and superintendents should treat us decently and that the examiners should not be so "stuck up."

Someone in the audience asked him what we were going to do in case some of our people would not abide by the decision and would work tomorrow. He answered in an even louder voice than before, raising his fist, "If they work we'll break their heads for them." Our younger fellows thought it would be quite fun to have a fight with those that would work and before very long there was quite an understanding amongst the young fellows as to where and when they would meet, early in the morning, to visit shops and see whether or not they were closed.

On Sunday morning I got up quite early and with quite a mob we spread out to the numerous shops in the neighborhood. Most of them did not work, but we did find some that did; they were afraid that if they stopped working the employers would not give them any work at all, and we threatened with violence, took off the thread from the machine, shut off the fire in the coal grates, abused them very vigorously, made fun of them, and stationed a committee there to watch right in the shop and see that nobody worked. In those days there were not shops separated from the homes; they were all in homes; homes and shops were all together. The casual entrance of strangers into one of these shops was quite a normal proceeding; we had as yet not acquired the habit of knocking at the door before we went in.

Later on Sunday we met again in the same hall and selected spokesmen to visit the manufacturers. I remember that we had great difficulty in selecting the spokesmen; everybody was afraid that he would be considered by the manufacturers as the ringleader of the fight and, therefore, wished to be excused from the appointment. Those that were the most vigorous spokesmen, though, were the men who did not get work to do directly from the manufacturers but were working for the contractors in their outside shops. They did not mind going because the manufacturers would not reach them individually by boycotting them.

After great efforts a committee was constituted; it wasn't appointed by anybody nor was it self-appointed. Simply the consensus of opinion formed itself on a group of men who, while they represented the people and knew the interests of the people, were at the same time not within the reach of the employers for purposes of employers' retaliation. The point that the committee itself might be bribed by the manufacturers was quite an item of discussion in our group. It was said that, as for the contractors, they might be offered more work and better work and be induced to line up on the side of the manufacturers. The element of personal honesty was an item of consideration, and after a great deal of haggling and discussion, the committee was formed.

By that time the manufacturers themselves [had] organized into a group to fight the strikers, and when the committee appeared before the manufacturers, they were told that in the judgment of the manufacturers the people had no grievance to complain of, that they had better go back to work. And after that report was brought back to our mass meeting we felt quite forlorn and bitter, and resolved to continue the strike. When I say resolved, I don't mean that a vote was taken, not even a pro-and-con discussion. It was simply a sort of consensus of opinion to continue the strike without anyone in the group questioning its being so.

This situation took place in the month of April, 1886. By that time the preparation of the Knights of Labor for the eight-hour strike in May [had begun] and the agitation was conducted very vigorously. Someone in our group had invited the authorities of the Knights of Labor to appear before our meeting and advise us to join the Knights of Labor. A delegation from the Knights of Labor did appear before our meetings and advised us to join their organization, and we did join their organization. All I then knew of the principles of the Knights of Labor was that the motto of the Knights of Labor was, One for All, and All for One. I think they did require us to pay in a dollar per man for membership and when we paid our membership fee we were all initiated with great ceremony, took an oath of allegiance to the organization, and were made full-fledged members.

All this was done while the strike was going on and we had plenty of time to elect our officers, formulate our demands for the manufacturers, and establish some kind of an organization. As I think of the matter now, I am still very much puzzled. As I said before, nobody knew who called the first meeting, nor did anyone know who called on the Knights of Labor to send us a delegation. Prior to our entry as members of the Knights of Labor we had not even selected a secretary or a chairman of our meetings. None of us knew that an organization must have a chairman, a secretary, rules of order, a mode of proceeding by which one man will get the floor while the other man will have to sit quietly and wait until he is through—all of that was unbeknown to us. When we went out on strike we didn't have a vote; when we agreed to join the Knights of Labor we didn't have a vote; when we sent a committee to the manufacturers we didn't have a vote. This whole thing was done in a way that appeared to us spontaneous with no objecting voice. In rare cases somebody did say something; nobody knew whether he agreed or dissented with the established public opinion, but there were no men or issues discussed. As I think it over now after so many years have elapsed, I am satisfied that there must have been someone who did, with premeditation and intent, help to cause that whole movement; first causing the rumor to be spread that the meeting was to be held; after that meeting was held, he must have so informed the authorities of the Knights of Labor and caused them to send a delegation to our meeting. It must also have been the same party that suggested that we join the Knights of Labor, but if anyone did all these things at all, he did it very cleverly, because up to now, our people do not know how it all came about.

Under the rules of the Knights of Labor, the only people authorized to negotiate with the employers were those selected by the Knights of Labor themselves, members out of their own central committee. It was those appointed who undertook the job of visiting the employers again and negotiating with them the settlement of our strike. I remember the personnel in that committee, a bricklayer and an Irish blacksmith and a man that was in business of some kind, not a working man at all. The rules of the Knights of Labor were that every man was entitled to membership except a saloon-keeper and a lawyer, so that there did belong to the Order, storekeepers, landlords, clergymen, and all kinds of people. It was not a labor organization in the strict sense of the word. Its claim was not made based purely on the claim of labor and their interests, but it was based on the claim of ethics, morality, justice, etc.

When this commission went over to our employers, they were received very well, but were informed that we were being led by a lot of anarchists, men who do not know what they want, and since this commission didn't understand our trade nor the nature of our complaint, they came back quite converted to the side of the employers. There was a complete misunderstanding between ourselves and the committee of the Knights of Labor. As I can formulate it now after so many years have passed, I think the following would set this complicated situation in some order. We wanted to establish a regular day's work; while there was a movement for an eight-hour day, we would have been glad to agree with the manufacturers for a ten-hour day, because we were working unlimited hours and we would even give in to a comprehensive regulation of overtime, but we knew we couldn't do it ourselves, we couldn't establish a uniform work day by our own authority and wanted the manufacturers to agree on the justice of our claim and co-operate with us to enforce that regulation by failing to send or give work to the shop that failed to live up to that standard.

The manufacturers made fun of us and the delegation of the Knights of Labor saw it in the same light. They claimed, which was true, that we were not working directly for them at all; they said, we give work to a contractor and he can do what he darn pleases; he can work four hours a day so far as we are concerned. But we knew that unless there was an agreement between manufacturers, contractors, and working men on this standard of ours, competition among ourselves would cause in the future, as it did in the past, a condition making for an unlimited working day. On that point this committee of the Knights of Labor ridiculed us, saying, "Can't you fellows take care of yourselves, establish your own rules in your shops?" so that they even made some of our own people believe it was true. The argument was: if you want to work ten hours, work ten hours; don't work any more if you don't want to. But since the work was distributed in a large number of separate shops, especially homes where a union cannot possibly keep control on the time their members work, we knew we were right, but at the same time, we could not possibly convince the authorities in the Knights of Labor of the justice of our claim.

Substantially the same argument was made in reference to wages. The argument was made by the employers in something of the following manner: it isn't us that make you work cheap; you're working piecework. If you don't want to make a certain garment for a certain price, don't take it out from the shop; we don't force you to take it. And that was true. They couldn't force us; this was a free country. But our poverty, our want, and our need did force us and we ourselves competing with each other reduced our wages below a living point. It was the intention, through the organization, to enter into an understanding with the employers to mutually cause contractors and working people to set the price for labor before the merchandise left the factory so that the price for the labor would not be subjected to competition between ourselves, but that a standard of wages would be set and maintained in the interests of all concerned. It was this point that the manufacturers would not agree to and made our committee themselves believe they were right.

There was another point at issue and that was, we claimed that work should not be given to anyone in a shop that did not belong to the union. The manufacturers maintained that meant they were to become organizers for our union and they said to the committee, if these fellows want to organize a union they can do it themselves without calling on us to organize them. On this point we were even more vitally interested than on both of the previous points because we sensed the intent of the employers. We knew that unless that point was acquiesced to on the part of the employers, shops that didn't belong to the union would get all the work; union shops would be left in the cold, which would disintegrate our organization and destroy whatever we had accomplished. On this point, too, the committee agreed with the employers. They said, if you fellows want to belong to the Knights of

Labor, nobody interferes with you—this is a free country. And it is. Except that freedom to starve militates against freedom to belong to a union, and that the right to be a member of a union must be accompanied by the right to get work and earn one's living while he is a member.

The Knights of Labor commission did not convince us, but did encourage materially the scab element amongst our people; it encouraged the contractors; it encouraged such relatives of the contractors who were working in the shops and constantly, by agitation and persuasion, threw cold water on our enthusiasm. But the bulk of our membership was solid on all these three points, and after four weeks or so on strike, we did take a vote on the subject and the majority in favor of the strike were more than three to one.

Something else happened in the course of the life of that strike that may be recorded now as being of significance. A mass meeting was called to explain the nature of the strike and encourage our membership. By that time there were already a great many of us that were in actual want for food, house wants, etc., and when that meeting was called a man was invited to speak to us in the German language and he made a wonderful speech. August Spies was his name. He was the editor of a German socialist or anarchist newspaper. He was then engaged in the agitation for the eight-hour movement, but he didn't only advocate an eight-hour movement. He advocated something much more significant. He told us that we were experiencing now in the modern industrial life a class struggle; that we, all of us, were on the side of the poor; that the capitalists, the employers of all kinds, traders and storekeepers of all kinds, the government, legislators, judges and policemen and clergymen were all classed as either capitalists or their henchmen and were arrayed against us; that humanity was suffering because humanity was disinherited, that the property of the country belonged all to that one class and their henchmen; that the great body of the people, the working man and the poor, had no property, and depended for their living only on wages that they received from the employing classes; that under the present economic order of things there was such a thing as an iron law of wages which meant that no working man got more than bare subsistence for his work so that he might be able to live and work for his boss and reproduce, in his children, working men for ever after to keep his employer in wealth, nay, he said, even in riotous luxury; that the employers were maintaining their horses and their dogs in better houses than their men; that the employers worked their horses less than they did their men and that was because when a horse died because of being exhausted the employer lost something, while if the working man died, he was easily replaced with no damage to the boss.

August Spies went on to say that we are now living in an industrial age that keeps on developing itself, that working men are acquiring more and more significance as the real producers of all wealth; that the employers, tradesmen and their henchmen, clergymen and government officials, are all a useless lot, bound to be overthrown by labor in the course of time, and that historically labor was assigned the mission to overthrow the capitalist class, and that while he wished us good luck in our strike to establish a regular working day, raise the price for our work, and enforce decent treatment on the part of the employers, he thought that this was only a minor effort and that the real effort to be made by us [was] to destroy root and branch the present capitalist order of things and establish a co-operative commonwealth. He advised us to read anarchist and socialist newspapers and books on the labor movement; there were then and there in the hall a number of German socialists and English socialists and anarchists who distributed amongst us appeals, leaflets, newspapers, in both German and English, and we were advised to read them so that we might educate ourselves in the cause of labor, the theories of socialism and anarchism, and on the general labor movement. He spoke in a very plain German, and since Yiddish is only a dialect of German, I understood almost every word he said and it made a great impression on me.

On that night when I went home I was aflame; the whole argument struck me like lightning and went all through me. I had heard ideas that I had never heard before in my life and they seemed to express the very thoughts that were in my inner consciousness. He's right, I thought; we are disinherited, the property of the country does belong to the rich; all we get out of it is a bare living for very hard work; there must be a chance to improve conditions; there are so many of us, there ought to be no division of opinion amongst us; we ought to all unite, all the working people from all trades, and support what he calls the Labor Movement for the purpose of getting redress. But as I was analyzing his speech in my own mind, I discovered something that quite surprised me and worried me so that I did not sleep all night. In substance, after all his complaint, agitation, and what not, he theoretically agreed with the employers; he said they were a separate class; we hadn't any right to impose on them the function of organizing our union: it was up to ourselves through the strength of our own union to enforce all these standards as formulated by us and demanded to be given by the employer; it was up to us to set rates of wages and do no work until those rates were paid. But that was a difficult and almost impossible task because the styles that we were working on of different kinds of women's clothes varied; there was more work to be done on one than on the other; it wasn't so easy to ascertain the amount of work on a given garment except by actual trial and experience, and once you tried and did the work, it was up to the employer as to whether he would depend on your judgment or not as to the amount of work there. It was impossible to set the price for work except through negotiations on the part of both the employer and the help and the contractor, and for this purpose it was necessary for the employer to recognize the union and negotiate collectively instead of individually. When they said negotiate between yourselves, settle the prices between yourselves, enforce same through your own authority, we all knew that that couldn't be done; that it was all rot; and yet, according to the Knights of Labor, the employers, and this socialist anarchist speaker, we were wrong. Some solution must be found to the problem, I thought, and I am going to study and find the solution if I can, and the subject matter worried me very much.

In the meantime, the strike must be kept up. Those that went back to work must be stopped; otherwise when the bosses won, the future in store for us would be even worse than it was before, and our experience in the past was enough for us to make it clear what the future would bring us. After four or five weeks our strike was quite demoralized; some of our people said we didn't know what we wanted, and there was practically no leadership. The Knights of Labor did not influence our thought; it was common talk amongst our people that storekeepers, bricklayers, and blacksmiths don't know anything about clothes, that they don't know what they were talking about. We paid very little attention to the socialists and anarchists; we weren't ready to overthrow everything and didn't want to engage in any such effort; all we wanted was to work normal hours, receive decent wages and be treated fairly by our employers, and let it go at that.

But conditions were all against us. The way we were employed, we couldn't do a thing except with the co-operation and sanction of both the contractors and employers, and while the majority of contractors were with us, yet a few of them, the biggest of them, we knew we couldn't trust; they turned to the side of the employers as soon as there was a break in our ranks. There were a good many of us that felt very much demoralized because of the want in our own families; that was particularly true of the women-folk in our population; they didn't understand anything of our strike and urged their husbands very vigorously to go back to work. In the synagogues, too, the authorities were not very friendly to us: according to pious Jews, the economic fortunes of the life of each individual were ordained by God long before a man was born and to unite for purposes of rebellion and strikes was to do something against God's wish and could not be sanctioned by religion. Every life's factor, the family, the church, the employer, and even the socialist and anarchist were essentially against us and we were demoralized indeed.

On May the fifth, 1886, an event happened that had a great influence on the fortunes of our strike. It was known to us that the manufacturers had taken into their own downtown shops a number of our own people to do the work inside instead of in the outside shops. In doing so, they were able to satisfy their trade and prolong the strike for an indefinite time. When we got together in the hall in conversation between ourselves, it was made clear that unless we could go downtown and stop those shops, we would be obliged to lose the strike; but that was a big job. The manufacturers had their factories on the upper floors of great big buildings. To break into these buildings it would be necessary to have a great many men. It was necessary to overawe the non-union people in the shops, and make them come down in the hope that we might win the strike.

A consensus of opinion was formed that in this special case the committee to stop those shops must be composed of our entire membership. About six hundred of us left the De Koven Street Hall, which was about a mile or more distant from the factory, and walked in a body downtown. When we crossed the Van Buren Street bridge, something happened that we had not expected to happen at all, namely, patrol wagons came in on us from all sides of the city in large numbers; hundreds, probably thousands of policemen were unloaded in very short order in the cloak district; every policeman had a billy and they began to chase us and beat us unmercifully. Within ten or fifteen minutes the whole neighborhood there was cleared; none of us were arrested, none of us had time to do anything that would warrant an arrest. We simply were there, but a great many of us were beaten up very badly, and we ran for our lives.

When we finally got back into the hall, and got over our astonishment at the treatment we received at the hands of the police, we bound up the wounds of those of us that were badly hurt and tried to find some explanation for what had happened. We found the following. One of our men was able to read German. He said that he read in the newspaper that there was a great big factory about a mile away called the McCormick Harvester Works; that the people over there were out on a strike for an eight-hour day; that two or three days past they had had a meeting near the factory; that the policemen had tried to disperse them and they killed a number of men; that yesterday these men held a meeting at Haymarket Square and the policemen there, too, tried to disperse them; that someone threw a bomb under the policemen's patrol wagon, which killed a number of policemen and wounded a great many more; that the police were out to stop those gatherings and were looking for the men who threw the bomb; that it was said in the newspapers that the men who threw the bomb were anarchists; that one of them was this same August Spies who had lectured before us, and because of that, any assembly on the street by working men was prohibited, and the fact that so many of us had gone downtown at the same time made the police think we were anarchists prepared to throw bombs and make riots and therefore they treated us the way they did. Now if this man that knew German had told us about it before we went, we probably would not have gone, because we were not a fighting crowd in the real sense. Most of the people were elderly tailors who had never had a fight in their lives, but we didn't know anything about it and therefore got ourselves into trouble. That event, too, demoralized materially the strike.

After May 1st, 1886, picketing became absolutely impossible. The police arrested all pickets, even two or three. The attitude on the part of the police was practically the same as though the city was under martial law. Labor unions were raided, broken up, their property confiscated, the police used their clubs freely. Arrests were made without any cause, and the life of a working man was not quite safe when out on strike.

In a great many of the downtown shops where American girls were working, they did not go out on strike at all. In fact, they were satisfied that the Jews were out on strike. Most of them wanted the Jews to lose their jobs; they felt as though the Jews were encroaching on their special industry and rights; they were here before. And then again, we couldn't very well talk to them; not many of us could speak English and besides, our appearance and our attitude of mind were completely foreign to the American women working in those shops.

American women were really better paid than we were, and they had the better class of work. They were making what is called in the trade "samples," special orders, rush orders, and very seldom worked on stock. They also had the advantage against the Jews in that they didn't need to support families and had steadier work inside the factories, so that we had no union of interests and no sense of solidarity.

After the strike had lasted for eight weeks, we were obliged to give it up and lose it. It so happened, though, that year that business improved materially, and while we lost the strike, we made more money that fall season than we had ever made before. The character of the merchandise began to improve. In 1882, when I first began to work in the trade, outer garments were mainly what was called "circulars" and "dolmans." A circular was a plain shawl cut in the shoulders and with a narrow standing collar put in, hanging straight from the shoulder, which wasn't much of a garment at all in the modern sense. A dolman was substantially the same thing, with two large cuffs on each side and a plain three-quarters of a yard of cloth sewed in, called sleeves. But from season to season those shawl coats were modified, shaped back, regular cuttings out for sleeves and with sleeves in the garments, pockets, stylish lapels, and collar, so that it began to formulate itself into a regular more-or-less tailored garment. Garments of that kind require a good deal more work, better tailoring, and we had developed the skill and the taste so that as time went on, the women's garment-working trade, which was formerly only a girls' trade, began to be developed into a skilled tailors' trade requiring, at least partially, tailoring skill.

I was again required to increase our shop. We bought additional machines so that we had five machines in our flat and had six or seven girls working and I began to earn more money. We paid for more transportation expenses for our relatives, some of whom we put to work in our shop. Our shops became even worse from the point of view of sanitary conditions as business increased. The family was living in the five-room house; the man and his wife working, several children, and one or two helping. He was still able to use the dining room and kitchen without having the shop there, but he had to have the shop in his bedroom and living room. The same rooms were used to sleep in and to live in. When the shop increased, there were finishers' tables in the bedroom; the living room was crowded from end to end with sewing machines; in the dining room there was the press of work and it was chuck full of bundles or merchandise, so from the point of view of sanitary conditions, the more work we had, the worse they became.

To tell the truth, the crowded and filthy sanitary conditions didn't bother us at all. We weren't used to anything better in the old country, but from the point of view of the American shop in the American factory, we certainly had rotten places to work in, crowded and dirty, a large number of garments lying all about the house, on the beds, on eating tables, any old place along with rags and dirt in every part of the house. In slack seasons, which were about six months of the year, we had almost no work at all and the little work that there was, we received very little pay for. A great many of us were out looking for other classes of work during the slack season, but few of us found any; after a fellow works in a tailor shop he cannot do any more coarse, common labor, and he has no skill to do any other kind of work. The same was true of our women-folk; we all had to live the whole year on the money we earned in six months, and while the season in 1886 was a little better than it was in previous years, there wasn't enough money earned to decently carry us across the whole year, and we still suffered great poverty and want.

The experience I had during the strike and the speeches we heard in these six weeks left a great impression on me. The vision of a united labor party and labor unions held out to me great possibilities. Life was very hard then; in busy season we worked almost to death; in slack season we suffered great want; the American atmosphere influenced our people much. As we became more and more Americanized we noticed the difference between the standard of living of the Americans and that of ourselves, and we suffered by comparison. The stores were full of merchandise, the streets of downtown were filled with well-dressed crowds, healthy-looking, neat-appearing people, while we, during our busy season, were unwashed, unkempt, ill-dressed and overworked and, during the slack season, underworked and underfed. The housing, too, we noticed was much better amongst the older emigrants and the American families. They didn't have to keep their shops in their houses; they were able to keep their homes straight, while we, who had the shops in our living room, had pretty poor places to live in. We had to rent poor houses, too, because for shop and business purposes they wouldn't rent us any decent houses, and so a sense of rebellion found its way into our minds. We didn't know much about the labor movement except what we learned from the strike, but enough was left from the strike to cause us a great deal of thinking and dissatisfaction.

Two years after the strike, in 1888, the sense of this dissatisfaction began to take shape. The more intelligent of us, especially the younger people, began to talk when we visited each other about the labor movement. We didn't know very much what it was, but we talked about it anyway. In those two years I [had] learned to read English and had already read a number of radical papers and some pamphlets on the labor movement. Some I got in the public library, and some I got from friends.

There was a young doctor in the neighborhood, who I was told was a revolutionary in Russia, named Knopfnagel. It was to his house that I went to ask him what socialism was and what was a revolutionist. He gave me some pamphlets and some explanation which frankly I didn't understand very well. He spoke to me about the French Revolution in the eighteenth century; about the nobility and bourgeoisie; how the nobility had outlived their usefulness and through the development of the town, and the merchant, the bourgeoisie had acquired social power; how they had become able to function in social life in competition with the nobility when a struggle ensued which made for the French Revolution, and modern capitalism was born; that modern capitalism now is outliving its usefulness; that the proletariat is acquiring social significance and social power, and that there will be a revolution in the immediate future overthrowing capitalism, expropriating the expropriators and establishing socialism.

What is socialism—a co-operative commonwealth, a partnership of all people, mainly the working people, the abolition of rate, interest, and profit, the establishment of a brotherhood of men, and that may only be done through the class struggle. Something in the line of the same thing was the talk that August Spies delivered in 1886 and for which he and his friends were tried and sentenced to be hung, and were hung on November the 11th, 1886. Somehow to me the social problem wasn't as simple as all that, and I said to him that I only vaguely understood what he was thinking about, and that I would have to read up on the subject. He advised me to read and study the science of political economy, books by Adam Smith, David Ricardo, Karl Marx, Proudhon, and others. He also advised me to read up on natural science, Darwin's books and Herbert Spencer's. He told me to read the history of the world and special histories of Rome, England, France, Germany, and Italy. He suggested to me that I form a club to be called an educational organization by which we would invite lecturers, establish a reading room, and establish a center for labor unions, etc.

There were about seven or eight men, friends of mine, to whom I first submitted the idea of forming that club. Most of them felt like myself about life; the work was too hard, remuneration too small, and general living conditions unbearable. We got together one night at our house after work and formed an organization called the Workingman's Educational Society. We taxed ourselves some thirty-five or forty dollars to rent a floor of rooms on Canal Street, painted and hung out the sign on the front door, had circulars printed both in Yiddish and English announcing the formation and establishment of that club, and on the back of the circulars was a statement of its aims and objectives. All eight of us circulated around the Jewish community and distributed about a thousand copies announcing a meeting on a certain Saturday night. We bought forty chairs all told and we had a mob of several hundred people on the first night. They couldn't all get in and they crowded themselves into these rooms so that we were almost choked. Knopfnagel made the first speech; honestly, none of us understood a word of what he said, but we appreciated the spirit in which he said it and were quite enthusiastic and applauded him to beat the band.

After this response we were very much encouraged; we took in forty members on the first night; each man paid a dollar initiation fee and promised to pay twenty-five cents a meeting. We thought we had lots of money. We formed all kinds of committees; a committee to reorganize the coatmakers, and a committee to organize a branch of the Socialist Party, but some of us disagreed right then and there on the Socialist Party. They were inclined to be anarchists by saying that political action was all a mistake; that it was simply a sauce for corruption; that the state was the property of the capitalists, was in the hands of the capitalists, was the tool of the capitalists, that we couldn't get it even if we had a majority, that the institution of the state could not be for purposes other than capitalist purposes; that labor didn't need a state; that labor simply needed an industrial co-partnership, a brotherhood, for purposes of living and producing together, only for needs and not for sale. And so a discussion arose that lasted for months and months, until finally we separated, the anarchists separate, and the socislists separate, and some in between, but others neither anarchists or socialists, were desirous of belonging to our club for purposes of education and sociability.

The nature of our industry was such that there was almost constant reason for irritation. In the beginning of the season there was very little work, and before price for labor, which was by piecework, was stabilized, there was very great competition and the price for labor was almost nothing. Two and a half up to four dollars were a week's wages for very hard work; the same was true at the end of each season when the work slackened down. In the busy season we knew we had to make up enough to support us the balance of the year and so even if we were paid fair wages or what was called fair wages, we were never satisfied because they weren't quite equal to the money we needed to go on for the whole year and the sense of dissatisfaction was brewing amongst our people almost constantly.

The group in the Educational Society assumed upon themselves the duty of advance guard and considered it about time to organize the coatmakers again, because in 1886 and 1887 their union was destroyed. I remember once some such experience as this: "Moisha," said I, to one of the men working in the same industry, an operator, "over in the Educational Society we are going to have a meeting tonight on Canal Street right near Bunker. You'll see a sign at the door, go right up about eight o'clock at night."

"What's the meeting for?" said he.

"We are going to increase the membership in our socialist society," I said to him, "and I want you to be a member."

"Socialist society? What do these fellows want?"

"Well, we want to establish a co-operative commonwealth; we want to make a revolutionary change in society; we want to abolish rent, interest and profit; we want to have the working man acquire the entire property of the country and abolish private property and other means of production and distribution; we will then be able to work shorter hours and earn more money and live better. You know how you live, now. When your children are sick, you haven't any money for a doctor; you very seldom can pay your rent on time; you always owe money to the grocery store; you're damn glad to get credit; both you and your family never are well clothed or well dressed or well housed. The people who employ you think of you as just so much labor power; they care for and are interested in you less than in their cattle; the same is true of your landlord and the entire class of parasites; hangers-on, etc. That's why we want working men to join the Socialist Society, to establish a condition of things making life worth living."

Moisha listened to me patiently and when I was through he said to me, "Tell me, will we have to convert everybody to that? All the Jews?"

"Yes," said I.

"What about the Germans? Them, too, won't we?"

"Yes."

"And the Irish, the French, everybody in Chicago?"

"Yes."

"And then the people all through the state, won't we?"

"Yes."

"And the people of all other states, won't we?"

"Yes."

"You're crazy," says Moisha.

"Why?" says I.

"You won't live long enough to see it and your children's children won't live long enough to see it. Why should I worry my head about the distant future when I've got all I can do to take care of the troubles I am facing today? Haven't I got enough worries now? So that you want to put me next to some more. You're crazy, I tell you, I won't come." And Moisha didn't come.

Some weeks afterwards, I met the same Moisha. "Moisha, over at that Educational Society on Canal Street," I said to him, "there is going to be a meeting tonight. I want you to come."

"What's it for," says Moisha, "socialism? To take care of my great-grandchildren?"

"No, Moisha, this time you're wrong. It is to organize the cloak-workers into a labor union."

"A labor union, what's that?"

"Well, you know the season is approaching; those manufacturers pay almost nothing for work, and when we have no union, even when the season is in full blast, we won't get enough out of it to be able to live decently. Then we work too damn hard—fifteen to eighteen hours a day. But if you organize into a union now before the season is on, we will stop work just before the season develops and make the manufacturers give us decent prices for our labor and establish some rules in the industry under agreements with the manufacturers making for our benefit—work less hours, get more money, get better treatment, and what not."

"Are we going to do it this season or wait like you socialists will?"

"No," I said, "we'll go to it right away."

"That sounds reasonable," he said. "You can count on me; I'll be there."

Conversation with Moisha and similar Moishas was a lesson to me. When I was reading in socialist literature about the class struggle and class interests it was all words to me, theories. But in trying to organize a union or the socialist movement, those words acquired live meaning and the men responded to what voiced their immediate and real interests, even if it was necessary to make considerable sacrifice or to risk the well-being of themselves and their families.

We had then organized again the cloak-workers and the subject of affiliation was considered at our meeting. The old Knights of Labor sent a delegation to us again, and after carefully going over their constitution and by-laws, we saw that the authority to contract with employers and our labor union was lodged in their central body. We were obliged to be represented in our negotiations with men engaged in crafts other than our own. This convinced us that the Order of the Knights of Labor and its laws were not suited to our needs.

We then appointed a committee to take out a state charter and establish a union of coatmakers independent of affiliation called the Chicago Coatmakers' Union, of which I became the president.* I think the initiation fee then was a quarter, and the dues were five cents a week. We appointed a committee to visit the manufacturers and have them raise our wages, and establish a ten-hour day.

During that time, I was already reading and studying quite vigorously. Every spare minute of time I used to read: I learned to read well. There was a Hebrew library in town wherein there lived a young man who was a great Hebrew scholar. He earned his living by peddling matches, etc., but

* The union was formally chartered as the Chicago Cloak Makers' Union by the State of Illinois on March 5, 1890.

he only peddled one or two days a week. He occupied a cot in the kitchen of a very poor family for which he paid in rent only fifty cents a week. His meals consisted mainly of a cup of coffee, and bread, occasionally a plate of soup or some potatoes and vegetables, for some of which he paid his landlady. Other meals he had by simply buying food at the grocery store and eating it on his own account. All told, his expenses were no more than $1.75 up to $2.00 a week. But he used to sit in that Hebrew library day and night and read the most difficult books on economics and science that were read by any of the people in our neighborhood.

He was well acquainted with my oldest brother, and it was with him that I began to study. He explained to me different passages in books of political economy—Adam Smith, Ricardo, Malthus, and Marx. We spent nights up to as late as two and three o'clock carefully going over the laws of population as explained by Malthus, the laws of rent as explained by Ricardo, the laws of wages and market price as explained by Smith; economical and theoretical premises one after another, which involved the most comprehensive and intricate thought, were studied and discussed by Wernick and me.

Wernick was an anarchist; I got to know him in the early part of 1887, the time the anarchists were murdered by the authorities of the law. Both he and I, in our rooms, went over every item of the evidence, discussed the law, reflected upon the ultimate effect of the execution, its relation to the social problems, and it was from these studies that I developed the capacity to lecture upon social questions, was able to address large meetings in the year of 1888, making for the formation of labor unions amongst our people.

We had another strike in 1888 and were defeated again, but we didn't feel our defeat then as much as we did the defeat of 1886. The reason for that was that I had begun to understand the nature of unions and strikes somewhat differently than I understood it at the first strike in 1886. I had been reflecting upon the nature of industry. Somehow, I felt, by either defeat or victory of a strike the essence of the relationship between the employers and the men was not changed very materially. The lesson that I acquired in 1886 was when the employers told us it was not up to them to organize a union, or to send work only to union shops. If you want to be organized, do it yourselves through your own initiative. If you want to get a ten-hour day, don't work any longer than ten hours. If you want to get high wages, don't take any work out from the shop unless you are paid your price. You have to stop your competition amongst yourselves through the strength of your own union and not make the employers a party to carry out your own schemes for improvement. The members of the central committee of the Knights of Labor acquiesced in that theory. Even August Spies, the anarchist, stressed the fact that improvement for labor could only come from labor itself. That made me think that while it was better to have contractual relations with employers, and establish some standards in the industry sanctioned by all concerned, yet since the employers wouldn't give in, to a union shop, the standards for which they would be responsible, we would have to formulate standards ourselves and enforce same by our own will and authority. So we passed a resolution that we would work no more than ten hours a day; that we would do no work unless the price of labor had been previously agreed to before the garment was made; that we would permit no one in the shops except members of our union; and other reforms, and opened an agitation of mass meetings to formulate that sanctioning of our industrial consciences. This was the year of great activity on my part and others that I knew.

4

The Russian Jewish immigrant population in New York was a great deal more than that of Chicago, and the movement to organize educational socialist and anarchist societies began earlier in New York than in Chicago. The so-called intelligentsia resided in New York mainly—that is, those who came to America already ready-made socialists, anarchists, and nihilists, and those who left Russia because of their convictions. The garment industry was developed in New York a great deal more than it was in Chicago. Around 1889 there were in New York over ten thousand cloakmakers among the Russia Jews; while in Chicago there weren't any more than seven or eight hundred, so that the organization in New York was much stronger and also older.

A man named Joseph Barondess was the main leader in New York and it seems that he quarreled with the socialists and a fight ensued for the control of the union. The socialist group who [had] heard that I had made a success of the union in Chicago, that I had modified the hours of labor, and had had some influence on the price for labor, negotiating with manufacturers, etc., thought best to send for me to put me up against Barondess in the struggle for factional union control. In the invitation that they sent me they failed to specify the particular work they thought I ought to do. The letter simply read, "We have a great movement and problem in the city, and we have heard of your devotion and experience and we, therefore, invite you to come and help us in the campaign for organization and leadership."

I was glad to take advantage of the opportunity since I was confronted with a problem of competition between the two cities in the American market for trade. Already in those early years manufacturers in Chicago complained that they were being underbid in the general market by the New York manufacturers and that the ability of the New York manufacturers to sell merchandise cheaper was because most of the immigrants first settled in New York and they had a larger supply of labor at smaller wages. It was then necessary for us to influence the New York market to raise wages so that we might be able to hold our established so-called standards.

When I came to New York* I found the conditions in the industry chaotic. There were no standards there at all. There was no conception of the principles of a union. There was simply a general unrest. The price for labor was very cheap, the hours of labor substantially not limited at all, but a very vigorous campaign of slander was carried on by one group of the cloakmakers against another group of cloakmakers—they were divided on the subject of leadership. The great majority of them lined up and believed in Barondess as the only savior of the cloakmakers, while a small group, the more intelligent ones, formed within the organization a rebellious group against Barondess.

I had a meeting with my followers, those that had sent for

* In 1897.

me, and listened to what they expected of me. And this was their proposition: They would go out amongst the masses, they said, and make agitation in my favor, the motto to be, "Give us an experienced leader," and the agitation to be, that I was experienced, that I had [led] successful strikes, that I had modified the hours of work and raised wages, that I was honest, devoted, intelligent, and mainly that I was a socialist. On the other hand, naturally, they would say the opposite about my opponent.

As I said before, in my experience in the movement, I found myself up against an industrial situation that I didn't quite know how to handle at best and I, therefore, suggested that before the subject of leadership be passed on, the subject of issues be considered: what it was that we wanted; how we could formulate our desires; and what we should do to realize them. Based upon a set of these principles, we could make a campaign for organization and take up the issue of leadership after we had prepared the ground so that we might have it clear what the leader should lead us on to.

It seems that my plan of campaign was considered quite impractical and visionary by my co-workers. They said, "Our people don't understand what unionism is at all; we haven't got and never had a real union. It's a mob that only flocks together at the beginning of the season so that they may scare the boss into giving them better piece rates and threaten him with the strength of the union even when the union is non-existent." To make that threat more effective, the people believed that Barondess was the best man, because he was a good speaker, and as they claimed, a big bluffer. What they wanted me to do was to meet him on his own ground, make better speeches than he did, and bluff more effectively.

But I had those labor issues at heart, and I decided that I would go and hear Barondess speak, and since in a day or so there was a meeting, I postponed a conference with our men until after the meeting. I found the sentiment of the meeting very strong for Barondess. Barondess himself didn't come to the meeting, but he sent a letter which was read by one of his lieutenants. The letter submitted the sole issue to be himself and his persecutors. It was filled with braggadocio as to what he could do for his people, and with abuse against his enemies, charging that his enemies were also the enemies of the people, and made his plea purely on personal grounds. No industrial complaint was contained in the pleas, no indication as to what he wanted to do if allowed to attain authority, no premise or form of organization or anything on the subject that was germane, but personal praise, and abuse for his opponents, and I noticed that the people were almost unanimous in their approval of what he wrote. His sentiments received very vigorous applause and endorsement almost in every sentence. The more vigorous the vituperation against his enemies, the louder was the applause.

So I found myself completely out of cahoots with both the people who were with Barondess and those that were against Barondess, and didn't want to work with either of them. I had called together my group and laid before them a form of campaign that would interest me, namely that we work out an appeal to the cloakmakers asking them to join our union and to engage in an effort to improve conditions, formulate our demands, devise means and ways whereby we could have those demands realized. On that I found almost no co-operation whatsoever; either you make a successful personal campaign or none at all. I then told them that I couldn't work with them, and that I would have to go back to Chicago.

Before I left, I asked some of my comrades to take me through the shops so as to get myself acquainted with the actual situation; wages, hours, shops, kind of merchandise, competitive and non-competitive so far as Chicago was concerned, etc. I found the industry much more developed than in Chicago; the system of trade tailoring (fine tailoring work) prevailed much more than in Chicago. While in Chicago a great deal of work was done by girls, girls had very few places in the industry in New York. It was all tailoring and some of it was very fine tailoring. In a number of factories, the tailoring required a higher class of skill than men's tailoring.

The manufacturers, too, were much more prosperous. Some of the factories were owned by immigrants of our own class, not the German Jews and Americans of Chicago. I also took notice of the mode of production, which was considerably advanced compared to the Chicago manufacture. That was in the better shops, but the major portion of the work was done in sweatshops and in hovels, in dark tenements where the people lived, and living in New York was a great deal worse than in Chicago. The rooms in the old buildings that the people occupied were small, two rooms in each flat had outside light, while the balance of the rooms led to very narrow courts and were dark and stuffy. The places were very crowded, no attention was paid to sanitation at all, and like in Chicago, the merchandise was used as bed clothes, for both adults and children. The people worked day and night and looked like galley slaves.

In those years the American Federation of Labor had its headquarters in New York, and while the organization that I belonged to in Chicago did not belong to the American Federation of Labor, yet I saw fit to go up and see Brother Gompers and had a long conversation with him. He received me in a very friendly way, willing to consult with me on the problems that I submitted to him, but after three hours' conversation, it seemed to me that I had made no headway. He felt no different than the people in New York—that just now the subject of leadership was the most germane subject. It was very simple to him—"The people want Barondess, give them Barondess," he said, "since no one else of you fellows have the confidence of the people, why shouldn't he be the leader?"

I told him that our union was not effective, had no interest in the industrial lot of our people because we had failed to formulate a premise by which all the people in the industry, manufacturers, union, the people, etc., should sanction formulated standards and that the first thing for a leader to do was to formulate standards and get the people to agree to those standards, make a campaign for same, and if necessary, go out on strike to enforce same, and who the leader was should be a secondary consideration. Gompers and I did not understand each other at all. He was right in with the mob spirit; every point I made was answered with, "Well, if they want Barondess, give them Barondess. They have confidence in Barondess, that's the man to elect." I had no better fortune in visiting Barondess himself. I spoke of problems, issues, manufacturers, and almost at every point he spoke of his enemies, of his so-called just sense of resentment. We spoke different languages and I left New York in disgust and in despair.

A year later, under the leadership of Barondess, the people of New York carried on a vigorous strike that lasted for ten or more weeks and were finally defeated. A number of their men went to jail; Barondess, too, was arrested and sent to jail on some sort of trumped-up charge. And the Barondess following had lost courage; the union was disorganized and very weak. The people suffered great hardship, while in Chicago we had maintained our organization, had effected an understanding with the employers, and while it wasn't a very satisfactory understanding, not being with all the employers, yet the union was fairly well organized and a ten-hour day was tolerably well enforced.

That situation was effected at no small cost; in all our strikes we had had victims; men were boycotted and were obliged to leave town, for they could get no work. In strikes, the police treated us shamefully. There was already the beginning of the gangster system; some of the employers hired men to beat up our pickets. We, in turn, used to retaliate by beating up scabs and those who violated the standards that had been established. For instance, we made it a rule that no employee working in the inside shops be permitted to take work home at night. This rule was generally violated by the

97

older tailors. The younger men formed themselves into groups of committees, stationed themselves in the manufacturer's neighborhood, and would make the tailor take the work right back to the shop or open up a quarrel which eventually ended in a fight. The argument in the last analysis was violence with some people. However, the great majority of our people honestly endorsed and lived up to those standards as best they could. In some cases an exception had to be made because of the exigencies and needs of the industry itself.

In the meantime, we kept ourselves very busy in the educational club. Socialist and social logic and anarchist and economic speeches were made twice a week. Occasionally we had prominent speakers of national fame address us in large halls. Pamphlets and booklets and circular letters and appeals and statements were constantly printed and distributed amongst our people so that we made ourselves felt and were talked about in almost every family and on every occasion. We made an agitation against the Jewish clergy a very germane part of our work. We got the religious part of our population aroused against us with great vigor. Is there a God, or isn't there a God? Is the story of Genesis true, or isn't it true? We succeeded in making these topics the subject of conversation amongst all families so that on one occasion we invited a speaker, a socialist and a Jew of national fame, to address our people on the subject of religion. He gave us a lecture in which he spoke very disrespectfully of the Jewish religion, assaulted the veracity and authority of the Bible and all its teachers and teachings, cited authorities in his favor among the most modern thinkers, such as Huxley, and others, and when he was through, the religious portion of our people was so aroused that a riot ensued. The intent was to beat up the speaker. We members of the Educational Society surrounded the speaker to protect him, and there was quite a fight. Some of our membership was beaten up very severely, and the other side didn't fare much better. Several of their men were beaten quite badly, and one of the religious group had several of his teeth knocked out.

Next day I and two other comrades were arrested on charges filed against us by the religious group, and after a hearing lasting for very nearly a month, Judge Eberhard decided that this was a free country, that the constitution of the states provided for liberty of speech under the law and that, therefore, the religious group had no right to interfere with our meeting or threaten or engage in violence, and, therefore, I and the other two comrades were set free. The Judge took occasion to reprimand me especially, because according to the testimony, in the fight I was the worst of the lot.

The subject of modern matrimony, too, especially the religious ceremony in connection with marriage, was quite an item, and on that item, too, I considered myself quite an authority. In a lecture I held on that subject, I maintained the right of the relation between men and women based upon the nature of their being, natural affection, instead of the authority by the church and public opinion. I even questioned the authority of the state to interfere with the conduct of individuals pertaining to so intimate a relationship between men and women. I thought that [was] modern capitalist barter, and while there may be some sense in it for the capitalist who had dowries and property rights to apportion and protect legally, us poor devils had only our love lives to bestow upon each other. It was after this speech that I became quite famous—rather, infamous, amongst a great many of our people, especially our married women-folk. They said I was preaching free love and sex license, and I was hated quite cordially by all my relatives, and even a great many of the people in our own trade and industry called me a libertine, etc.

In those years my earning capacity had materially diminished. Employers normally had very little liking for me. They were especially afraid that I might make trouble in the shop, and while, as a matter of fact, I behaved as normally as any other workman in the shop, since I was known as a public character and agitator, no employer wanted to employ me. I didn't have the choice of working for the best shops, but had to work for some of the poorer ones, and besides, I tried to honestly enforce the union standards, and in competition with men who failed to live up to union rules, particularly as to hours, my yearly earnings were small indeed. But we did have a considerable effect on the trade in general. The hours of labor were materially modified and while there was no general observance of the ten-hour day, by the largest proportion of us, it was actually enforced at great sacrifice and money losses to ourselves.

A great many of our people in the industry had not been tailors in the old country. They learned the trade here in America, became cloakmakers, or men's tailors. But from the old country they came from a stock of traders, merchants, professional, and, generally, bourgeois classes. After a number of us had learned the American language, the call of property and trade made itself felt amongst our people, so that the more energetic and intelligent of our people, especially those that were in active business in the old country, left their work benches and went into business after the saving of the first hundred or two hundred dollars.

It is true, all had to begin in a very small way; with a hundred or two hundred dollars they were able to start grocery stores, markets, cigar stores, cigar stands, newspaper routes, etc. Ordinary cigarmakers opened small cigar shops, mattress makers opened mattress shops, and so all along the line. The mechanic and the peddler in a small way became merchants and manufacturers. Rag peddlers opened up rag shops wherein they sorted, renovated, and in a number of cases, mended and repaired torn clothes of their purchase. The mechanic would open up a shop of his own. Men who collected old iron, for instance, would open up iron yards, in a number of cases, remix and remelt old metals of all kinds, and sell them to the different foundries. The spirit of business and trade found its way immediately after we learned the language and had got ourselves acquainted with the nature of the country and its people. It became natural and possible for us to assert our own inclinations.

"What will become of us," my mother used to argue with me. "Look," she would say, pointing to one of my cousins, who opened up a store of general notions and peddlers' supplies. And she would point to another one who went into the ladies' tailoring business, and a third who opened up a grocery store. "Look," she said, "they're all making money; they are improving their condition, while you and your socialism and your ideas about labor unions and your heresy in relation to religion keeps you poor, an underling, a menial, never certain where your next month's rent is coming from, not even certain of your next meal. Is that what your new wisdom teaches you?" And from a practical point of view, she was right. All my relatives thought I was nuts, and when I was very proud and they knew it, they wouldn't even talk with me or recognize me.

My affiliation with the Socialist Party upset me considerably in my thought. As I understood the teachings of socialism, its estimate of the social problem, its studies in sociology and history, it stressed what it called the materialistic conception of history and the class struggle. It claimed that it was not an ethical doctrine, but a scientific doctrine; it claimed that it was not Utopian, but scientific, meaning practical. Now that attitude meant to me that its social science was not only an estimate of the economic and industrial development of the age, but also a scientific estimate of the nature of man. Since it claimed to be scientific, it followed that it must be practical; that is, that working men would align themselves with the socialist movement because in the industrial development of the present age, working men had no other recourse to political and social conduct except through the avenues of the socialist movement. But in my Socialist political campaigns, I found that the working man voluntarily voted the Democratic and Republican ticket and paid no attention to my so-called socialistic political and scientific wisdom. It therefore followed from my reasoning that the doctrine I was preaching was not scientific, and according to the teachings of socialism, an appeal for the Utopian ideal, even if converts could be made, could not be effective in the effort to solve the social problem. So I was what is called "stumped."

To my mind, education and agitation to recruit membership into the labor movement must be effective or the philosophy was erroneous. I therefore partially gave up working in the political field and centered my attention very largely on the economic field, where I found it easy to recruit membership into our labor union. Where the class struggle, in terms of strikes and boycotts and [the] public was effective, [it] made for material reduction in the hours of labor and increase in wages.

I found collective bargaining, that is, bargaining for wages, hours, distribution of work, rights in the shop and treatment on the part of the employers, foremen, examiners, etc., to have been much more effective in the interest of labor than the bargaining of the individual working man and woman with their employers. But there were numerous obstacles in the way of effectively carrying out of this collective thought in our special industry, and that worried me very much.

The industry was a seasonal industry; between the months of November to part of February there was almost no work at all. The latter part of October was slack and the month of November was even more slack, say two days a week. In December, no work at all. In January, no work at all; February, only work for the sample men, not 2 per cent of our people; in March duplicate samples, 7 or 8 per cent of our people; April, stock made of odds and ends to be sold very cheap; May and June a little more stock; July the first orders; August busy; September and October busy; November again slack.

We worked about three and a half months busy; about four months before and after the season part work, and three or four months no work at all. It was during the slack season that the union was not effective at all, and the manufacturers paid such small wages people had to work a week for three or four dollars. It is true they were glad enough to do it, because we never saved enough in the busy season to carry us comfortably through the slack season. But we couldn't live even half, not even a third, on what we earned in the slack season, and strikes wouldn't be effective, because the manufacturers said that they didn't need our work.

But as the years went on, our industry did increase in volume. Manufacturers had saved enough money to begin to make stock, say a month ahead; they would begin to work heavily, say in the month of June; some even as early as May. It was in these times that while there wasn't enough work for all, there was some room for effective bargaining, and since I was the main member of the union, I was invariably appointed to head the committees in negotiating with the employers.

In those years, our people had received quite a training in the union-strike business. In the year 1892 we had already experienced three or four very severe strikes. Some of our men had penitentiary sentences hanging over their heads. One of our men was shot, another killed by a non-union man. Employers had learned to hire gangsters to beat up our pickets. Over and over again we had serious fights on the streets of the sweatshop district. We had succeeded in effectively assaulting the business prosperity of our employers and some of the most stubborn ones we had ruined in business. Employers found that we were fighting with a desperation that they hadn't counted upon in their estimate of our weakness, and the reason for that was because we were in despair during the slack season, and overworked in the busy season.

In those days we were driving machines by foot-power. The material we worked on emitted a poisonous dust assaulting the lungs of the workers. And since we worked so hard, using [up] our vitality, a number of us contracted the poor man's disease, tuberculosis. We had also acquired a desire for a home separate from the shop. The general American prosperity and culture, while very slowly, did penetrate our population, and a sense of resentment against these awful, oppressive conditions formed a sense of loyalty to this union cause that was real indeed. For instance, during one of our strikes that we had against a part of the employers, those that were employed in shops where there was no strike voted half their wages to support the strike. I have known cases where families allowed their sick babies to die for want of money to pay doctors or for want of proper nourishment and care while they were offered good wages if they would only scab on the balance of us.

Employers found that it was in their interest to recognize and negotiate with members of our unions. And in negotiating with employers I had begun to learn something of commercial problems other than only the class struggle. I found that the problem of the employer as a merchant must be taken cognizance of by the representative of the union before a real understanding and agreement might be had between them, making for the establishment of standards for labor through[out] the industry which could actually be enforced and lived up to.

Take a conversation like this: "What do you think," an employer asked me, "that I have to pay for this garment?" I looked it over and set a price. He sat down and figured out the amount of cloth it would take, lining, trimmings, overhead, and cutting, all expenses outside of the cost of making the garment, and then said this: "You understand, don't you, that I'm not in business for glory. I will cut up merchandise and employ you fellows only upon condition of my ability to sell same and make a profit on the transaction. Well, the truth is that in slack season I would have to sell the merchandise at such a small price that I would lose money if I paid you what you want. In busy season I may be able to pay you what you want, and even more, but we are not making the price in busy season, we are making the price now, and, therefore, I can't pay you the price that you ask."

"Well, then," I said to him, "all right, we won't make the price now at all; we'll strike with every garment if we have any strength to strike at all, but we will have you where we want to have you when we become busy; then we will treble or fivefold what we are asking and make you pay in the busy season for everything we've lost in the slack."

"That," he said, "could not work out because our busy seasons are short, we are entering into contracts for sales of merchandise long before the season comes around and unless we know what we'll have to pay we can't make our prices, and if we make them and you strike on us in the busy season, we will be ruined. We must be able to settle the price for labor with you for the entire season and you must be able to deliver labor to us during the busy season with no strikes; otherwise, we cannot employ union labor and we will be obliged to destroy your union or your union will destroy us. But in order that we may enter into an agreement with the union for any kind of standards, the union itself must be strong and control the entire market and protect us against competition which makes it impossible for us to maintain the price for labor and sell our merchandise."

"For instance," he said, "just now I can buy merchandise in the eastern market, New York and other sections, the cost of which will be much less than the cost for garments made by your members. And so you can do as you please; either cooperate with us to formulate prices for labor and standards for employment, commensurate with the nature of the competitive market, or enforce standards which cannot be lived up to. And I'll simply record on paper an agreement with your people that can't possibly be lived up to."

Membership in the Workingman's Educational Society stimulated my social consciousness to fever heat. There were lectures three or four times a week. Discussions on social problems would continue after the lectures until two in the morning. Every lecture was an agitation speech in substance. The iron law of wages as formulated by La Salle was itself a premise that quite upset me. Would I have to live all my life and receive as compensation barely enough to live on while my employer rolled in wealth which he could not exhaust? Dogs and horses were to have better lives than I. Did such a premise apply to all the workers, my friends, my relatives? Such a question entirely absorbed my mental and emotional capacities. The group with which I was associated felt as I. We would agitate each other to fever heat, and were willing to make all sorts of sacrifices to bring about industrial, economic, and political changes.

During the winter of 1888, I went through the entire gamut of doctrines on the social problem. I became anarchistic in thought and read Tucker, Kropotkin, Proudhon. On cooling off a bit, I embraced the doctrine of the Socialist Party, which seemed much more reasonable in policy. Among our members could be found a number of students who attended professional colleges or were about to enter them, some university men, and one physician. We were all inspired with the missionary spirit to convert everyone to whatever our doctrines might be. We did unite on the trade union movement. The theory was that trade unionism was a preparatory school for the final conversion to socialism or anarchism, and we were bent upon organizing into labor unions the industries in which our people were employed.

The first union we organized was the Cloak Makers' organization. We were at once confronted with the situation whereby men joining the union were immediately ousted out of their jobs. Therefore, it was up to us to call a strike both to protect our men and preserve our right to organize a union. This problem, dating from 1886, when we were out on strike, presented itself again to my mind. I asked myself: What are we striking for? What means have we by which we can enforce our victories?

So before we called a strike, I called a meeting of the officers together and told them that I would lay before them the difficulties before us, which I had learned from practical experience through the previous strike. Should we win, how could we preserve the fruits of our victory? That depended on the nature of our demands. Should we demand a reduction in the hours of labor, and increase in the price for labor, and nothing more? The employer would say again—"You can regulate your own hours of labor in the outside shops, and as for the price of labor, it is piecework. If you don't get paid enough, don't work." Therefore, our whole strike would dissolve into nothingness, since the employer would send his work to shops working longer hours and at cheaper rates. I therefore moved that no strikes be called in our industry unless we first got our demands formulated in terms of a closed shop; that the strike cannot be settled unless the employers agree to send no work to unorganized shops, and that this be the cardinal demand. The subject of wages and hours does not need to be stressed upon as much as this—that of the closed shop.

A committee was appointed to draft resolutions upon which a call for a strike could be made. At the next meeting when these resolutions came up, there developed quite a difference of opinion among the members. Some who in theory agreed with the employers said all they demanded was higher wages from the bosses. We will take care of the hours through the union alone. In fact, we will take care of the wages too. We won't work until we're well paid. The reason for striking is not for the employers but for ourselves. We would like to stir up our people, create opinions making for high wages and regulated hours. We must form a union morality among our own people, sanctioned by our own authority, enforced through our own members, in the main. Emissaries from the bosses, who already had opinions on the strike formulated, were present at our meetings.

So it was necessary for me to carry on quite an agitation on the subject of the nature and structure of unions. In my version, the workmen alone could enforce standards. If standards were not enforced completely, the best union members were not benefited by the union. On the contrary, they were hurt because work was sent to shops which violated the provisions of the union, that the only possible redress was to get employers to agree to co-operate with the union on the enforcement of strike provisions; that is, send no work to violators of the provisions. This difference of opinion was discussed at numerous meetings, and the great majority in the end decided to strike for a closed shop, and we did.

After a prolonged strike of six weeks, we lost out again. We went back to work on the old terms, but by that time the season in the industry was in full swing, we had ourselves established a ten-hour day in the outside shops, and since merchandise had accumulated during the strike, we were quite busy, earned fair wages, and partially enforced a ten-hour day. But in slack times, the union again began to lose its hold, disloyal shops received most of the work, since they lowered their union standards, and the membership in the union petered out. The same thing was true a year later. The union was reorganized, during the season better wages were enforced, some control was established, and in the slack season, while the union still existed, the membership was very small and we were obliged to wait for the next season to reopen an organization campaign again.

During those years, particularly in 1888, the subject of whether the union should be composed of both employees and the contractor was vigorously discussed, and it was finally voted to oust the contractors and to form the union of wage-workers only. It was then that I made up my mind that I was going to give up my shop and become an operator working for others instead of being an employer. I had done well, comparatively speaking, as a contractor, having made enough money to send for a number of my relatives, to pay for eight or nine machines, and to establish myself and my family quite comfortably.

When I gave up the shop, not only did I have to go to work for others, but Father had to do so, and my brothers also. We all reverted to the condition of being a proletarian family. There was quite a difference of opinion between myself and our family, especially Mother. She pointed to the prosperity of her relatives and neighbors who were contractors. She argued with me that I had no business to destroy our livelihood, to subject my old father and brothers to the necessity of working for others. My attitude of mind was distasteful to her on other grounds outside of my proletarian loyalty. In that Educational Society, religion was quite a subject of discussion. The agitation in the main was from the point of view of atheism. Mother said I was not only a Goy myself, but I was also converting others to my heretic notions; that nice boys, who went to *shul*, prayed every day, and were properly religious, were through my subverted doctrines converted to doctrines of heresy to become "Goys."

These were years of great struggle. I was obliged to fight with the employers in the shops, with Father, Mother, and all my relatives at home, and since I understood the principles of unionism better than most of my fellow workers, I had to fight a great deal in my union, and in the Educational Society. I was a zealot, a propagandist, absorbed completely by my social consciousness in the campaign for what I called "a better day."

I read every spare minute I had and I improved my understanding of social problems, and learned a great deal of political economy, sociology, and natural science. I did not understand in detail the doctrines of biology as taught by Darwin, but I read a great deal of it, and heard numerous lectures on Darwinism, Spencer's doctrines, and on Sunday mornings, I attended lectures delivered by the Ethical Culture Society headed by William Salter. The American Socialist had a branch and had meetings every Sunday afternoon where

Thomas Morgan was the main spokesman. I attended these regularly, also. I had almost no personal life. I was always at meetings.

With regard to my personal life, an event transpired which may have helped to form me along my lines of development. Three of the girls working for me when I had a shop belonged to a family of cultured and educated Russian Jewish immigrants. The family was way above our own, culturally. The girls could read in Russian, and they had all gone through the upper schools in Russia. Their father was a merchant, and, as I was told, quite rich until impoverished by the Russian pogroms, whereupon he came to America. At one time, these girls invited me to visit their family for an evening. On a Saturday night I went to see them. Among the guests who visited that family was a young woman introduced to me as Mrs. Regent. I was told her husband was a physician, and that she came from Milwaukee. Through Milwaukee relatives of these friends of mine, she had been introduced to this family she was now visiting. This young Mrs. Regent attracted me very much. I had never met anyone just like her. She was very beautiful, and dressed very neatly, more so than any woman I had ever met before. She combed her hair in [a] different and more attractive style than other women of my acquaintance and had a wonderful pair of smiling eyes. She seemed to be able to both penetrate and at the same time give volumes of human joy and happiness, and her body corresponded with her eyes, in being and movement. She seemed to me a sort of center for intelligence, joy, happiness, and good fellowship. Everything she said was appropriate to the occasion, brimful of humor. She called, with her vibrant being, for everybody to give friendship, joy, and happiness. Her attitude was the complete opposite of the immigrants with whom I had associated. She was different, different indeed, and this difference I felt keenly, so before I left I practically saw no one else besides her.

I don't know why, but she seemed to be attracted by me

too. Before I left, she spoke to no one but myself, and when we parted, she was extremely friendly, was glad she had met me, and expressed the opinion I was very intelligent, that I had the conversation to [bring up] intelligent topics of discussion. When I left, she squeezed my hands very firmly and that night I didn't sleep. Every movement of hers seemed to have settled itself on my mind, and the impression vibrated and re-vibrated itself in my memory. A hundred little instances, her manner of speech, the way of dancing, the way she sang, her pleasant ways, filled my mind. The difference between herself and all the women I had ever met pounded on my whole being like a sledge hammer. I was a house on fire to myself. The next day she left for Milwaukee.

The girls in the shop talked about her all day. I said nothing, but my heart was choking full with her and for a period of eight months I heard nothing from her. Then one of the girls from this family casually told me that Dr. Regent was going to divorce his wife, and that they were now separated. She came to Chicago to live then.

That information affected me like a streak of lightning. For a time I thought of nothing else and felt nothing else except Tillie. What a joy it would be to be with her. She would help me in all my difficulties. In this big campaign in which I was engaged, I could rest with her. I could be comforted by her. She was sent by God to me to help me carry out all my ideals. I took it for granted that such a woman as she was could not be anything else but a socialist, since I could not imagine an intelligent being of any other doctrinal feeling. Even if she knew nothing of socialism, I felt she would of course fall for the justness of its reason for being. I asked one of the Shoenbrod girls to invite me again to her home to meet Tillie. I met her, walked with her, told her of my feeling for her, did not even ask her to marry me—simply took it for granted she would, since, I reasoned, we were born for each other. She, too, seemed to acquiesce in my opinion on the subject. Our only practical conversation was about the length of time it would take for her divorce. That, she thought, would take a year, or less, and it was understood between us at once that we would marry as soon as she got her divorce.

[Publisher's note: At this point in Bisno's original manuscript, there is a gap of five pages. As the continuing discussion makes clear, there was a very brief and tempestuous marriage in 1890.]

I loved Tillie. I loved her to distraction, but I hated quarreling more than I loved Tillie. My estimates of quarrels were the same as my estimates of criminality. It was against the essence of my conception of human relationships. With me, quarreling and violence were on the same plane. Quarreling and falsehood, treachery and deceit, were on the same plane. I could not conceive of two people quarreling unless they had a sense of animus toward each other. Love between two and quarreling could not have coexistence in my mind, and so good breeding was not in the same class with quarreling about it to me. Good breeding was of much less significance in life, and while I admitted in my own mind that it would have been better for me to be well bred so I could comply with Tillie's demands, I also considered it much less significant and felt she was wrong in her demands, forcing them with violence and temper.

In our long discussions, I made it quite clear that while I meant to improve my conduct, yet I did not mean to allow her to fuss because of it. I was to be changed slowly, and she would have to understand my mind was occupied with far more vital items. These quarrels, coupled with the differences in the standard of living and also the fact I had no money to meet her requirements even if she were right, made it clear to me that she and I were not suited for each other and that we absolutely could not live together.

After the third week of our married life, I planned to leave her. My love for her was battling with my ideals of living. I could not sleep or work or read. Nothing she did had had the least influence on me in modifying my life for her. I was still drawn to her as I had been on first meeting her. I yearned to be in her presence and I yearned to be away from her, and after a great deal of suffering, I finally decided to leave her, although I would never cease to love her. I might pay with my life for leaving her, but leave her I must. Six weeks after our marriage, we were divorced before a Jewish rabbi and suit was filed through a lawyer in civil court for a divorce. Tillie left Chicago and went to Milwaukee after our Jewish divorce and there married a man named Kaufman who was a baker. One of our friends who visited Milwaukee and saw her at her home testified later that she had committed bigamy. When I filed suit on these grounds, she left Milwaukee and I have not heard from her since. During the period in which I applied for a divorce and when I secured it, I suffered tortures on the grounds of my love for her. When she came to Chicago and I learned of it, I would stand near her home night after night hoping I would glimpse her as she came in—or perhaps I might see her through the window. I had to control myself but I did, with great difficulty. I never did approach her, but she did talk to me. At one time she asked me to come back to her. She said she felt I was very honest, that I loved her, that she might adjust her life to mine in time because she knew I would make a similar effort. While I was almost crazy to do it, I controlled myself and refused to do so.

One thing had occurred during our married life of importance in this story. One day, there was work enough to keep me busy only until two o'clock. I found the door locked. One of the men working for me who lived in the immediate neighborhood met me on the street smilingly and mentioned the fact that he knew Tillie had gone out. He told me about a young man, a furrier, who was friendly with Tillie, and moreover said that the furrier had told him that within the last week Tillie had been visiting her former husband, Dr.

Regent, in his office. She had personally confided to this furrier that Regent was not as bad as she thought him to be, that she was spending a great deal of time with him, and that it was his belief that she was once more living with Regent as his wife. I then went home and waited for Tillie. I sat and wondered why Tillie had never told me she was visiting her husband of other days, and formed the impression she was being secretive with me. She did not return until one o'clock that night.

I knew that she had no friends in town outside of our mutual acquaintances, who were really my friends, and so I was convinced she had been staying with Regent until that hour. Her behavior on her return convinced me absolutely that my suspicions were correct, and yet I cannot recall having had any sense of jealousy. If anything, I was very sympathetic to the idea of her staying with Regent, if only because we two had quarreled, had no sympathetic attitude towards each other, and I thought she might at least find some comfort with the other man. I knew I could not ask her about it because she might think me jealous, so I opened conversation with her on the subject of my theories with relation to married life. I told her that in my opinion the most significant right a human being has is to his own body, and that the highest authority of conduct to each human being is the language of his own blood and his own passion, and that when two people meet who have a sympathetic attitude toward each other, and human passion is aroused, it is in my judgment criminal not to satisfy those emotions. Real love to me consisted in the liberty which each human being had to satisfy such passion with the sanction of those who loved them. I, I said, would sanction her conduct in staying with any one she pleased—my friends or others—and that I held myself at liberty to conduct myself on the same plane. That night we were sleeping together and there was a great deal of love expression exchanged between us—the subject of Regent disappeared from my mind entirely.

5

In my reading about the labor movement, I ran across a book called *Conditions of Working People* by Frederick Engels, translated [into English] by a woman named Florence Kelley Wishnevitski. The book made a great impression on my mind and was one of the strongest indictments I had ever read against the present order of things, the strongest claim for the ideal co-operative commonwealth and socialism and for the strong class struggle, and was very informative on the nature of the labor movement in England. In lectures held in our Educational Society, this translator, Mrs. Wishnevitski, was spoken of as one of the greatest American socialists. It was said she was a Yankee from way back, that her father was the father of the system of protection in America, and that her father had also been a judge for a great many years. She belonged to the highest class of families in this country, and yet she had joined the Socialist Party and was held up as one of the great examples showing that the better class of people were with the socialists. Shortly after my reading that book and hearing about Mrs. Wishnevitski, I was told that she had come to Chicago and was living in our immediate neighborhood, namely at a place called Hull House, and since I was eager to learn all about socialism and about the people connected with it, I visited her, introduced myself, told her I was a member of the party, asked her whether she belonged to it, and was told by her she did not, that she had been thrown out by the General Executive Board because the Board had quarreled with her husband.

But nevertheless she was a socialist, loyal to the labor and socialist movements and even loyal to the organization of the Socialist Party. She said she had a number of friends among its leaders of whom she thought very highly. She mentioned the editor of the New York German socialist paper as a great friend of hers, as well as others, and spoke to me of her great desire to participate in the activities of the labor movement. She would be willing to speak before party membership, labor unions, or labor educational societies. I invited her to address our meetings, and I had quite a discussion with her on the meaning and interpretation of socialist dogma. Her interpretation of socialist dogma was what she called English. She believed in the development of the labor movement along the lines of what she called English socialism, namely, the realization of socialism step by step, that as industry developed, the labor movement would develop, and through that force, laws would be enacted in the interests of labor. Single and individual industries would be nationalized in the interests of nations as well as labor, and the sense of the social revolution was centered in the main in this progressive wresting of power from the capitalist classes and its transfer to the working class. She was in favor of labor legislation limiting the hours of labor, insuring conscientous work in the factories, prohibiting the employment of children, limiting the hours for the employment of women and younger people, establishing municipal ownership of transportation, of our light and telephone systems, of our water works, in extending the function of a municipality by way of playgrounds, parks, and the extending of our school system, giving working men's children the benefit of an education equal to that of the best in the country. She was interested in legislating on the subject of dwellings and houses for the poor, prohibiting the building of dark and crowded tenements, allowing more air space by law for buildings, and also interested in giving the poor the benefit of more expenditures on street cleaning and alley paving, etc.

She believed most strongly in propaganda and education, considered herself a missionary for the cause in the labor movement, and offered herself in these efforts. Her criticism of the present order was sharp, bitter, vigorous, with a finely developed sense of humor always present, as well as enormous erudition. She was well informed on political science, economic and industrial science, and also the natural sciences. She was educated in Geneva, Switzerland, and over there had married a Russian Jew, an artist, a young man who ran away from a Russian prison, a revolutionary from early days, who was the original cause of her becoming a socialist. She talked with me as though I were her equal. The fact that she was a Yankee and I a Jew seemed to make no difference to her. When I described the poverty, suffering, and oppression of our people, she took a great deal of interest. She was very sensitive to suffering, and appreciated very much people who had public spirit, social consciousness, and were willing to make sacrifices for them. The world of the rebel and the student was her world completely.

She introduced me to other members of the Hull House group—to a woman named Jane Addams particularly. She also was an American for many generations back, a very refined person who in conversation I found to be a person charged with moral and ethical principles. In agreement with

Mrs. Kelley Wishnevitski,* her indignation ranged along the same reasons for indicting society, but she disagreed with her on the nature of the class struggle. Jane Addams believed in democracy, in the people; she had an unbounded faith that things would work out well, provided people were given a chance, and she was the originator of this place called Hull House for the purpose of sharing her education with her neighbors, the common people. She wished to help them in every possible cultural way. She had organized lectures and invited people of all sorts, and of various political, industrial, ethical, and religious convictions to lecture there. An open discussion was encouraged after the lectures. Moreover, she had organized a kindergarten there, and a large number of classes to teach foreigners school subjects; classes in music, in painting and fine arts, spinning and weaving, as well as a shop, where boys might learn carpentry.

There was living in their group a young woman named [Ellen Gates] Starr, who was very religious, Episcopalian by faith. She was also a university woman, and was teaching English classes and participated actively in all of the efforts of Hull House. I met her and arranged that she give me several hours a week in reading, writing, and arithmetic lessons. I remember my effort to learn to write was rather unsuccessful. We spent our time mostly in trying to convert each other. I was all charged with the burdens of the labor movement and my effort in the same. She, I believe, learned a great deal more of the labor movement from me than I learned about reading and writing from her. She was a great comrade, very sensitively honest, wonderfully well bred, and as true as they make them. Julia Lathrop, too, got to be a friend of mine. She, too, lived there. She left a great impression on me of the sense of cautiousness in agitation and in inquiry about the

* Bisno here added the name "Wishnevitski" to the original manuscript, but he usually refers to Florence Kelley as Mrs. Kelley, the name by which she was known during the years he worked with her.

labor movement. She was both progressive and conservative, but brought to the subject always a great deal of knowledge and a great deal of energy, and especially a wonderfully clear, calm, and balanced mind.

My acquaintance with the people at Hull House was an eye-opener to me. People who did not belong to our class took an interest in our lot in life. This was very new to me. I had heard of such people when lectures were held in our club on the subject of the Russian revolutionary movement. There, I was told, young members of the Russian nobility and rich members of the aristocracy had thrown their lives in with those of the poor, and went around as crusaders for democracy and the abolition of private land-holding. They threw their lives in with the poor and were arrested, held in jail, exiled to Siberia, even killed in a great many cases, all on the altar of their missionary spirit to help the poor and abolish despotism, to overthrow the Czar, assault the authority of the army, and give the people a voice in determining their political and economic status in life. But all this was said of Russia.

In this country, the venture on the part of Jane Addams and her colleagues was something new, and while I did not agree with their Anglo-Saxon estimate of the nature of the social movement, I appreciated cordially the nobility of their characters, the integrity of their effort, and I prized my acquaintance with that group very highly. I participated actively in those public discussions of the lectures given at Hull House. There was freedom of speech over there. It was indeed free. For instance, one of the great preachers of the Episcopalian Church was invited to speak on the subject of how to ameliorate the conditions of the poor. He was quite a reformer and quite a liberal. His indictment of the order of things was as vigorous as that of any socialist. His honesty and integrity could not be questioned, but he submitted that 'the great hope of mankind was to believe in the aid of God, that

Jesus was the example set to mankind as to how they were to conduct themselves—love your neighbor as yourself—and sacrifice yourself on the altar of your love for mankind.

I was then very atheistically inclined and when I took the floor, I denounced this doctrine as a hypocritical shield to protect the interests of the clergy who were in league with the capitalists to benefit by the unequal distribution of wealth, the oppression of labor, and who sanctioned the disinheritance of the major part of the population, who sanctioned the private ownership of the largest part of this country's property by a comparative few of our population. I said that since the church did not take the revolutionary position of free inheritance, they were part and parcel of the ruling and governing classes and their very pretense of an honest attitude toward the poor and the labor classes was a fraud making for fooling the people while they were engaged in the business of stealing their substance. Some of the audience thought I had made a very ill-bred attack on a man who was the guest of the house, and that I should have been more gentle and less personal in my talk. Since I was not acquainted with manners such as the better-bred people speak of, I felt that they might be right, that while what I said was true, yet my language might have been too strong for them. Perhaps I really did not belong there. I might speak in such brusque fashion at my own meetings, but had no business to inveigh in such manner at others' meetings. Later I asked Miss Starr about it because I knew she was very religious and had a great deal of personal friendship, regard, and veneration for this particular divine. No, she said, our meetings are free, and it is our intent that everybody attending should speak his mind honestly and freely, and since I believed you to be honest in your convictions, I think our friend the clergyman would consider you right in speaking as you did.

At one of the meetings, Isaac Horwich was the lecturer. He was a refugee from Siberia, a Russian Jewish nihilist, of great erudition, known to be a great rebel and socialist. He was lecturing at the University of Chicago on matters pertaining to Russian economics, and his lectures found a great deal of sympathy both in the audience and the residents of Hull House. Mrs. Kelley, Miss Addams, Miss Starr, and others entertained Mr. Horwich, asked him in the minutest way about his complaint against Russian authorities, and expressed [the] greatest friendliness towards him and the movement in which he was interested.

There was one lecturer who had a special significance for me. McLaughlin, a teacher of political economy at the University of Chicago, was that man. He lectured on the doctrines of Malthus, and spoke sympathetically of the idea that we were increasing our population at a faster ratio than our production of food was being increased; that poverty was natural because of our increasing population; that mankind had no hope in any of the alleged changes for structural society, but believed that the solution resided in the individual, and that the only reform possible lay in the reformation of each individual by himself. The center of his theory of reform was that a poor man had no right to get married and procreate since he could not support them, and that it was in the very nature of things that he should not be able to support them. He got me mad. When I had the floor I asked him whether he was married, had children, and whether it was the practice among his people to be married and to have children. When he answered in the affirmative, I charged that the rich not only deprived the poor of their rightful inheritance, access and ownership to land and utilities, but did not even want them to have access to their women-folk; that these rich wanted to assault human nature, to turn the labor population into eunuchs, sterilize them—both men and women—and since he represented his class honestly, that is how capitalism wanted us to behave ourselves—to labor hard, be poor, and hold our women for the benefit of capitalists—that men of that kind generated a sense of hatred among the poor as no socialist could possibly do.

I considered such an attitude atrocious. I did not even favor, through the social revolution, a reciprocation of such an attitude whereby the males of the capitalist class would be sterilized and become eunuchs. The subject of the right to be married, the need to have children, to mate with a woman, seemed to me to be ingrained in the essence of our lives, and it provoked in me a severe reaction against the attitude of mind of the capitalist class against our mode of living. I sanctioned then in my own mind the idea of getting married for myself, of having children so that I might produce soldiers for the social revolution. I did occasionally reflect upon the helplessness of the individual to determine the lives, fortune, and ideas of his children, and confess now I was somewhat skeptical with relation to my own power to make socialists out of my children or to get a socialistically inclined wife who would stay put in that belief as the years went on. But, all things considered, I felt that getting married, having children, had the best of the argument.

There were coming to these meetings several young men and women who belonged to rich families. They participated in the discussions. Lovett Hunter, William English Walling, Ernest Poole, and others came. Gertrude Barnum, who was living at Hull House, was the daughter of a judge; she was young, graceful, well-bred and enthusiastic. She participated in these labor discussions eagerly. Florence Kelley was active in these meetings. She would lecture from time to time. I wasn't satisfied alone with the speeches at these meetings. I made it my business to carry on my missionary work with individuals; I became intimately acquainted with Hunter, Walling, Poole, Miss Barnum, and Miss Lathrop, and tried to convert them. I succeeded with substantially every one of them in a measure, so that years after, many of them testified in public [to] my agency in their conversion. A group was formed composed of Henry D. Lloyd, a prominent physician named Bayard Holmes, Florence Kelley, and Ellen G. [Starr] to engage in a campaign for legislation to abolish sweatshops, and to have a law passed prohibiting the employment of women more than eight hours a day, prohibiting the employment of children under fourteen, registering all under sixteen, and to expose to the public the unsanitary conditions of the tailor shops and to protest against low wages, long hours, and oppressive conditions as experienced by the people of all varieties in the clothing industries.

It was Mrs. Kelley who introduced me to Mr. Lloyd. Lloyd was a great personality. At that time he had already written several things on labor problems, and a book called *A Strike Against the Miners,* wherein the story was told that mine owners had themselves by design caused miners to go out on strike so that the scarcity of coal might raise the price of coal and give the mine owner opportunity to rob the public of millions of dollars; that the mine owners used the agencies of the state to oppress and defeat the miners. It was a great document in those years, written by a man who himself was rich, had great learning, and was looked up to as a model citizen by all classes. He was not the same sort of socialist I was, but befriended me and invited me to his home. We spent hours and days together discussing the social problem, and while our union made the first public movement to denounce sweatshops at Turner Hall, it was Mr. Lloyd who had me hire the Central Music Hall, a public hall at State and Randolph streets, one of the largest and best appointed in the city. There, we had a number of clergymen of great reputation speak in favor of this reform legislation. Lloyd made a great speech; so did Bayard Holmes, Mrs. Kelley, and others. We packed the hall to the roof and the newspapers took up the shout, to the extent of column of type after column, reciting the speeches, reporting various shops, standards of wages, picturing the lecturers, etc. It was not long after, that the legislature appointed a joint commission to investigate sweatshops in Chicago. Through these same people, especially Mrs. Kelley, who with myself and Mr. Lloyd were in the heart of the movement, in 1893, a law was passed prohibiting the employment of children under fourteen, and that of women for longer than eight hours a day, ordering employers to furnish the addresses of all their shops, and sanitary measures were taken to protect the consumer from contagious diseases. Employers were prohibited from employing people in their homes.

The industry I was engaged in—that of making women's clothes—was what we called a piece-worker's industry, the men and women doing the work by piece. The price for labor, before a union was established, was made by the employer. Occasionally when a man or woman couldn't earn enough at the price set by the employer they would complain and have it modified or not, depending upon the judgment of the employer in the main. Employees without the union had no power to enforce their own views on the price for labor, and normally the price for labor was set by the employer. Very seldom would an employer admit that he erred in judgment in setting a price. But when a union was organized, the spirit of the people rose and the price for labor was increased materially. But in this trade every new garment had to have a new price and a standard had to be set for labor, and there were three ways to settle those prices.

One was for each employee to settle the price for the garment they were working on with their employer individually. Another was that a committee in the shop was selected to settle the price for labor for the entire shop. The third way was that a representative of the union, in consultation with the committee of the shop, settled the price for labor with the employer. In case each individual settled the price for labor with the employer, the price was poor because the individual was afraid he would be fired if he insisted upon a high price for labor. Even if the union should protect his or her job it wasn't safe for an individual to insist upon a fair price for labor because it was so easy to find fault with the work, or sometimes a person came in late, or numerous other ways to find cause for discharge. It was the business of the people individually to be in the good graces of the employer so that they might hold their jobs. It was much better in case a committee settled the price for labor, because in that case they didn't settle the price for labor only for themselves, but for the entire shop and they were also people who were more trained in knowledge as to the amount of labor to be done on a garment. But the better way was for a representative of a union to be the spokesman in settling the price of labor.

Originally the employers insisted upon settling the price for labor with each worker individually, and after they had acquiesced in letting a committee from the shop settle the price, they still wouldn't allow a representative from the union [to] represent them. And finally, after a great many controversies, strikes, boycotts, and what not, employers were agreed that the union could have its spokesman along with a committee to settle the price for labor. The knowledge, intelligence, etc., that were necessary to a representative of a union to settle the price for labor were very great. He had to be a good mechanic, was supposed to be an expert in all classes of merchandising and in numerous callings such as pressing, tailoring, machine operating, cutting, etc., and had to be able to speak well and represent his people effectively. He had to be honest so that he might not be unfairly influenced by the employer, and had to have a powerful, authoritative personality and strong will power in addition to all that, because in negotiating the price for labor for large numbers of people, every move or judgment of his was of great significance as affecting the lives of the people.

Now the more vigorous and capable a representative of the people was, the more effectively he was feared and hated by the employing class. During these years when I was obliged to represent our people in entering into contractual relations with employers, settling prices for labor, defending assaults on the part of employers in case of discharges or other forms of discipline, I had a great deal to do. Every issue that arose between myself and the employers had to be brought to the shops—a constant campaign of education and agitation on each special issue in all the different callings. Standards of employment adopted by the union could not be enforced except with the active aid of all our membership; it was necessary that they understand clearly the issues involved, and a great deal of education had to be given them.

In those years I was obliged to make a great deal of sacrifice for the union. The union was not as yet strong enough to employ regularly a representative. The people hadn't steady work and didn't pay steady dues into the union, so that while I did a great deal of work for the union and occasionally got some money paid for my time, I didn't have a steady job from the union and I couldn't hold a job in a well-paying, responsible firm because employers were afraid of me. So my earnings as an operator through the year were much less than those of other members of our union. I had not been as good a workman, either, as the other men; I spent too much time reading, attending meetings, making agitation, discussing, etc., so there wasn't enough time left for me to acquire efficiency as a working man, especially since the industry itself kept on being improved right along, and better and more efficient workmanship was required. So that while I was at least partially successful in raising the standards of living for our people, I was at the same time very effective in assaulting my own standard of living and that of our family. My people, to whom this whole labor movement was a new and strange innovation, and who only knew it as it affected the income of the family, considered me crazy, had [no] sympathy with me, and at the same time, I was a sort of an outcast, outlandish, a man not to be reasoned with, and one who affected the fortunes of the family deleteriously, so that I was quite estranged from my family.

At that, all things considered, we had made considerable advance. Most of the shops belonged to the union, most of the manufacturers recognized the union, dealt with us collectively, and my reputation as a loyal, devoted, energetic, capable organizer of the union grew extensively amongst the people in the industry, so that when the union in New York was weak, when the few loyal members that still remained in the union found that they needed someone to reorganize the union, the executive board voted to send for me and employ me to help organize the union and to do in New York what I had succeeded in doing in Chicago.

It must be borne in mind that the apparel industry was a great deal more developed in New York than it was in Chicago. In the year of 1900 there must have been about twenty thousand people employed there while there weren't more than a thousand in Chicago, and so I acquiesced to go to New York and help their union. One of the main reasons why I went was because almost every manufacturer told me that the union in Chicago couldn't set the price for labor, since that was decided in New York, and because in case we wanted work at competitive prices for labor, we'd get no work at all to do during the greater part of the slack season. Chicago manufacturers would buy from New York, and they did. I went to New York mainly for the purpose of raising the standard of living over there so I might be able to maintain a union standard of living in Chicago.

I was interested in the people of New York too. But my real interest was my Chicago friends whom I knew and whom I had struggled together with and whose standard of living I actually affected, whose raises I raised, whose hours I reduced, whom I saw living in better quarters, and who together with me had made personal sacrifices on the altar of this cause during strikes and other efforts. It seemed that when you are engaged jointly in a social effort on whose altar you are obliged to make jointly great sacrifices, a human attachment is formed something like the attachment of one's family. It gets to be inculcated in one's very being and becomes a part of one's character. My character then was "union movement" and I went to New York with the enthusiasm that had been formed from a number of years of very live activity in Chicago and with a fair measure of knowledge of the nature of the problem.

The day I arrived in New York I called a meeting of the executive board of the union and consulted with them upon the nature of my office. I was told that I was going to be paid eighteen dollars a week, that while the union was weak, there was still enough money to pay me those wages, and that I was to help organize the union, adjust matters with the employers, enter into agreements with employers, etc. I then drew up an instrument providing for the employers to recognize the union and to enter into contractual relations with same, establish a principle of collective bargaining and numerous other provisions, making the agreement effective. I was then given a list of employers whom I was supposed to visit and negotiate a union agreement with.

One of the firms I was supposed to visit was a firm named Rosenshein. It seemed that the firm employed about a hundred people inside of the factory and some three or four hundred people in the outside shops. It was a very prosperous concern and I was told by my fellow members of the union that it was a very difficult firm to deal with. "This Rosenshein is a smart fellow," I was told by one of them. "He always gets the best of you." That didn't worry me; I considered myself as smart as any of them. And I went to introduce myself to Mr. Rosenshein in full confidence that I was an able match in knowledge of the trade, in general intelligence and ability, so that I would compare favorably with him. After I introduced myself to him, told him my name, who I was, what I was there for, he asked me if I lived in New York. I told him that just now I was, but that I had come from Chicago. At that he was rather surprised. Weren't there enough men in New York to do that work that they wanted to import a man from Chicago, he wanted to know. I then told him that I had had more experience in Chicago than the fellows in

New York had and that I did not consider it out of place for me to come from Chicago to work for the people in New York. Then he wanted to know what I made my living on, and I told him that I was getting eighteen dollars a week. He was rather surprised to find that there were people willing to pay for that kind of work. Sticking their noses into other people's business, he called it. And being paid for it, besides. "What do you want from me?" he said. "Well, I want you to read this document, it's a general form of agreement to be entered into between your firm and the union, covering the subject of the standards to be set in the industry, hours, wages, distribution of work, rights of employers and employees, etc."

After he had read the document, he told me that he would not sign it. I then told him I was authorized to order a strike in his factory and in his outside shops, and that I meant to do it at once. After he had heard that, he modified his attitude, confessed frankly that a strike would materially injure his business, and wanted to know why I picked on him rather than someone else. He pointed to a number of shops that he said had much worse employers than his, paid worse wages, employed their people irregularly, and that I was probably sent to make a strike in his place by some of his enemies that egged me on to it, that he couldn't understand for the life of him the reason why he should be singled out from all the rest of them, and more of the same kind. After a great deal of explanation on my part, and after he was convinced that I had resolved to call on his people to leave their work, he finally agreed to sign the agreement, but when he took the pen in his hands and before he actually signed it, he burst out laughing, a long and continuous laugh, almost hysterical, and after some little time, he finally stopped laughing.

I said to him, "Rosenshein, what are you laughing about?" He turned to me, and he said, "To tell the truth, it's a little more than I can stand; it disgusts me. I am a pretty good hand at lying myself, but this business of unions and union agents, men coming here from Chicago, getting eighteen dollars a week and fooling and cheating the people, is a little more than I can stand. I have been a party to making these promises on more than one occasion, but before the union agent has barely left my factory, the people working for me in the outside shops begged me for work, agreeing not to comply with any of the terms of the union, cheating each other for my benefit; but it seems that the fraud has got to be kept up and so they send for a man from Chicago, pay him wages, sign agreements, violate the same continuously, and the farce is carried on. I don't want any strikes; I'll go along with you in this strike as far as you want; I'll sign up and before the ink is dry on my signature, there'll be another agreement entered into between some of the people working in our outside shops and our firm, substantially nullifying every provision in this agreement that you want me to sign."

"Under these conditions," I said to him, "I don't want you to sign the agreement. Give me that paper back. I will go back to the union, verify what you say, and if what you say is true, I promise you not to molest you any more so far as I am concerned until such time as I will be in the position to honestly enforce the provisions of this agreement." I bid him good day, took the agreement, and went. I then decided to call a shop meeting of all the shops working for Rosenshein both inside and outside, tell the story as I had heard it, and devise a plan by which union standards on those agreements might be enforced.

The first outside shop I visited was that of a man named Spiegel. That was a room about 25′ by 60′, employing some fifty people; about fifteen or sixteen machine operators, and the balance, pressers, finishers, tailors, buttonhole makers, etc. I found the shop to be in a very old building, a good portion of the plaster of the room was missing, the windows covered with dirt, almost none of the paint that had once existed on the woodwork was visible, and the whole place was partially dark, dirty, and very crowded. There must have been at least fifteen hundred garments in the place; in one corner the bundles were piled up clear to the ceiling. The people working in the shop seemed to be completely absorbed with their work, no one noticed me when I came in, no one raised his head from his work. They had the old foot-power machines. The noise in the shop was so great that one had to shout in order to be heard. Everyone in the shop was simply absorbed with attention to their work. I went up to the first operator on a sewing machine, told him who I was, told him that I was calling a shop meeting, and asked him to come to same immediately after work. While I was talking to him, he kept on running his machine, even failed to turn his head to look at me, but after I was through he turned his head, stopped for a minute and said, "Yes, I heard about you, they sent for you to come from Chicago, didn't they? Well, please speak to the next man." He turned back to the machine and began to work.

I did speak to the next man and finally to the third and fourth until I got to the fifth. They all sent me each to the next. When I got to the fifth, he turned his head even before I had begun to say anything—"Yes," he said, "I heard what you said to the other men; frankly, we will not come. Let the other dirty bastards go to meetings; we have gone to meetings long enough." I then found that this shop had been out of work for a period of four months, that Rosenshein was discriminating against it, sent work to other shops, but failed to send to this one, and gave the contractor as the reason why he didn't send them any work that there was too much union in his shop. He indicated that if the people in the shop would sober down a little on the subject of their union, pay no attention to authorized agents of a union, do the work at the price as settled by Rosenshein himself, he was going to send them work. One of the men in the shop—it happened to be the very fellow that had told me they were not going to come to a shop meeting, and who was a relative of the contractor— had arranged with the contractor that the people in the shop were going to lay low on the subject of unions so that they might get work.

The price for labor was outrageous; the people in the shop worked practically an unlimited number of hours; they got in before daylight and worked until late at night. They asked no price for work at all. They were exhausted in their long, protracted idleness and lack of activity; they were beaten and they knew it and they looked it. They looked like a set of galley slaves very determined to stick it out in their loyalty to their contractor and to Rosenshein.

I then visited a number of other shops. The men who had no work were perfectly willing to come to the meeting, in fact, they were very enthusiastic in their loyalty to the union; in most of the cases it was the very men who paid no attention to the union when they received the work. The shops that had a lot of work were very lukewarm on the subject of attending the shop meeting. They each had their story to tell, their complaint to file. And in substance it was this: "Go to meetings, no work. Stick to your work and don't go to meetings and you're likely to be employed."

There was a great scarcity of work generally, and a very depressed attitude of mind. I then instead of calling a shop meeting called a meeting of the executive board in which I submitted to the board, first, the statements of what I had found; next, a modified form of an agreement in which the authority to distribute the work amongst the several shops was to be lodged in the hands of both the employer and the agent of the union so that whatever agreement might be entered into between the employees and the union, it would be possible for the union to enforce the same. Next was a statement to the people in the industry, reciting the experience I had had at Rosenshein's, Spiegel's and other shops, and ordering all the people employed at Rosenshein's factory to come to a shop meeting and ordering the people of all our other shops to come to a general meeting in which the new instrument, as drawn by myself, would be taken up, considered, discussed, and if possible, adopted, and standards established in the industry reducing the working day in all outside shops to ten hours, increasing the pay, and providing for a machinery making for the enforcement of the terms of the agreement. This was what the president of the council thought a big job and asked me how I was going to bring it about in life; how I was going to get the employers to agree that the unions join in with the employers to acquire the authority to distribute the work, and that the employers would recognize the union and acquiesce to all the terms as formulated by myself.

The only answer I had was that this was my notion of the nature of labor unions; that it was the business of a labor union to establish and maintain union standards and that these standards were limiting and defining the number of hours I might be employed in the industry, setting rates of wages for work, and mainly, to establish the power that would effectively eliminate competition between one union man and another and between one union shop and another so that the standards as agreed on might be maintained. Unless this was held as the first condition for the organization of the labor unions there was no reason for any working man to join, pay dues, go to meetings, go out on strikes, and allow the union authority over him personally.

To this, the answer was in this line: there is no one way to Rome; that what I had said was the end and not the beginning of a union; that a union is not only an accomplished fact, but also an educational institution; that while what I said was true it was also true it could not be done in a day and that just now the most significant thing was to keep the union at all, get the employees to join, and not to enforce standards, but to agitate standards, to educate the people to some form of machinery which would make it possible for us to do something about the evils in industry. I then asked him whether he thought that he would tell the people the whole truth and nothing but the truth as Rosenshein had told me. I wanted to know whether he would tell how one shop was allowed to scab against another shop; that it was allowed to have violations on the subject of agreed standards of wages; that while competition had been eliminated in the same shop between one man and another, you do not eliminate competition between one member of the union and another in case they work in two different shops.

In my judgment, I said, scabbing as practised here in New York by shops instead of individual employees bears down on the lot in life of the ordinary working men more than ordinary scabbing does; that scabbing in teams, scabbing and finding justification for it, assaulted the sense of solidarity among working men much more directly than ordinary scabbing on the part of individuals. It was vicious, criminal, I said, and [I] felt I would rather work in the industry without a union than be employed, be a member of the union which did not answer this first significant problem for a working man—Thou mayest not scab against thy neighbor. This was particularly true of our industry because there was not enough work for all, and the need to scab against your co-worker was pressing constantly against the consciousness of each working man and his family. Competition between one shop and another for work was so keen, all made for the whole tragedy of our present industrial life for working men. The elimination of all this must come in the first line of defense in the formation of a union.

"Well, what will you do about all this?" asked the secretary at last. I answered, "You must agree with my formation of a union or I cannot team up with you at all." "What will you do with those who will not agree?" he asked. "I will not accept them as members of the union and will throw out those who are members and do not live up to these standards," I said; "I will go in for agitation just as you wished it. I will help to establish an industrial morality. I will wait patiently until I can form a union capable of meeting these problems. I will go in with you into significant strikes and will contribute personally my share of the sacrifice necessary to be made. But I will stand for no deceit, no cheating. I will be open and above-board in pronouncing every assault on the sense of solidarity, and will make the principles of solidarity binding on each man joining us, and will organize a machinery willing and able to cope with our industrial problems, especially this one. Along with the standards we desire to establish on the subject of hours of labor, wages, rights in the factory, etc., there must go with it, the principle of a man's right to his job and the right of a shop, when engaged and employed, to its pro-rata share of work so there may be no competition between shop and shop, which assaults the standards so keenly."

"But," said the secretary, "people do not understand this." "Then we don't want them as members," said I. "And those that are members?" they asked. "I'll throw them out," I said, "and punish them by a boycott in which I will allow no member of our union to work with them in the same shop." To this the secretary answered that if it came to throwing out members from the unions, of his personal knowledge the whole membership would have to be ejected. I then asked every member of the council whether in their judgment what he said was true. They all acquiesced by saying yes. I said, "Fellow working men—as I see it, I do not belong here. I'll go back to Chicago." And on the same night I took a train and went back to Chicago.

The experience in New York upset me considerably. I found myself engaged in a struggle which seemed hopeless by its very nature. I could not make harmony for our people through the agency of a union with competition between shop and shop going on with their permission. I could not abolish this competition unless the union had authority, along with the employer, to distribute the work equally among shops as well as among men, and unless the employers acquiesced in the principle of the right of a man to his job.

135

The employer had no right to discharge a man from his job, or to discharge a number of men by failing to supply their shop with work on his own motion. The work in the factory must be distributed by authority lodged mutually in the employer and the union at the same time. I knew none of the employers agreed to that. I knew they would put up the strongest possible fight in case we even asked for it, and I was willing to engage in the effort to force the employers to see the justice of this claim, but I found myself against an even worse situation—our own people did not see any objection to competing shops. Even those who did failed to see the significance of it and did not feel as if they could support me in this crusade. I felt that unless these provisions were embodied in our demands, our strikes were purposeless and wasted.

I felt extremely discouraged; in fact, I despaired. I did have some consolation, and that was that the people in Chicago were at least partially willing to agree with my view on the subject matter and that there was quite a morality established in the matter of scabbing against each other. Committees in our union would go around from shop to shop making comparisons of the price for labor, calling strikes on shops agreeing to work for less than others, carrying on a very vigorous and active campaign for an industrial morality making itself felt in the industry to a very large extent. But I knew that unless this morality was established in the East where the market was ten times as large, the more active we were in the West in improving our conditions, the less work we would have.

I found the labor movement to be not as simple as I had first conjectured. The sense of solidarity, as I projected it in my mind, among working men did not quite work out. Our membership was not as loyal as I thought they should be. Competition between men and men, shop and shop, continued. In every shop there were a few much more loyal to the employers than to the union. Some of the members of the union opened up shops and became contractors themselves. Meetings during the largest period of the year were unattended by the workers. They were too busy to attend in the busy season; in slack time they found they had no occasion to go to meetings. At the beginning of each season, there was a little flurry in attendance and then I would make great speeches for loyalty to the cause of labor, for the great ideal of brotherhood and solidarity, but the only effect I caused was—let us settle the price of labor, and we're off. We have no further use for speeches. The rank and file were practically unscrupulous, had very little idealism, and whatever ideals they may have had were personal and selfish. They had very little social consciousness and were only touched by a sense of social interest when an extreme enough event occurred which would move the whole mob. A catastrophe seemed necessary.

The predominant sentiment I found to be cynical. After a speech, the average man would say—this fellow is looking for a job. He has some ax to grind for himself. It seemed to me that almost everybody was fighting to shield themselves from the assault of social consciousness. The reason seemed to be that social consciousness did not seem to pay. The ordinary working men were the worst offenders. As I found it, the leaders whom the ordinary man disbelieved were much more honest and had much more social consciousness than the ordinary man ever gave the leader credit for. Social consciousness evidently had to be implanted and could not be effected by lectures or speeches at all. It could only be effected in the average man through great hardships and long experience of bitterness. The ordinary working man was not good soil for the growth of social consciousness. He conceived of the idea very slowly, and it failed to grow often and in many different individuals because some would become contractors themselves, were given special privileges in certain shops where they earned more than others; in fact, much of their practical experience militated against social consciousness and made for a cynical attitude on the part of the individual. In the case of many it made for a feeling which might lead to betraying the social cause since the cause of the individual seemed of supreme importance. The more intensely I looked into the whole subject matter, the more difficult the problem seemed to be in my mind's eye. The more fanatic I became, the more loyal I became, and [the] more eagerly I studied it. Every conceivable theory on the subject of social problems and the individual nature of man and his problem filtered through my mind. Events and experience came back to mind recurrently to be thought over, measured, compared, and used to draw definite conclusions from.

These were years when I was burning alive with life problems and social problems. I got accustomed to my work as an operator and performed it automatically, without thought in its accomplishment. Habit set the pace so efficiently that each garment I made seemed to take about the same length of time to finish. The quality seemed about the same in each garment. The work was automatic and I did not have to spend any thought on the subject. I did not go to sleep at the same time every night, but I arose at the same hour each morning. There must have been reserve enough in my body to be able almost automatically to arise at the same hour no matter what hour that had to be. I would enter the shop each day at the same hour and would work automatically except when there was a new garment to work on, which would take a couple of hours to become used to. So I would study my social problems and my human problems while I was working.

My problem of Tillie occupied a great deal of my mental activity. She stood out before my mind's eye vividly. I would speculate on where she was, on what she was doing, on whether she was happy and comfortable. The labor movement too took a great deal of my thought. As I conceived it, it meant to me a sort of social building—people would pile social brick on brick, until an edifice of industrial solidarity was erected. I saw these bricks fall apart as fast as I laid them on, and my interest in the building always was so intense and germane to my life's happiness that I was constantly provoked, agitated, and in a state of fever over my non-success.

My family, father and mother, cousins and others would also constantly bear weight on me. I was always a target for argument and jibes. The cousins who had been my former partners in contracting ran their shops and made money. They showed evidence of their wealth and comfort. Other cousins who began poorly made enough to open up a store. All along the line each was personally successful and afforded additional argument for a life of selfishness and money-making, while I was labeled the fool who worried about other people, talked a socialist language they did not comprehend, and was misunderstood, misrepresented, and sneered at, as well as ignored constantly. I remember that at a family gathering, I was the subject of discussion. "He is no different than we are," said one of my cousins, "only he wants to show off. When he remarries, he'll change quickly." Another said, "He threw religion overboard because it's easier to be irreligious." They even resented the fact that I had to be a subject matter for discussion, but I was. I worried them. They worried me and bore on me with all possible weight.

I needed a rest and found I could not very well rest alone. I was hungry for a woman friend. In the movement I had a number of male friends. Some greatly enjoyed being with me and learned from me social, political, and religious interpretations of life. Others who had studied more and had better minds than I afforded me the same kind of joy in turn. All these, however, gave me no rest. If anything, they only increased the tension on my interest more. I had no balance, no comfort. My attitude of mind was romantic, so I was drawn to women. I formed an attachment with a very stupid girl. She fell in love with me at once and very vigorously. She would not let me alone for a minute. She did not understand a word of what I told her, knew nothing of my problems except that I was a very nice boy and she loved me, and when we were together I responded by way of hugging and kissing her and pawing her. That suited her splendidly, and [she] was cocksure I was hers. She told the world we were engaged, which I did not deny—but in a couple of weeks, she herself became a problem for me which, added to my love for Tillie, my troubles in my union, and in my socialist society, and my family, made an unbearable burden.

After four weeks, I broke off my relation with her in a very simple manner. I was still hungry for a woman, but looked for one who might have some sort of spiritual life in common with me, who would understand me and would fill my life with rest and understanding. So I began to go about with another girl whom I believed better suited to my needs. On a certain outing of our union, this former sweetheart, Fanny, had a racing match with me. I tried to run away from her, she was hotly after me, seeing that I did not get a chance to talk to the latest girl I knew. We kept this up all day, until at four Fanny fainted. All my friends considered me brutal. I had to get a doctor to bring her back to consciousness. I spent the balance of the day and night with her. She understood not a word of what I was saying; I had no sympathy with her pain. It was a combination that did not fit. She got the impression that we did not belong together, and did not pursue me further.

Only a few months after, I had another similar experience. I could not live without a woman. In this case, the woman was much more intelligent. She had gone through high school in Germany, came of a very fine family, her brother was a university man, her father was well cultured and learned in Jewish lore. Her family objected to me strenuously, but she hung on to me for dear life, and found me very difficult because I was so completely absorbed in the labor movement and had such erratic, anarchistic attitudes toward life. I would approach, play with, kiss other girls in her presence, or attend meetings and not see her for weeks. Should she come to see me for an evening when men connected with the labor movement were present, I would give all my attention to the men. Yet I needed her to modify my intense distraction with my labor thoughts. I needed sympathy and comfort and womanliness. I liked this girl fairly well. She loved me almost to distraction, but we gave each other nothing but pain; she with her claim on my time and attention, and resentment because of her sense of jealousy, and I with my continuous effort to ward off any strong hold she might get on me because I desired to hold myself apart for the labor movement and any individual desires I might have. Again we lasted only a few weeks together and separated in a flame of resentment, pain, and worry.

I was left with no confidence in my ability to adjust myself to women. I was stumped. Prostitutes were the only comfort I could take. I knew it was artificial, unreal, a mercenary affair. My moral sense revolted against it. My physical sense was drawn to it. My life in these times was a constant discordance, and the more it was so, the more I became devoted to social problems and the labor movement, socialist enthusiasm and science.

I loved Tillie, and was looking for a woman. I approached and felt out almost every woman I knew. There was an Irish girl with whom I worked in the shop, whom I was trying to convert to unionism and to socialism, and away from Catholicism and cheap literature. She was young and very beautiful, sensitive and enthusiastic. Her feeling was—marry me and I'll become all you'll want to be done by me. She said, "You are wonderful—you speak so nicely even though you are a foreigner." She tried to seduce me, too. But I was afraid of her. It seems I had sense enough to understand that an American-born Irish Catholic would not fit in with a Jewish socialist and atheist, who was moreover engrossed in the labor movement. My habits and ideals were completely foreign to hers. Our flame lasted only a short time. I think it was her mother who saved me. She made her daughter leave her job, transported the girl to an aunt in a small Wisconsin town, and again I ran around like mad looking for another woman.

141

I don't believe I was very popular with the women in the Educational Society, where I delivered lectures regularly. Firstly, I paid no attention to personal appearance. I seldom took a haircut, and never combed my hair, shaved seldom, wore ragged, dirty, and old clothes, never shined my shoes, wore them with open scars and holes in them, in fact, I was a sight. One time, I delivered a speech on the subject of love and sex relationships in connection with my interpretation of what the socialist movement meant for the future. Like every other socialist, I charged modern matrimonial relationships with being on a cash basis. I said that modern woman was bought by easy livelihoods furnished by the husband. Those relationships smacked of prostitution; that the only decent sex relationship was where the financial background as consideration was absent. The love relationship should count alone. I said that I found within myself a yearning for the women I knew, in toto, and that my notion of ethics with regard to them contained no sex morality. If I had any morality on the subject, it was the morality of obedience to the sex nature of my being.

My own sex urge was the highest authority for my conduct. A taboo on sex urges and conduct I considered stupid, crazy, and immoral. Girls said of my behavior with them that I was a wild Indian. A girl showing any sort of leaning toward me I would embrace in public without any feeling of shame. The older women called me a savage, and when I wooed my present wife, both her brother and her friends advised her vigorously against me. They said I was unreliable as a family man. As I recall now, I wooed my wife because I wanted to get away from Mother, and from my love for Tillie, from my discordant, distracted state of being. I felt I would find it in a woman—any kind of woman, especially one who needed the same peace as I; a woman who was not only unhappy but really miserable.

Sarah was troubled. She was a young immigrant living with her brother, who was loaded with a family, and was studying a profession in order to make a living. His wife kept boarders. The home was crowded, and the earnings of all were small, so that in slack seasons they had barely enough to live on. She was a sickly girl and distracted because of her poverty and absence of adjustment, and so naturally fell into my lot, as I into hers. I was convinced that this match fitted both our needs, but I soon found out that I had erred in judgment. We had come of different stock from the old country. She was the daughter of a prosperous bourgeois family. Her home knew no want; the family had servants and stood high in the estimate of their village. While in this country, as an early immigrant, she was poor and sick, her raising had left a clear mark on her. Her need for a higher standard of living was severely taxed—much more than I was. Anyway, I married her* and found my wife served the purposes of my life much more effectively than any of the other married couples I knew then.

* In 1892. Between the years 1892 and 1906 six children, one of whom died shortly after birth, were born into the family.

6

After a number of public meetings denouncing sweatshops, the legislature of Illinois appointed a commission* to investigate the shops. Along with Florence Kelley, I was appointed to prepare information, and I took members of the commission through numerous factories and sweatshops. I testified before the commission, suggested witnesses, and did what I could to make the inquiry a success. Our little group had prepared a bill, at the initiative chiefly of Florence Kelley, prohibiting the employment of women longer than eight hours a day, the employment of children under fourteen years of age, and prohibiting all employers from using any help outside of their own family in their homes. It also provided for establishing a department of factory inspectors including one chief inspector and several deputy inspectors.

John P. Altgeld was then govenor of Illinois. He was a lib-

* In 1893.

eral, rather a radical, very sympathetic to the cause of the labor movement and a man independent in character, powerful in will, and a great and intense student of the social problem. His party had a majority in the legislature and our bill was passed, made a law, and the Governor appointed Florence Kelley as chief inspector, Mrs. A. Stevens as assistant to the inspector, and a number of deputies. Some of the radicals were Mary Kenney, myself, and a few others.

I think it must have been that Educational Society which I had joined in 1888 that had inspired me with a desire to investigate everybody and everything bearing on the social problem because in 1891–92, when Mrs. Kelley was given permission by the Federal Labor Bureau to investigate prostitution, I made it my business to hang out in their haunts to learn as much as I could, even though I was in no way connected with the investigation. I loved to chum with the lowest portions of the community: tramps, drunks, prostitutes, etc.

As our union developed, this struggle with non-union people and scabs, especially during strikes, became a very germane part of the entire union movement. For that purpose, the low classes in our union generally volunteered to participate in a melee. We had in the union irresponsibles; some even criminal in nature. Boys would hang out at prize-fight centers, or with drunkards. These would always volunteer to fight scabs and since I took an active part in all the strikes, I naturally teamed with that class of people and frankly, I suspect myself to have been not much different from them. The laws did not have a morally binding effect on my consciousness; capitalist laws, [as] I called them, made in the interests of the privileged classes, ought not to have a binding authority on poor people. So I did not look upon these semi-criminal people as men and women who violated or intended to violate laws which I was honestly supporting. To go into a scab shop and violently destroy some of the merchandise or machinery, beat up the scabs if they insisted on continuing their work, didn't seem wrong to me, so in the investigations I made about prostitution and its causes, I did not honestly do it as a man might who was above the people he was inquiring about.

A tramp was my kind; one of the disinherited in modern capitalist society. A prostitute was my kind, belonging to the same class. I was interested in the profession not as an assault on the laws of God or men, but whether or not it yielded a living and the risk of contagious diseases involved in it, and the hardships to which it subjected its members and the opportunities as well which it offered its inmates. The fact that it was immoral or illegal meant nothing to me. To me it was not at all immoral, but indirectly it gave me an opportunity to make quite an inquiry on the subject of biology, physiology, psychology, and character of the tramp and prostitute and the semi-criminal in my group. I tried to ascertain its cultural level and to find its significance as an economic factor. The information received was so disjointed, so discordant, so many-featured, and so shaded that I was quite upset and bewildered.

Before I began the inquiry it was very clear to my mind that all social evils were arising out of the capitalistic institutions and that the disinherited portions of the people did simply all they did to serve capitalism; otherwise one could not earn a living. But in this inquiry I found that individuals reacted differently to life because there were physiologic, biologic, and sociologic causes motivating conduct along with economic forces. While the economic cause was the dominating one in a great majority of cases determining conduct, there were exceptions. These exceptions may have only been seeming. One has to take into account different types of mind and different levels of culture in the study of economic and social problems. We did have a problem of men's minds along with the problem of unjust economic and social structure.

The development of industry itself was not purely an industrial and economic product; that too was intimately related to culture levels of manpower engaged in the formation of that situation. For one instance, I noticed that it took a certain type of human character to build up a successful sweatshop; that while normally the successful contractor was supposed to be a rather conscienceless person it had to be a man with industrial vision and forethought, organizing capacity; a man with the will to stick and suffer great hardships in order to satisfy what was at the same time his greed and vision. Some who were more capable actually developed great inventive and organizing capacity as well as an artistic sense and appreciation of skill in the industry. Therefore, the charge that the contractor or sweater had as his motive greed was not altogether true. As a result of his conduct, he was not the only beneficiary, because he developed the industry. People were better dressed, and a larger proportion of the people were engaged in the industry. He helped to maintain low standards among the employees, he was greedy and unscrupulous, he was always the direct agent of the capitalistic employer, he used his talents to deceive, cheat, and oppress his immigrant countrymen, labor, even his own relatives. But along with all this he developed the art among his workers of producing fine clothes and helped to open up a source of revenue making for the support, poor though it was, of a larger and larger part of our population. While my sentiments were very strongly for labor classes, I was not completely blind to the agency of the larger needs of our population even when it came to the sweaters and manufacturers who were my social enemies.

I think it was this attitude of mind which made it possible for me to more successfully negotiate with employers than any other man in the union. The provision prohibiting the employment of women for longer than eight hours a day is a law which we take on the face of it to be a hygienic provision. It was said that modern industry charges the vitality of working men and women much more severely than in former years; that the hours must be limited so as not to stretch their vitality in too short a time. In the case of the employment of children, the same theory was submitted. The children were obliged to work too hard, and therefore could not be raised into the proper sorts of citizens. The educational factor was also introduced. Children working in factories cannot attend schools, and grow up ignorant, and so add to the total of our ignorant population. Moreover, they would not be robust and healthy. Our union and myself had none of these motives in mind. We believed that the longer we worked, the more we produced; and the faster we completed our work, the keener the competition with each other for work. Therefore we would get less money and have less to live on. So the factor of industrial competition was paramount in our minds, but the factors of citizenship and health were paramount in the minds of the legislature. Normal public opinion thought as did the legislature.

The assault we made on home work, too, was inspired by different motives. The public [s]ought to guard itself against contagious disease, normally prevalent in the homes of the poor families doing the work. In our case, we wished to abolish home work because it was possible for us to organize our people much more efficiently when large numbers of them were working in the larger shops. So while the newspapers and churches were agitating for one set of motives, the unions who supported the bill were mainly inspired by the economic motive.

When I was a deputy inspector I was fanatical almost to blindness with regard to the law. My impression is that Florence Kelley felt the same way I did. The same was true of most of the radical group with regard to factory inspection. In those years labor legislation was looked on as a joke; few took it seriously. It was considered that such legislation was passed mainly as political fodder. These laws, it was believed, were not really to be enforced. Inspectors normally in those days were appointed from the viewpoint of political interest;

men and women operated who had no social consciousness, and in most states this class of legislation was not enforced. There were very few, almost no, court cases heard of, and it was left to our department to set the example of rigid enforcement of labor laws. Since I participated in the framing of the law, in the propaganda to enact it, I was considered to be the proper person to take it up with the larger industrial units. So I had an opportunity, while an inspector, to report violations to the courts and to have the courts assess fines for violations. But also I would educate the parents who sent their children to work, and the employers of these children, the women who were employed longer than eight hours a day, and their employers. Since everybody took the law as a joke because of a lack of interest in industrial legislation and because of a contempt for politician-made laws, I found myself charged with a mission requiring a great deal of effort and application, knowledge, and intelligence about the subject matter, and moreover persistence and vigor.

These were years when I studied the labor problem as never before. Not from books but from actual industry. Industrial development, machines and quality production, concentrated capital, the nature of immigrants working in the industry, the industrial moral levels, all these were items coming under my observation, and they all gave me a great deal to think about, not only about what happens in industrial life but where the whole thing was leading to. I tried to ferret out its effect on life, health, security, culture, and citizenship, as well as its effect on the opportunity to organize labor unions.

A great proportion of the people employed in the industry were foreigners, and my own people, the Jews, were employed largely in cigar and clothing manufacturing, millinery, gloves, and other light industries. They would work for cleaner, larger, and better appointed stores; factories and shops were to be more efficiently managed; better machinery was to be installed; production to be better organized, and quality and quantity of production constantly improved. The men in social life almost constantly talked earnings. An improvement in one shop would travel speedily through to all other shops. There was a bent of mind to succeed in the business in a manufacturing way that took possession psychologically of practically all our people, almost from childhood up—all, the poor, better-to-do, the rich, all. Even the most inefficient tried vigorously over and over again as long as they could save a few dollars.

The business of investing in real estate, too, in those early years, began to tell on the minds of our people, and we progressed much more rapidly by way of acquiring the goods of the world than our immediate neighbor immigrants of the Slavic races: the Bohemians, Poles, etc. For instance, just south of the Jewish neighborhood, I found as inspector that buildings without gas remained without gas; oil lamps and soft-coal stoves and toilets in the back yards were the rule, while among our people, old buildings once not equipped for gas, were remodeled; houses where the toilets were outside were remodeled for modern plumbing, long before the same improvements were put into effect among our Slavic neighbors. We antedated these improvements by at least ten years, taking them neighborhood by neighborhood. So the theory of the poor becoming poorer and the rich richer, and that of the poor man never changing his class, I found to be not quite true, especially among our people.

It was very largely true, however, among those of Slavic descent. In inspecting stockyards, I found quite a change in the personnel of nationalities employed in the yards. In my early immigrant days, I used to visit the yards from time to time because many of my friends and neighbors worked there. Most of the employees then were German and Irish. I also went there during the strike of 1886; went to their meetings because of my interest then in strikes and labor meetings. Most of the employees, immediately after they lost the eight-hour strike at the end of 1886, after having had about six months of the eight-hour day, which was finally lost on a lock-out, could not stand to have their new standard assaulted, and left the employment of the bosses and were replaced by Slavs. So when I inspected the yards in 1894 I found that most of the stockyard neighborhoods which were formerly settled by Irish and German were now settled by the Slavs: Croatians, Rumanians, Poles, Bohemians, etc. When I tried to find out where the Irish and German workers had gone to, I was told they had moved south and had changed their employment, having become the saloon-keepers, storekeepers, and professionals of the stockyards neighborhood. The fact that they had been replaced by these lower Slavs had not hurt them. In fact it had shoved them up in the economic scale. That too was an additional argument dislodging my conviction about the poor being always poor, and the rich being always rich. My conception of capitalistic development making for a constant assault on the prevailing standard of living by capitalist society was materially modified. But I was still very loyal, generally loyal to the principles of the Socialist Party and those of labor unionism.

I found the class struggle expressed just as vigorously as before in efforts to enforce the child labor law. Almost all manufacturers vigorously fought this law. Governor Altgeld was overwhelmed with protests both against Mrs. Kelley and myself. In going through the stockyard factories and other places, I had broadened out in my knowledge of industry, the nature of business, and of American life. I used to visit a number of American factories, and then filling out schedules among American families, I would be constantly estimating and was interested in the respective cultural levels. I found quite a difference between American homes and those of the immigrant Jewish homes. They had cleaner, and better appointed, homes. The same was true of the German and Scandinavian people. In their case, they were much older immigrants, and were probably wealthier, and composed mostly of better-class mechanics and professional people, etc.

In the years of 1894–95 there was a smallpox epidemic in the city that raged most severely in the Polish and Bohemian districts, and since there were a great many home tailor shops, our inspection department was obliged to visit these homes and either burn or disinfect the clothing being made in the homes of smallpox victims. I then noticed that the epidemic was largely confined to the Slavic immigrant families who did not believe in vaccination, or modern hygiene and medical care. In one case where a woman and her small children were visiting a family where there was a patient lying in bed with smallpox, swollen and festering with pox, at the point of death, I asked this woman why she brought her children to such a dreadful place. She answered in her broken English that if God wished them to die, they would, and if God did not wish it, they would not die. Almost a riot was caused every time the police tried to remove a patient to the contagious disease hospital, or enforce quarantine rules strictly according to the health department. In our struggle against sweatshops and home shops, we were not only obliged to struggle against the employers but against the ignorance of the very people who might suffer because of it—as well as their stubbornness. Almost invariably when we got a report of a case of smallpox in a home shop, outside of the regular immigrant district, we found the family belonging to the same nationality as other stricken ones.

It was peculiar that while the Slavs lived only a few blocks away from the Jews and their shops, yet the epidemic did not cross the border line. There was no smallpox in the Jewish community. The Jews would vaccinate, and what other causes there might have been, I don't know. I merely observed the given ones.

I was then actively participating in the agitation for a Socialist Party. My experience in the factories made my view very comprehensive with regard to the problems of labor so that I was in a position to make quite a contribution in discoursing on the economic situation among our people, since most of our people had little opportunity to get acquainted much outside of the pale of their quarters. Visiting the homes of working people and the poor while I was gathering evidence in case of violation of the laws pertaining to child labor, I found my convictions as a rebel and socialist growing on me. In the years of 1893–94, there was a terrible panic, and I ran across families with no food in the house, no heat in winter, no shoes so children might go to school, and no clothes, too, unemployment in a great many homes, and with work either absent or too hard.

Men used to complain of the indignities suffered in the factories as well as women: in order to get a job, men had to bribe the foreman and pay him part of his wages regularly, and in a number of cases, women could hold their positions because they were good to their superiors. The sense of class animosity existed even amongst the most ignorant and poor, but it found no sane expression except occasionally in strikes. This simply meant fight and shedding of blood with the police, a great deal of radical and erratic speeches, and in most of the cases those strikes were lost. I have participated personally in a great many of those strikes. Though an officer of the state, I was very loyal to the cause of labor and I would search striking factories for the employment of children or other factory-act offenses such as employment of women for longer than eight hours a day, and actively agitated for socialism, labor unions, strikes, etc.

I was not especially persona grata among my own comrades in the socialist movement. Since I held a position under a Democratic administration, a great many socialists were rather skeptical among themselves of my real loyalty to the Socialist Party, and since I did not believe in La Salle's Iron Law of Wages, nor in the fact that the classes so absolutely exclude each other. By my experience I was even more convinced than ever before of the need for stressing the economic and industrial side of the labor movement, and the need of paying less attention to the political side. As I saw it, we were not ready for politics; also that politics was not ready for us. There seemed to me to be almost no relation between politics and the labor movement. The normal political morality of the average citizen was very shady, very meaningless, and personal. The politician of a given neighborhood had no social comprehension of any kind; it was personal—Vote for me. The politicians were men of nondescript character; saloon-keepers, shyster lawyers, and men who were normally in morality below the average citizen. Discussions at political meetings were invariably in meaningless phrases. The predominant shout was—The other party were liars, scoundrels, cheats, grafters, they were out for the money—which was all true. Both parties felt that way about each other and both were right. The most criminal group of men were the legislators. No one cared as to who was elected to the legislature—a lot of drunks. Public funds were squandered as far as the public was concerned. They were normally divided between the politicians and businessmen who made money out of municipal and state institutions and franchises. There was almost no social morality. The socialists who entered politics as a practical policy were looked upon as dreamers or as men who were in the same class as the other parties save that they were out of office and sought office.

The very fact that the men made political appeals caused the average working man to lose faith in them. That was not so in our appeals for labor unions. There was some belief in the morality in the cause of the labor movement. There was plenty of selfishness, dishonesty, and graft in the labor movement too. Most unions were organized for selfish purposes for their members; they had very little sense of solidarity, interest in each other or in the general cause. The trade autonomy principles of the American Federation of Labor formed no tie of solidarity between the respective organizations. There was very little discussion or understanding between one union [and another] or one industry and another.

The leadership was not quite so bad as the leadership in

politics, but it was bad enough. In the building trade, the leadership was in a number of cases a grafting one. They would use the union for purposes of extortion of money from the employer, and while the unions benefited their members, they did not have among themselves a coherent or binding industrial and legal relationship. For instance, in the building trade, no union had authority to pass upon wages or terms of employment of other unions, but they had a council among themselves which imposed an obligation on all affiliated unions to sympathetically strike with each other—so, the painters might call a strike and the carpenters on the job would be obliged to sympathetically strike with them and maintain a morality of not working with scabs. But they had nothing to say as to whether or not the painters should or should not go out on strike. There developed a sort of irresponsible and gang affiliation between the respective business agents of the respective trades in the building industry, and those leaders would protect the wages of their members loyally but would at the same time use the club of strike over the employers, contractors, and builders for purposes of getting personal graft. That put the building industry almost constantly in chaos and turmoil; very seldom did a job go through without strikes and violence and slugging and injunctions, with police violence and graft added to it all, and the leaders of the strike forming a gang with the politicians and crooked policemen forming a fellowship for dishonest purposes.

The initiation fee in all these unions was very high, and grew higher from year to year. To get into any of these unions became very difficult and each separate union formed a sort of monopoly in its own small group. Most members were continually bent on the idea of allowing fewer and fewer people to enter, making a scarcity of labor in their own calling and therefore making for the maintaining of their standard of wages—but these ideas militated for a selfish group idealism, and were against the sense of solidarity of

155

labor. They made for a sort of aristocracy in each special group. Certain phrases—such as the brotherhood of labor, the brotherhood of man, the solidarity of labor, an injury to one is an injury to all—were commonly used in propaganda, but they were meaningless as a real force and as a real social and industrial morality affecting the actual conduct of the average working man. The unions made very little propaganda anyway and there was an impotence felt in any of their general gatherings. The average man felt that any appeal for social morality was what they call bunk, since any really strong union was hard to enter, and in order to become strong it was necessary to get the actual support of a strong union, and normally each union was very selfish.

There was a sense of the need for social morality, but it was really felt more among the unorganized, especially among the unemployed and the poor, the immigrants, but these were very helpless. They would fill large halls in big socialist or anarchist rallies, where some eloquent speaker was advertised to address the meeting, but it always resolved itself into hot air. Economic conditions seemed to militate against the real sense of solidarity and industrial morality in labor, and yet there was more of that in the labor union movement, in the sense that it meant something, than there was in the political arena. The average working man did feel it was wrong to scab and strike, but did not feel it was wrong to vote for either the Republican or Democratic parties.

Even among the more intelligent working men, there were discordant currents running through. Nobody was satisfied. The panic hit everybody. There was either complete unemployment or very partial employment, so that almost everybody was worried about his lot. There was a great deal of actually intense want and suffering, but there was a chaos in the mass of social opinion. The farmers and debtor class who had their property taken away by the foreclosing of mortgages pleaded for a debased currency, charged the bankers with [being] the cause of their troubles, said that the bankers and monopolists owned the government, and ought to be thrown out of power. The single-taxers charged that land ownership and land monopoly were the causes of all the current misfortune. The anarchists wanted to abolish government and charged that the seat of all trouble was the existence of any government at all. The social thought of the day had numerous currents and cross-currents. There were a great many public meetings, meetings of unemployed, fights with police, suppression of free speech, persecution of agitators, but to no coherent purpose. There was mass chaos, and misery.

The Debs Pullman and railway strike,* which went [on] under the name of the American Railway Union, held out some hope, but the federal government interceded, arrested all the leaders, stationed federal soldiers in Chicago, and the federal judiciary issued drastic injunctions, assaulted vigorously the ordinary guarantee given to each citizen by the Constitution, and while it did not openly declare martial law all over the country, martial law did exist as a matter of fact, and the strike was defeated. About the same thing took place here in Chicago in the clothing industry. A big general strike involving thirty or forty thousand people was defeated after a very fierce contest in which many made severe sacrifices; an atmosphere of wholesale hopelessness and pessimism made its way through the morale of most of the working people.

In these years I was active in participating in the labor movement, made speeches to railway men, to tailors, to unemployed, to socialists, and to ordinary educational and radical organizations. My sense of loyalty to the labor movement and the idealism for a better day absorbed all my energies, and I worked for it day and night. My condition of being married and being at the head of a little family ran along fairly well,

* In 1894; the strike was led by Eugene Debs.

but not quite as well as I had hoped it would. Up to the time I became a factory inspector, I had not earned enough to live on decently, went into debt, occasionally had to sponge on my friends, had period after period of unemployment, could not get a job even when there was work. In our industry, slack seasons were a regular institution, and I cultivated the idea that I might live poorly and yet be satisfied. I knew I could not be both in the labor movement and earn a decent income, and my loyalty to the labor movement was much stronger than my desire to have untorn shoes or a decent place to live in, or fine clothes, or even expensive food. I was perfectly willing to live on almost nothing and be satisfied because that did not disturb me at all.

My wife had been raised in a middle-class family so that in the old country she was in the habit of living in [a] fairly good manner—certainly much better than I, and she was hungry for a decent home, fair clothes, and good food for her children, as well as an airy and comfortable home. So, while I did not mind it at all, she did, and when I became a factory inspector and got in a steady and fair income, I planned to still live on terms of small expenses and to save money for a rainy day, while my wife planned nothing of the kind. She wanted a better home, more expensive furniture, and improved conditions of living all around. So my sense of economy in the family was not realized, and my financial worries did not stop; if anything, they were increased.

I also worried about my lack of education. I wanted to read and educate myself, to acquire the technique of writing and spelling and grammar—but between my job and the labor movement, my time and attention were all occupied. My hopes of better education in the rudiments of the three R's were not realized. So at no time was I comfortable, or in any way able to enjoy my personal living. While I did not have what the ordinary man calls pleasures, either in person or in my relation to my family, I did enjoy intensely my active participation in the social movement; speeches, agitation, debates, leadership, and reading on economics, social science, and natural science, occasionally on philosophy and ethics and sometimes good literature, were quite a spiritual satisfaction for me.

I was not much worried in those years about the problems arising out of matrimony and problems arising out of love. I was too busy to think about them, and yet occasionally the subject would arise in my experience. In a strike of skirt-makers, there were quite a number of women, and when I went to meetings and worked together with the women leaders in the group, I ran across the problem of the unmarried women, mainly those who had participated in the labor movement or those who did not succeed in establishing themselves in homes. While these women were intensely interested in their unions, they, at the same time, seemed to have felt a need for a personal life in relation to men, and [in] our joint social work, which kept us at meetings late at night, [we] formed a sort of admiration for each other because of our loyalty to a common cause. That association made for a feeling toward each other which was different than the feeling which men might have who admired each other in the labor movement; comradeship between men and women had a character all of its own. When a girl was tired, sleepy, and hungry, and exhausted, I always felt to her as though I should want to express my sympathy in a more intimate way than I felt toward men; and my women friends [felt] that they needed that sort of sympathy, and in return would feel they must express their sympathy to me in a more intimate way than towards each other. They flocked around me as a leader of their cause, but also because I was young, vigorous, and enthusiastic, and they admired my enthusiasm, and capacity to express my feeling for the cause they were struggling for. Over and over again, there were situations which forced the idea—why did you marry?—why that strictness with regard to a monogamic morality? Some women did not say it in so many words but would indicate it by their behavior. I am tired and uncomfortable, they would say—humor me, comfort me, embrace me, show me some sort of intimate personal affection; and the same held true with regard to me. My heart went out to them, and I felt as though I wanted to express in a physical sense some form of my attitude of mind —namely, a strong affection by way of embracing, kissing, etc. —and in the case of one girl particularly, neither of us restrained ourselves and after a very enthusiastic meeting, when we were alone, expressed a considerable body of love for each other. And while we did not commit adultery in action, I am quite sure we both did commit it in thought and somewhat in behavior.

The same was true in our socialist meetings. In our discussions of the social problem, we assaulted all institutions of capitalist society. We went to extremes to tear down every sense of morality which was highly considered by capitalist society, law, and religion. Along with our criticism of capitalistic institutions, capitalistic matrimony would enter as an item of discussion. We charged those matrimonial relationships with barter and sale. When women members of the party who were not successfully married and felt strongly against it were discussing the subject with me, there was every motive to do violence to the present assumed monogamic sex morality, and while we were all absorbed with the social problems and paid little attention to our respective sex urges, yet the fact that we had not any redress for present-day matrimonial morality made for our feeling of freedom with each other. There were occasions when girls who were greatly disappointed in love and were active in the movement felt a need for men in the movement whom they admired, and I was much admired.

7

The subject of the nature of labor unions was vigorously discussed in our socialist groups. The Pullman strike absorbed a great deal of interest. Should there be trade unions or industrial unions? Individual trade unions found it impossible to maintain their organizations because in dealing with each separate unit the employer had it in his power to set one craft against the other and, in the end, to defeat them all. So those of us who studied the subject of labor unions and their nature considered the industrial union to be the only form of organizing labor which would be able to efficiently measure up in power and strength with the employer individually, and if need be with the whole class. The Pullman strike came about just in the nick of time to give this theory a chance to assert itself in a test case between the largest corporations in the country and the labor unions.

There were several thousand people employed in the factories of the Pullman Company manufacturing sleepers, passenger, and freight cars. There was rigid discipline in the factory. The workers worked ten hours a day, the wages were very small, and the managing part of the factory was unscrupulous in their treatment of labor. Working men felt that all their foremen and superintendents were hard taskmasters. Week-workers were driven like slaves, and whatever piecework was to be had, had the wages on it constantly cut.

About that time, Eugene V. Debs organized an American Railway Union. That union was organized because of numerous defeats prior to 1894 of railway men in their efforts to form a real organization. So that Debs and a number of leaders and co-workers conceived a scheme to organize an industrial union in the railway business; namely, a union composed of the numerous trades employed on railways—engineers, conductors, telegraph operators, switchmen, signal men, machinists, molders, and numerous other crafts. The principles of the union were something like those of the Knights of Labor—an injury to one is an injury to all—and authority to legislate and contract was lodged in industrial unions instead of in trade unions. Organizers were sent out into the numerous shops and brickyards [freight yards?], and the organization grew by leaps and bounds. Based on that scheme, several strikes were undertaken on southern and western railways and the men were victorious in a very short time. A new wind of labor solidarity blew through the railway centers and inspired working men with a great deal of hope. Debs and his friends were held in great esteem. Branches of the American Railway Union were organized all through the country with feverish speed and intensity. "We've got them," the men used to say at the meetings. "When we are all together, they can't beat us."

Among the groups which the union was trying to organize was the group employed at the Pullman car shops. The complaint of the people at Pullman was the company was too tyrannical, too overbearing, too despotic, that they charged high rent for the houses furnished their workers, paid small wages, worked their people unreasonably hard. People used to say, "We are driven like slaves." So it was easy to organize them. They flocked to the union driven by that irresistible mass impulse which at certain periods in the labor movement ran like wildfire and set social consciousness at a premium over and above all ordinary human interests. Every working man became an agitator, and every agitator a prophet. It was a sort of inspired movement where the atmosphere was teeming with enthusiasm, self-sacrifice, and boundless hope.

When the Pullman Company failed to recognize the committee of the union, would not negotiate with its men or listen to their complaints, would not bargain for employment collectively at all, insisted upon their right to individually bargain with each man, then a strike was called by the American Railway Union in the Pullman shops. The men were poor, very few had enough money saved to live without working, the organization was young and poor and could not support the men out on strike, and it was necessary to end that strike on short notice because there was no money to be had either by the members or the organization. It was then that the American Railway Union requested the railroad companies to abstain from using the Pullman cars on their roads, so [that] the Pullman Company would be forced to give in to the demands of its men. The railway companies considered it to be none of their business as to how the Pullman Company treated its own workers. The Pullman Company was a separate corporation independent of the railway companies, and only had contractual relations with the railway companies to carry the Pullman cars for certain stipulated payments. They [the other companies] said—we do not wish to be made party to a boycott against the Pullman Company because it is not legal, and it's none of our business, anyhow.

The very novel demand on the part of the union which was trying to force co-operation of one interest in order to bring to terms another industry was resented by the entire capitalist class. Commercial associations, manufacturers' associations, bankers' associations, voiced their sentiments unanimously against the union. The entire press stood for the capitalist side of the controversy. Every public gathering of either employers or commercial men, politicians, and in some cases, well-to-do clergy as representing the church, voiced their disapproval of this innovation on the part of labor. This is not a strike, was the consensus of opinion, but a revolution, a test of strength, an unlawful use of the power of boycott and strike. The newspapers were full of this assault, but the members of the American Railway Union paid no attention to them. They declared a strike on road after road and before long, every road entering Chicago from the south or west was tied up. In some cases they succeeded in reaching a considerable portion east of Chicago. The atmosphere was charged with the mystery and significance of a great national class struggle. Yet, there were many who lined up with the employers—this was true of the better-paid help in the railroads. Stationmasters, the older engineers and conductors, office help, men who had been employed for many years and were waiting for promotion or pension, remained working. The old-line labor unions, too, did not fall into line; the leadership resented the encroachment on their sphere of authority and did not advise their members to join the strike, and while many of the members did join the strike against the authority of the organization, yet there was a significant dissent making for a division in labor itself.

It became necessary in certain communities to stop the movement of trains by force and violence, and this was done in many cases. Moving trains were blocked and stopped; in some cases, in the fever of the struggle, irresponsible men set fire to freight yards and cars. Individual scabs were assaulted and beaten up, large numbers of arrests were made, and when in Pullman the people began to starve because they had no money, especially women and children, the atmosphere became tense and hot. I offered to speak and made several speeches, went around from hall to hall, talked and encouraged men as I went around my duties as factory inspector, and while, as a public official, I had no right to make myself conspicuous, I did the best I could to speak in favor of the industrial instead of trade union, and also to speak in favor of the leadership of the American Railway Union, and for the idealism implied in the sacrifices of the railway men employed in the Pullman works.

Because railways are considered an interstate industry, the federal judiciary were called on to prohibit the men from carrying on their strike and boycott and the federal executive committee* was put in motion to line up with the employers against the strike. Orders were sent out by the judges enjoining the men from interfering with the movement of the trains and with the business of the railroads. At one period, federal troops were stationed in Chicago to protect the scabs in their work and because of that, after a long, protracted strike, it was lost. All the railway, shop, and Pullman shop men went back to work. The union was materially weakened, the men were told that membership in the A.R.U. would forfeit their jobs, and as a result membership dwindled to a very small proportion of its original numbers. Debs was sent to jail along with several others of the leaders, and a lesson was given the struggle of labor which had its marked influence on the men and gave them a great deal of food for thought.

It gave me food for thought, too. And as I went around from factory to factory, and in my investigations on child labor, from workman to workman, I could not help but form estimates of the relative strength of the two sides; compared to the large corporations with their enormous funds, labor unions, if they used the strike weapon only, were almost helpless. Every large employer had a big reserve of merchandise on hand to protect him against a possible strike. Every

* What Bisno meant by "federal executive committee" is not clear; he may have been referring to the men who were President Cleveland's advisers during the strike; or possibly "committee" should read "authority."

large corporation had large sums of money specially accumulated on purpose to be able to meet any situation arising out of the sentiment brewing and being formed in the labor movement. Big scab organizations were formed, calling themselves detective agencies, and from time to time being authorized by county officials, given sheriff and police authority, to be able to take the place of, and to use violence against, working men in case of a strike. Thousands and hundreds of thousands of dollars were spent to organize and marshal criminal classes against any effort made by labor.

The labor movement degenerated into a small, favored trade group that here and there were able to get favorable agreements with employers because of their serving the employer in case a general and all-around effort was made to establish a standard for the general labor situation in any given industry. Defeat for labor was written in the air. In our department of factory inspection, too, the employers made it their business to cripple our efforts. They did this by appealing to the courts, saying that the *law prohibiting the employment of women for longer than eight hours was unconstitutional. The Illinois Manufacturers Association openly instructed their members to violate this law, to pay no attention to the factory inspection department in its effort to enforce the same, and in due time got the Supreme Court of Illinois to declare the law unconstitutional.*

The political organization, the Socialist Party, made some headway in those years, increased its membership, but not enough to really tell in the distribution of power between the two classes. Every election was a new defeat for labor. The employers' side had too much at stake to allow labor to organize any telling power in any part of the field of its activities. Both of the political organizations, with their enormous funds and their enormous hired manpower, centered their fight against the working men; votes were bought, labor votes

* In 1895.

were not counted, labor votes were stolen, the press and other agencies of public expression lied vigorously, competently, and effectively. In the fight against labor no measures were illegal or unfair. The employers were effectively organized as a class. They were loyal to their class interests. In meetings of manufacturers' associations, instructions were given: "Give no quarter to labor." Every little strike was suppressed, every resource at capital's command—especially the courts, and our police and hired sluggers, newspapers, the magazines, and every possible public voice—persecuted and prosecuted men who had any public conscience and dared to line up with labor, until their finances and reputation were gone, all were used. Labor had an uphill fight. There was a panic in the years between 1893–97. There was a great deal of unemployment which helped the employer in his struggle against labor and made the struggle of labor an unequal and almost hopeless fight.

My family was increasing during those years. My wife gave birth to a child about every two years and my expenses naturally increased so that the wages I received as an inspector were barely enough to get along on. My wife had a higher standard of living in the first place than I did. She acquired it since her family had been well-to-do, while I had been very poorly raised and hence my standard was very low. Already in those years, I began to see that I had probably made a mistake in my selection of a wife. It was my wife's desire to measure up favorably in her standard of living with such of her friends who belonged to middle-class society instead of the ordinary tailors and cloakmakers, and while she tried her best to get along on my wages, she failed to save any. We consumed every dollar I earned and I was always at the ragged edge. I worried to save for a rainy day and I knew one would come. My reputation as a union leader and socialist made it impossible for me to get a good job at my trade and the average earning in my trade was small because of the slack season, and because during those panic years, it was impossible to establish an effective organization or raise materially the price for labor. So I was constantly worried and there was constantly a difference of opinion between myself and my wife on the expenditure of money. I warned her about a rainy day and she as consistently paid no attention to it at all. But in other fields she was very loyal. She allowed me to spend night after night in public meetings and very seldom interfered with my being out, took the entire burden of the care of the children and the hard work necessary to keep up the household and family.

I was a free-lance and had a great deal of opportunity to participate in the labor movement and also an opportunity for cultural development. I attended public lectures, did a great deal of lecturing myself, chummed and mixed with people of a higher level of education. There were in our neighborhood a group of people who had lived in one of the new buildings just erected, composed of settlement workers, reformers, artists, writer-folk, and literary people. They came together several times a week to visit with each other, in one of the bachelor apartments. One of the men took two apartments, broke the connecting wall and so made one very large apartment of it. We had, therefore, a very large living room which easily allowed the meeting of fifteen people. All these people lived in this poor neighborhood for substantially the same reason one lived at a settlement house—to know the poor, and to rub shoulders with them. There was something doing among the poor. There was a live, teeming labor movement, the social problem was discussed much more intensely, in fact lived by the population, more so than in the better-to-do neighborhood. There was material there for the artist, writer and poet, for the student of social problems, and for the scientist interested in the nature of man. There were numerous social problems, so that these gatherings were extremely interesting—every possible subject was discussed. The latest thing said in science, in social science, the news of every significant movement and labor events, were constantly the themes of those people. Art, too, was discussed, and a general sharing of opinion was part of the procedure of the evening.

Most of the people there were university graduates, some with Ph.D.'s, others still students. I was invited there because of my acquaintance with the Hull House people. Frankly, while I was interested in the subjects discussed, I was more interested in the personnel of the group. The men and women who gathered there were unmarried and I found none of my experience in my own group when unmarried men and women got together. The subject of the difference between men and women was seldom discussed. While the subject of equal rights and woman suffrage were occasionally talked of, it was discussed so impersonally that one could not notice there were both men and women in the group. Every subject was discussed abstractly and impersonally. There was a play of human intellect and occasionally humor, even sarcasm, was evoked, but it was all impersonal. They did not discuss the subject matter disinterestedly but it seemed their breeding and reserve made for the behavior there.

One evening I went home with one of the men visiting there. He was a country lad, rich, attending University, interested in social problems. He was invited by one of the girls, and was a regular visitor of the group. "What happens?" I asked him. "These bachelor men and women do not behave in relation to each other in the same way as men and women of my circle when they visit each other. These people seldom sing, almost never dance, and their attitude towards each other carries no sign of their sex life. They never talk of marriage or behave as if there were such an institution existing. They treat each other as though they were not men and women." That, he explained to me, is in their education and breeding. While very vigorous wooing does go on with some of them, some are not so constituted; and he named some who really had a bachelor view towards the future of their lives. "Take H——," he said, "who invited me here. We have known each other since we were children. She isn't rich, and was depending for her living on her work in the settlement. She is very beautiful and has had any number of well-to-do, cultured, educated admirers, but she seems to feel that married life allows no woman to expand along the avenues required by modern life, and she wants to be a free-lance. She wants no children, and wants to actively participate in social life, in the numerous movements; she wants to have an experience other than that of a mother; she is hungry to assert herself in other fields than that of a family. While some women can do it, though they are married, they are few and far between. Most women are too busy taking care of their children and husband, and the ordinary life of a mother and wife is obnoxious to her. My impression is that celibacy is natural to her. She has no desire to mate with men sexually. She does need men because of the experience and culture men possess. She derives opportunities from men to participate in the vocations she is interested in, such as social movements, politics, and education, and the practical experiences of mankind—those relating to science and politics and general business knowledge. But she does not wish to pay the price of marriage because then she is excluded from the world of men and confined to a single man."

"How do you know she is a natural celibate?" I asked.

"There is no one more intimate with her than I," he said. "We are friends. She even has the ordinary woman's feeling for affection. She loves to be embraced and kissed. She reciprocates. But that is as far as she goes. Her taboo is strong enough to actually influence her nature. She is comforted enough by that experience to satiate her, I think, to the very bone. No man can know a woman better than I know her. I have been wooing her for years, but can't change her, and it really seems as though that is her nature. Others of the group are hungry for children but they are more hungry for votes for women, for labor legislation, for an improved educational system, for an opportunity to lobby for better legislation, for public meetings, speech-making, improving our jails, collecting money for political prisoners, making meetings, and passing resolutions on all sorts of social ills. It is the spirit of human and social assertion which seems to have reached these women, and modern education opens up new vistas to satisfy their new urge. This is a new species of women and we must take them as we find them. They are natural celibates."

"What about the men?" I said. "I suppose," he said, "that [that] is a great secret. There are any number of mistresses to be had and there are even occasionally among these very women those who are different, and are glad to be mistresses, but that sort of conduct is not public property. What is public in their conduct, is their public conduct. That is as far as one can go."

I subsequently found that my new friend was not acquainted with it all. There was intriguing and wooing in the group. In one case, the wooing led to driving one of the most intelligent members to losing her mind, but it was all done in such a polished manner to completely secrete it, and under the taboos created by themselves, that I could not think of them even today, as men and women with natural sex impulses. As for me, this group was a great find. Items previously incomprehensible to me were clarified in that group. The philosophies of our great men accessible only to university men were there explained to me in such [a] way that along with my reading I possessed myself of the most significant and comprehensive thought of the age. While I acquired only a smattering here and there of the respective sciences, I got enough to be able to apply my knowledge efficiently in my researches on the social problem [and] to be quite a help to me.

I also acquired personal friendships there but somehow this friendship was different than my friends among the shop workers. My friendship was real, but it was a sort of touch-me-not friendship; it was a friendship arising out of a large group which one contacts socially—it was not a personal association. It was between men and women who have a common religion, common social aspiration, and are suffering in a common way because of a cause—but it was not personal, it was not intimate. There was a lack of that touch of human approach and sentiment which is the only real thing in friendship. There was an intellectual mutual understanding and need for each other's company, a joy in each other's efforts, a reverence and respect for each other, and sometimes great admiration for each other, but it was intellectual, it was understanding, it had no quality of blind devotion which asks no questions, reasons about nothing, without a demand for explanation.

I enjoyed the contact in a way, but when I met a fellow operator from the shops whom I had known for years, his troubles and personal problems, and we had a chance to share intimate and personal experiences relating to our personal worries and passions, and enjoyments and happiness relative to our families and relatives, somehow that sort of friendship contained a larger body of the meat of human life. When I picked up friends in these cultured groups, I decided that culture in itself chills intimate friendship. The kind of friendship I like to experience and the kind of passion I was in the habit of experiencing were almost completely absent in that group, even among themselves. It is probable that one of the reasons was [that] they were all well-to-do and needed to make no personal sacrifices for each other. Anyway, to me it was all strange and awkward, and while I fitted in as best I could and participated, I was really never part and parcel of the group. Was it because of the class distinction, because of a difference in culture and education, because of racial differences—I do not know, but there was a difference. To this day, I feel a sense of sorrow that I did not become part of that group in my own intensely personal way.

At this time an effort was made by representatives from the Russian government to make a treaty with the United States by means of which political prisoners might be extradited to

Russia. A group of us former Russian citizens organized protest meetings to defeat that project. The people at Hull
House—Jane Addams and her friends, a number of whom visited this Langdon group, actively participated in the organization of the protest meetings. We filled one of the largest
halls in the city. We had the best speakers and the most
influential, and the project was finally defeated, and we gave
ourselves credit for its defeat. I remember the enthusiasm
with which we hailed our success in defeating this measure.
A sense of reverence of appreciation grew about these people.
I looked up to them as human cultural giants and social souls
of great historic significance and my work with them was a
real satisfaction to me. My work in the Socialist Party and in
the labor union brought me in contact with both men and
women in a much more intimate relationship. There I had
friends with whom I would share occasionally the last crust
of bread or the last dime. There normal human affection was
paramount in all relationships. While we had not accomplished feats governing the conduct of the people of the state
or nation, we were at heart much closer to each other and
our labor was much more significant and related to the
meaning of our lives as compared to the Langdon group.

In my factory inspection department I was the big cheese.
There was a factory in Alton, Illinois, that employed some
three hundred children under fourteen years of age. I was
sent out through the state and visited Alton, and after a protracted fight and several law suits, succeeded in enforcing the
law. In my gathering evidence to prosecute a company, I was
obliged to visit a great many of the families from which came
the children employed in the factories, and I was strongly impressed with the great poverty of the families called in the
South "white trash," and the extremely low level of culture.
Alton has streets lined up along the Mississippi River which
are low and unhealthy to live in. Youngsters who worked in
the factories came from very poor families and it was com-

mon to see that children suffered from chills a good portion of the year. Some of the children would be ill at home, others would be working—then those who were working would become ill, too. The people had a calloused attitude of mind toward life, parents would have no sympathy with their offspring, men would have no sympathy with the problems of their neighbors. Wages were very low, the houses were shacks, and the poverty and suffering were extreme. The glassblowers, who had a union and had good wages, were just as much out of sympathy with my efforts to enforce the child labor law as were the employers. The same was true of the tailors.

Even if the children were sent to school, there was not enough seating capacity to accommodate 3 per cent of the children living there. They were ignorant, undernourished, worked hard, and had comparatively no care when they were ill. There was no sense of responsibility on the part of the employer. Nor was there a conscience on the part of the average citizen of the town. I ran across a wall of opposition and hatred because of my effort to get the children out of the factory into the schools. Some of the children were as young as seven or eight. A great many of them looked emaciated. They were all from pure American stock, no immigrants there at all. When I compared them with immigrants' children, even of the most backward country of Europe, I was impressed by the fact that they made the worst showing. My appeal to the union glassblowers found no response. I visited people with public property, the clergy, etc., and found very little response to my complaint and appeal. The people were proud of the industry in their city. The owners of the factories were looked up to as great benefactors, since they had condescended to choose Alton in which to develop their industries.

A great many of the families of these children lived in boat houses on the Mississippi River. These were some of the worst shacks, and malaria prevailed even more than on the land. They were tramp families who followed the river and would come into Alton and put their children to work for the period they stayed in Alton—three or six or nine months. The turnover of those children was great and the company had agents along the river constantly seeking new children. They constantly ran advertisements within two or three hundred miles of Alton, making all sorts of promises to have parents bring their children to Alton to work. Children working in these factories were subjected to a constantly changing temperature of the air, since their chief labor was to bring the bottles from the glass-blowing rooms to the chilling rooms—going from intensely hot ovens to a vastly cooler room.

I visited a church which the employers frequented, and found it to be a very rich institution. The clergy in their membership made great pretenses at religious piety, but their pretenses in religion did not keep them from murdering small children by industrial and economic ill-treatment. The class distinction between the rich and the poor was so inbred in their bones that they had no human relationship with each other nor did they have a human sympathetic attitude. I am under the impression that young cattle would have been treated better, with a larger measure of care, than were these children.

The justice of the peace was an old soldier from the Civil War who still retained memories of the struggle that the North carried on for the Union of the States and the abolition of slavery. He owned his own home and happened at one time to have been employed by the company as an attorney. I am under the impression that he was not even admitted to the bar but was elected by the community because he was respected for his integrity and because he was one of the oldest living residents of Alton. He did not care nor was he afraid of the company, nor did public opinion count very much with him, and be it said to his credit, that he was one of the very few in the city of Alton who co-operated with me in at least somewhat modifying the outrageous conduct on the part of the company.

As I went along in southern Illinois inspecting factories and brickyards, I gathered that in communities where industry was incipient, conditions of labor were worse than where industries were older. There was less self-respect on the part of the employees and a more calloused feeling towards the employees on the part of their superiors. There was very little of the labor movement and whatever little there was, was not inspired by the higher motives of solidarity that normally can be found where industry is older.

Governor Altgeld was appealed to by the factory to have both myself and Mrs. Kelley removed, and it is my understanding that he said, "Gentlemen, if you can not run your factory without the employment of young children, you had better close it." There were a great many children employed at the stockyards, and I had all I could do to effectively enforce the law. The owners of the yards were millionaires and yet they hired expensive counsel and fought every inch of the ground. In those communities the labor was mostly foreign, and children were employed by foremen and sub-foremen, straw-bosses, so that the employers almost never came in contact with the children or their families. There was a complete class separation and youngsters were employed under very disadvantageous conditions. Door boys were to open the doors of coolers and were exposed to hot and cold constantly. Boys cleaned casings where they constantly worked in wet rooms with refuse almost ankle deep, with an impossible stench of steam. Numbers of them worked in canning rooms with dangerous machinery, with no guards or protection to life or limb, with a constant experience of serious accident—cut off fingers, hands, killed. Some were caught in the shafts and belting and killed. Women, too, were employed to perform difficult and disgusting work in the yards, and they too were subjected to a treatment almost that of cattle. Tailor shops and sweatshops too employed a great many children. That was especially true among Bohemians and Poles of Catholic belief.

The children attended parochial schools and there was little discipline in such schools for making the children attend. They could leave the school almost at any age. Their parents were mostly peasant stock who were in the habit in the old country of having their children begin to work on the farm at a very early age. The Church authorities, parents, employers, all united in having children work in their early years —that it was better for their morals, they were not likely to grow up loafers hanging around saloons and street corners or alleys—and to employ them in those shops was not considered wrong at all. We had to fight the stubborn and settled public morality relating to children in order to get them to school and to raise the level of responsibilities of parents towards their offspring.

Wages were small. Manufacturers were very prosperous; their industries grew by leaps and bounds, but the employee failed to share in those benefits. There was striking in 1894. The strike was fought very stubbornly by the employees—a great deal of sacrifice was made on the altar of that cause, but since the employers were very rich, the strikers mostly foreigners, and the city and country co-operating with the employers as well as the courts, the strike was finally defeated. Our department did succeed in materially modifying the employment of children in that industry. We did, by numerous filing of complaints and arrests, succeed in calling attention to the condition—made it a subject matter for public discussion and exposure, and affected materially the public attitude of mind on this enormous industrial abuse. I took great interest in the work. Along with attending lectures, participating in socialistic and trade union movements, I was reading considerably, and improved my general understanding of the nature of social and industrial problems.

I learned to understand the problem from the point of view of the employee, the contractor, the beginner and the more prosperous manufacturer, and the large trust organizations—also from the point of view of the respective nationalities and the different cultural levels. When we were about to amend the law, I went through the labor unions of the city to have them co-operate with my department to improve the law—to enlarge its scope—and to make it possible for us to enforce it more efficiently. There I was obliged to discuss it in the councils of the different unions. Incidentally, the whole nature of the labor movement entered into my discussions. I had a window open for me both on the inside of each industry and from the outside of the respective unions who were organizing those industries, and also in the families which worked in the industries. It was a marvelous opportunity and experience. I saw the industrial and commercial and financial machine being formed from its incipiency up to its enormous development in each industry and I saw the industrial and social struggle and the influence on character in my daily life's experience.

As I understand it, there was a union of opinion in loyal support of that development. Women who worked in the factories, [who] came from peasant stock of eastern Europe, were in their hearts thankful for the opportunities to work at all. In their home village communities, they almost never had money or power to buy or to assert their own wills to realize any of their dreams. Most of them came from arid countries where the soil was not fertile, where life was hard by way of hard labor and ill-treatment, and they considered an opportunity to work in the factory where they actually got money, no matter how little, a great find. In a great many cases when I spoke to them of their lot being not so easy, they looked askance, and could not quite understand me. In a number of cases, they expressed great satisfaction—working at wages of four to five dollars a week, running machines by exhaustive foot-power, or sitting ten hours a day sewing, compared to the labor on their farms and the absence of opportunity to earn money there—so they found little complaint here.

The contractors knew that sentiment and used it 100 per cent. Tasks were constantly enlarged, wages constantly assaulted. I recall a few cases that throw some light on that situation. In one of the shops of the contractors where about sixty people were employed—in a small place—machines were so placed that when any of the girls wanted to leave her work, she had to get up on her machine, and walk over the body of machines to the door. There was a printed schedule there enumerating every special class of work such as seaming, sleeve-sewing, pocket-sewing, etc. Along with the enumeration of the classes of work, every hour of the day was recorded so that on that schedule it was to [be] recorded that between the hour of 7 and 8, a girl sewed 100 or 120 seams. The same record was kept for every hour of the day. If during any hour the amount produced was less than that of an hour previous, the forewoman was supposed to call her attention to her tardiness so that, in the language of her employer, the girls were continuously jerked up to maintain a speed in the slowest hour that they did in the fastest. Comparisons were made between the speed of one girl and another and the fastest was always held up as the standard. I asked the employer why he didn't employ piece-workers. "That's no good," he said. "Some of these girls don't care whether they earn much, and what we need is production, and the incentive of self-interest does not measure up in production as the threat to be discharged if they don't do just so much." That shop, too, employed a great many children.

I remember once a young man of my acquaintance asked me to loan him several hundred dollars. I asked him what he wished it for. He wanted to make a knee-pants factory on Noble Street. I knew Noble Street to be a settlement of newly arrived Polish immigrants. I said to him, "What will you do where there is no mechanic help—they are all peasants." "I'll train them," he said, "and once trained they will not leave my shop because they are green and helpless, healthy, hard-working peasants." I failed to give him the money and when I met him six months later, he told me he had lost all his money in training the help, but if he could get additional money, he could make it remunerative. When next I saw that fellow, he was employing forty girls and was rich.

8

I Lose My Friends.*—Between the years of 1893–97 there was a panic. A great many people were unemployed, small businessmen went to the wall, bankrupted, and there was general suffering everywhere. With the beginning of 1896, the panic materially subsided, and openings arose for small businessmen again. Many of my friends had, even prior to 1893, deserted our radical camp. The first radicals to desert were the peddlers in our movement. They seemed to have made money, even in bad times, and opened up stores of their own. So, a former violently enthusiastic union man, when there was no work in our industry, went out to peddle, opened up a small second-hand furniture store, and by 1896 was already fairly well-to-do. He was a friend of mine and during 1896, when I believed I was going to lose my position under a new administration, he advised me to go into busi-

* This is the only heading the author provided.

ness with him. He said, "You can't earn a living in your trade, employers will not give you work after you are through with factory inspecting, so you had better invest a little money with me and when you are through with your inspector's work, you and I will form a partnership in the furniture business."

Others had by that time set precedent in that business and made good. It was my understanding that if I went in with him, I could earn my living and make myself independent. But since I had given up business in 1890 for the purpose of staying in the labor movement, I did not want to take his advice. Three or four brother comrades had gone into the study of a profession. One particularly very devoted friend of mine had been studying law; another, my brother-in-law and an active member of the movement, was studying medicine; another became a pharmacist; still others opened up shops as contractors and small manufacturers or [had] gone into storekeeping.

There was a continuous migration from the group I worked with into the avenues of [the] profession[s], manufacturing, and merchandising. A neighbor of mine who was not a socialist, but was well known to me, once tried to persuade me to go into the real estate business. "Look," he said, "you can speak English so well. You've got a personality. You can go in and meet people. Speak to them on their own plane. Our people are beginning to buy up the real estate in our neighborhood. There is always a commission connected with a real estate deal and there is an opportunity to use one's intelligence by buying something yourself, selling it for more. You can't always be in the labor movement. Your occupation will not support you, especially since your wife brings you a new baby every two years, your expenses increase, and because of your intelligence and the people you mix with, and the kinds of friends you're acquainted with, even if you were an efficient cloakmaker and were able to hold a job as well as anyone else, the money earned in the trade wouldn't be enough for you or for your wife. Better take my advice—go into the real estate business with me. It is a simple business. All you must do is to be able to approach people and know them. You can make money."

What he said seemed to me reasonable. I was sure I could always make some money. There was a need for that kind of service in the community and I felt myself perfectly able to offer it. But the idea of becoming financially well-to-do, earning money without any labor, was repugnant to me. I thought it was true that socialism was only an ethical idea and theory, a religion, or a moral precept for conduct under capitalism, yet at the same time I knew how our people felt. Businessmen or men who are earning their money outside of labor were not trusted by working men, especially if he were a socialist, who would preach socialism, which was not consistent with this easy method of making money. I declined the offer. A profession would not be so objectionable. It might, though, but not as much as being a storekeeper, a property owner or a manufacturer, or contractor. When I tried to study in my off-hours, I was not able to accomplish much. My interest in mind was centered on the labor movement. Every now and then events transpired in the movement calling for my attention, and participation. Then again, I had no schooling and it was very difficult for me to study even ordinary school courses so I might study for a profession. So, while I at one time seriously considered the study of law, nothing came of it. The movement absorbed so much of my energy that I had to give up my enterprise.

The truth is, I did not know what to expect after I left my position. It worried me considerably, especially since my family was increasing and in 1896 I had already three children, expenses increasing, my wife's conceptions of a standard of living higher than my own—she wanted a fine home, a much better table, when I would have been willing to put up with a much more humble one. I was kept at the ragged edge and looked at the time when I would lose my position with a great sense of uncertainty, sometimes with horror. Still I held my own and would not be tempted by the conduct of most of my friends and by the suggestion of actual experience in my immediate social and money-making environment. Sarah knew, I said to myself, that she married a poor working man and I was not in duty bound to change my position into the businessmen's class in order to satisfy her higher standard of living.

Sarah never worried me about that; my position in the labor movement and in the community gave her a great deal of satisfaction. I was respected, revered, and admired by a great many people. I was known as the leader of the entire community in the labor movement. Every group to be re-organized addressed themselves to me to make speeches for them to help them re-organize. Those groups were numerous: bakers, furriers, capmakers, ladies' tailors, tailors of all kinds, and the union I belonged to, which made ready-made women's wear. I was also held in esteem by the membership of the Socialist Party, had a great many friends, was called upon to address meetings, and Sarah was satisfied with the position I held and did not crowd me to go into business. At the same time, I did not fail to observe the numerous avenues which a man might throw his energy into in order to make money. Occasionally, it was suggested to me by my friends [I] met as an inspector—people who belonged to both the Republican and Democratic parties, always on the alert to find men popular in their respective communities— that I participate in the numerous campaigns, become a politician. That I considered even more a betrayal in the interests of labor than going into a professional business. So I remained loyal to the cause I represented until finally a Republican administration won in the state and I lost my position as a factory inspector.

During the panic years, there was very little to do in our industry. Competititon for work was great. The union was broken up and wages were below a living standard. By the time I returned to the trade, I found an opening for a great

183

deal of work in re-organizing the union. Now, it was almost impossible to re-organize the union save through a strike. It was the habit of all contractors and manufacturers that once they had a non-union shop, they would fire the first man to join the union. When I called the men to re-organize the union, the employers responded in every case by firing the ringleader. So it became necessary to call strikes in a number of the factories. There was no fun[d] to carry on a campaign—no money for strike benefits and certainly no money to pay the leaders of the strike. There were a few in the industry, and only a few who participated actively in the leadership of the union. There was one young man who worked in the shop with me prior to my becoming a factory inspector. He was an apprentice in the trade then, a very capable young man and a very honest one. I helped to convert him to the cause of the labor movement and he was a very loyal disciple. It was both he and I who in 1897 began a campaign for the re-organization of the union, and the carrying on of numerous strikes. Prosperity returned about that time, but it did not hit our people any too violently, so that our earning capacities were very small and strikes required a great deal of sacrifice on the part of the men. It was not any too rare to find cases of actual starvation, of cloakmakers with large families sick in bed, with no money for doctor or medicine. There were even evictions where rent could not be paid. Under those circumstances, a strike was a very hard situation, especially so since the employers during strikes offered all sorts of inducements to our people to betray the union. I did know cases where men were offered agreements for three years of work with schedules of wages twice their normal earning capacity, and at the same time they had children sick in bed and doctorless. In one case I knew, a death resulted from that, and yet our people held out. We succeeded in maintaining a morale in the group equal to that of saints and martyrs.

I began to suffer great want immediately after I lost my position as factory inspector. While the union had assigned me some kind of a wage for my work, the fact that there were continual strikes and not enough money to take care of the most immediate needs such as lunch money, lawyers' fees, and fees for bail-bonds and fines, I did not have the heart to take any money from the union—or [not] enough to live on. My income from the union was very desultory and my family was continuously in want.

Some of our strikes were victorious, but they were brought about at great sacrifice. For instance, in the case of one strike, one of the members of the executive board deserted us, contracted with the employers to make a shop some place out of town where he could not be found, and scabbed on us. That was after we had already gone on strike for a period of over six weeks—some three hundred of us. The suffering in the homes of those families was unbearable, almost beyond human endurance. We knew this man was working with a number of New York scabs imported by a rich employer, and in this case I printed a circular describing the man and the form of his betrayal, pointed to the fact that he was one of the originators to call the strike, called him a Judas, and asked the peddlers and those who went around town to bring information to our headquarters as to where he was. It did not take long before one of the peddlers discovered the shop near a cemetery in an uninhabited portion of Chicago where it was almost impossible to ordinarily find him. This peddler passed by the shop with his wagon-load of rags, and noticed a cottage in the woods back of the cemetery, where an express wagon brought bundles of cloaks. One morning he informed me of it. I then had a bicycle and I rode out myself, and returned to Chicago. Within an hour, the entire shop was in the headquarters, offered to stop their scabbing provided they could be forgiven and taken back into the union.

There was another case where a man made a shop across an alley from the police station. We hired from a saloon-keeper the rear end of his yard, established headquarters opposite the police station, placed two or three hundred men to prowl around and pass by the windows of the shop. The intention was to overawe the people in the shop with the number and implied threat of violence of these men. That shop too came out and made peace with the union. Some of the men who scabbed inside the factory were met on the street or in their homes and dealt with violently by our picket committees.

In the end, the employer gave in and we won a great victory, so the union was re-organized and covered almost the entire industry. We then established a fair standard of wages, a nine-hour day, but there was one factory, the largest, that it was very difficult for us to get. We had trouble with the manufacturer all along during the life of the union. We were never really victorious with him. He was very stubborn. He hated the union, was spiteful and treated his employees like slaves, but they stood by him because of the fact that he had more work than any other in town. From a commercial point of view, his was a very efficient firm. They manufactured cheaply, and a great deal. They undersold their competitors, and the superintendent of the firm was very clever at designing, capable, and very treacherous. He was always able to defeat the union in all our previous contacts. Thus, year after year, we had been unsuccessful.

We had undertaken to organize this firm. It was a very serious job. It was necessary to have a great deal of money because we knew the firm to be very rich, and ready to make a tremendous fight. The firm had contractors' shops scattered all over the city among all the different nationalities, mainly newly arrived immigrants. The firm had a body of cutters inside who were very loyal and whom it was hard to get out. Their tailors were divided; some were scared to death, and others very loyal to the firm—hirelings, lickspittles, or relatives of men much favored by the firm. The policy of the firm was to divide and subdue. Some of its employees were well paid and treated well. Those in turn had many henchmen around them so a campaign to organize that shop was hard enough.

186

We published a great many leaflets talking to those men. We visited them in their homes individually. We conspired in a hundred and one different ways to get them, and we finally did get them to a meeting. Some thirty or forty out of two hundred came. The firm had spies at the meeting and some eight or nine of the oldest help and the most respectable and conservative help were fired next morning. The firm miscalculated, evidently, the influence that might have on the minds of their workers. That did cow them, but at the same time their sense of loyalty especially to these men was so great that this conduct generated a feeling of outrage that even a reduction in wages would not have produced. Our emissaries in the shops found a willing audience and in a few days we succeeded in calling the people out on strike.

We all knew this would be a hard strike. The firm never gave in to a union, they warned us. Once you leave, you never come back. The firm would rather give up business than give in to a union or rather to Bisno (it amounted to that, since the personal animus of the owner was directed against me). The first blow received in that shop [was] that one of our very loyal members was shot by a cutter working for the shop when he approached him in a desire to stop him from working, near his home in the early morning. The man was taken to the hospital, the bullet extracted, and an operation performed on his body through an opening in the back, and his survival [seemed] only possible. The next blow was given by a body of gangsters, some sixteen in number, men known to be criminals, prize-fighters, and even murderers. They successfully evaded the law. These, under the leadership of private detective agencies, assaulted our pickets around the contractors' shops and beat them up severely so some were actually sent to the hospital.

One day I was approached by a representative of the gangsters who offered to betray the interests of the firm for himself and his gang, conditional that the union give him a thousand dollars for the betrayal. He said, "We will make up a story that we missed the pickets and allowed them to prevent the entry to certain shops where stubborn scabs come." That proposition I turned down. On the next morning I ordered a committee composed of loyal men to come to my aid, and we opened up a street fight against the gangsters and defeated both them and the scabs in open fight. The most prominent gangsters we crippled; in one case, for life. He died within the next few months; others were severely beaten. So were our men. A committee of ours broke up a shop, broke the machinery, cut up the merchandise, and were arrested bodily with weapons in their hands as they left the shop, by policemen waiting downstairs with a patrol wagon backed up. It so happened that this committee was not sent by myself, but had volunteered that work themselves without my order or sanction. But, about fifteen minutes prior to their coming, I had gone over to see the contractor myself. I did this because this contractor was one of the members of the executive board. The firm had given him two thousand dollars to open up shop, contracted with him for a long period at high earnings, conditional on his betraying the union. He did. I advised him to give it up, told him that otherwise he would be fixed. I said that in the presence of some eighteen employees and when, fifteen minutes later, the shop was wrecked by this committee, the firm filed a complaint against me as instigator of the riot and I was charged with conspiracy, malicious mischief, violence with weapons, threat to kill, etc.

I was lucky then that because of my previous service as factory inspector I had friendly connections and influence in councils of high authority, and our people, including myself, were fined small sums which we paid, but which put us under obligation to the reigning political regime. While this conduct of mine was loyal to my union, it was a betrayal of conduct so far as the Socialist Party was concerned, and I was charged with disloyalty before the council of the Socialist Party and was thrown out of membership.

In that strike I worked myself to exhaustion, day and

night. I made speeches regularly in order to collect money for the strike, visited labor organizations, made general public meetings in our communities to form sympathy for our cause and a public morality for our standard, got people, even businessmen, to contribute to the maintenance of our people. We paid strike benefits, in food—small amounts to each family each day. Men who were working in other factories contributed as much as one-third [of] their wages and they earned little enough. The strike was defeated. The firm had their merchandise made in the cities of the East, bought ready-made merchandise, and carried on their business as though there was no strike, and while it may have caused the firm great expense, the firm was so rich and so influential that they easily weathered the assault and came out after our defeat with a chance to make even more money than prior to the strike.

The defeat broke us up. Hundreds of our men could not get back to work, and lost their livelihood. The union was much weakened. There was no money in the treasury. We had used our little credit, and were in debt. We needed money to support the families of the men out of work, and after the strike, when I went around personally to list funds and contributions, to pay fines for some of our members who had been fined, imposed by police courts, [to help] maintain the families whose men had been wounded, my own people responded very meagerly. I was a hero in their estimation, admired, reverenced, but a defeated hero; a man who had led them into a foolish venture.

It was my business to know beforehand that I was not going to win against this firm. Since my calculations were erroneous, I acquired the name of "Visionary," an honest idealist who was impractical, and therefore my reputation was materially assaulted, and the financial response was so meager that I could not meet even by one-fourth the expenses pressing on the union. In my own family, there was no food to spare during the strike, and almost none after. I remember I bought green peas, which were then very cheap, in the quantity of 50 pounds, and the family lived on them with no other food in the house for some time.

I lived in a very old, dilapidated, and crowded tenement house. There was scarlet fever in one of the families living there and since we had small children, it was advisable we move out in order to protect them. Well, I had no money for a month's rent in any other flat, nor money for moving, so we had to stay. Two of the children contracted scarlet fever and there was no money for a doctor or to give them any sort of care needed. The older boy contracted Bright's disease and only after he was swollen and half-dead I addressed myself to a physician whom I had known during a campaign for labor legislation years before, and told him my troubles. He took my boy into his own home, and both he and his wife worked on him for weeks and saved his life.

I could not find a job in the city. For eighteen weeks, I went around idle, pawned and sold everything we could. I pawned a forty-dollar overcoat for three, and lost the coat. I met the superintendent of one of the largest factories of the city. He had a friendly feeling towards me because after a victorious strike I had treated both him and his firm with great consideration. "How are you?" he asked me. "Well," I answered, "frankly I am down and out. Can't find any work." "Well," he said, "I'd take you into the factory, if I wasn't afraid of you." I said, "Well, I'll go back to my union, tell them that I'll agree to take a job with you, without participating in any way in your activity against the union or in the activity of the union against you. I will simply lay low, keep quiet and participate in no adjustment of any question that may possibly arise; the price for piecework, the disciplining of help, or what not. I want you to employ me at week-work so that the controversy for piece-price for labor does not involve me nor any of my personal interests. In case of a strike, I'll leave work together with the other men, but I will not encourage the strike nor will I help to settle the controversy. I will conduct myself in such [a] way as though I were not working for the firm at all, and I will do all this only on my receiving sanction from the union; not only from its authorities but from its membership." "Well, if you do that," he said, "you can come to work Sunday morning and I'll pay you eighteen dollars a week." That was a fair price at that time for week-workers inside the shop.

I went to the meeting of my union, told them my troubles, and received by almost unanimous vote sanction to carry out the suggestion as submitted by me to this superintendent. For three days I worked in peace; on the fourth, one of the men working in the shop came in late. He was reprimanded by the superintendent for disturbing the discipline of the shop and for disorganizing the work. The next day, he came in later. He was then told that unless he changed his behavior he might be fired. The next day he did not come until 11. He was fired. The men in the shop stopped work. Mr. Rosenthal needed the work badly. Every garment there was promised at a definite time and a stoppage of work would mean a loss of customers, the merchandise would not be accepted late, and he stood to lose a great deal of money.

"Bisno," he said, "put these men back to work." "I can't," I said. "I have no authority to do it. I haven't participated in causing this trouble. I have not promised to participate for either side. It is not right for you to subject me to responsibility for either the conduct of the firm or the men." He said, "That is true. You did not cause the strike. You did not advise that man to come late—but he comes late because he depends on your intercession in case of trouble. The men stopped work because they think you will adjust this for them. Your being in the shop encourages them to do things they would not do if you were not around. They know you, and they know and I know that you are depended on for adjusting troubles even if they have sanctioned your abstaining from doing it. I want you to put them back to work. I need that work. Harry, the late worker, is wrong in coming late regularly. It disorganizes the shop and I cannot run the shop unless Harry or anyone else subjects himself to the natural discipline of the factory."

As a matter of fact, the superintendent was right and I did intercede and adjusted the controversy. When I told the men to work again they did. I also arranged to put Harry back to work with a promise of no more lateness, and he kept it. I told him that unless he did, I would see he was discharged, and he knew the men would back me up if I did that. In a few days the men sought me out to settle the piece-price for labor. I did nothing to name the committee. I made no suggestions as to the piece-price. I attended to my work and the firm was satisfied, but after there was a considerable disagreement between the committee and the employer on the price for labor, the superintendent again turned to me with a great deal of resentment: "They are asking impossible prices. They're crazy. If it was not for you being here, they would be more moderate." One of the examiners, a woman, was not treated respectfully by one of the men. She complained to the superintendent and she felt, too, that because I was working in the factory, the men were disrespectful to her. I adjusted their complaint, settled the price for labor, my men were satisfied, but none of the shop authorities felt that my being in the shop was conducive to the well-being of the firm, so I worked under a severe strain. I knew it was simply a question of days before I would be obliged to leave the factory.

There was a man whom I had met at a socialist meeting who was the superintendent of a factory which was making sweeper cars. I asked him to put me to work at common labor there. They paid for common labor $1.50 a day—just one-half of what I was receiving at the coat factory—and he did. My work consisted of lifting and either carrying or wheeling large chunks of molds of iron, suited to the labor of one used to that strenuous type of work. My hands were delicate and so was my body. I was not able to lift the weights assigned to the other men who were used to that class of work. I was obliged to carry one side of an axle which weighed several hundred pounds, along with another man. The same was true with other weights. I was there to feed the several machines, lathes and drill presses, shapers, boring machines, etc. Occasionally I was put along with others to load cars with parts of the completed machinery for the sweeping cars. When there was no common labor to do I was taught to chip iron from the molds out of the molding shop preparing for their being tooled into the various parts. All of this was hardly my physical class of work. The shop itself was like a shed with almost no heat in winter so I had to stand severe cold, work extremely [hard] beyond my physical endurance, and every part of my body constantly ached. I was not able to sleep because of the pain. A night's rest was not enough for the next day's work. I did not recuperate as fast as I exhausted myself. I worked in that shed about five months until finally there was no more work in the factory and I was discharged. I had pains everywhere. One bruise healed and another was made. It was hard for me to chip iron without cutting myself, or straighten out strains of the muscles in lifting or carrying. I contracted severe colds from time to time and after I had somewhat adjusted my body to the severe strain, I was fired.

Through recommendations of friends of mine, I got a job as one of the station agents in the elevated railroad company. They paid $1.50 a day for seven nights a week—for twelve hours each night, collecting fares. One does not get steady work in this class of employment from the beginning. One must report as an extra for some time and get whatever days' work can be gotten, conditional on someone being sick or on vacation or absent for some reason. That gave me, to start with, about two or three days' earnings. I had to report to work seven days a week. When I got work it meant an all-night watch for twelve hours. After four months of service as an extra, I finally received a job as a steady worker—$1.50 a day, seven nights a week, and in due time received a day job. Here I earned $10.50 a week for seven days' work.

We then lived in four rooms above a stable in a house in the rear of another in the poorest neighborhood in town. We received the benefit of the smells of the horses and manure, and our own yard was filled with dirt and manure. The front part of the lot was covered by a butcher shop, which added to the filth, smell, and atmosphere of the place. The neighborhood was very crowded and this yard and the alley on which our building faced was a playground for [my] children, and my income was barely enough to fill their stomachs and keep them in school and clothed. Conditions somewhat improved in the industry so that during season our people earned twice and sometimes three times as much as I earned. While my wife said nothing it was clear that her desire for a decent place to live with her children, for food, clothing, etc., was not satisfied by my wage-earning capacity at that time. Even in those years I spent considerable time, whenever I had an hour, in the movement, attending socialist meetings or meetings of the union, making speeches, and reading up on the books on science, social problems, or good literature. I was respected by my friends and relatives, but at the same time, back of their respect there was a considerable contempt for my idealism and being what they called a visionary. My wife could meet none of my friends' families without being told that she was married to a damn fool who, from their personal knowledge, could, if he did some business, earn a great deal more money, but did not do it because of some fool vision about being a socialist.

A cousin of mine whom I was in partnership with before I gave up business to become a wage-worker had by that time a large shop as a ladies' tailor, earned $15,000 to $20,000 a year, employed a coachman and had himself driven around. He occupied a beautiful house on the boulevard, bought several constantly improving pieces of property, and whenever he did happen to meet in family gatherings, he spoke of me with a great deal of contempt. "That fellow," he said, "is crazy." He was particularly sore because I did not only fail to take advantage of this world's goods, but I had also prepared for myself a very severe punishment in the next world, since I had assaulted religious tenets and beliefs of the Jews on every public occasion I could do so. The feeling was I would be hung before long as a social rebel, and when I got into the next world, I would be punished because of my disrespectful attitude towards God and religion, because of infidelity and atheism.

The same was true of another cousin, also an immigrant, who by this time already owned two houses, lived on rent. His family was well sheltered and dressed, and were able to go to theaters, to hold family gatherings, to generally enjoy themselves, live and feel prosperous. These cousins were tailors like myself, but I had other cousins who began as peddlers and who had by this time acquired stores and were very prosperous. Then friends of mine in the movement had by this time become practising professionals, as lawyers and doctors, lived in streets where the well-to-do lived, earned much money, and were prosperous. Almost every man of some natural talent, either in education or trade, or in skill in this trade, all of my kind, men who originally were under my leadership in the labor movement, and who had held office on the union board, even those who had held paid positions, all had deserted the cause and had gone into making themselves prosperous. I was the only black sheep, both in the family and among my immediate neighbors. I not only did not go up, as they called it, but on the contrary had gone down, worked on common labor in one of the worst jobs in the iron business, and as a station agent at fifteen cents an hour.

Even in the labor movement, my activities were much limited these years. I was employed in fields where none of my people worked. There was no opportunity to organize people employed on the elevated roads and to tell the truth, if my desires had been to try to do so, I would have been fired. My memory of the eighteen weeks of unemployment, starvation, and sickness were yet too keen and held me in a vise. So I did behave. Whatever talking I did was outside of my immediate employment, and I did not have any chance at that. I was estranged from my opportunity to work with the people I knew, and with whom I was most effective in a social way. Where I was, my earnings were so small, so many hours per week to put in, that I did not blame anyone who called me visionary and a fool.

During the years between 1893 and 1897, the labor movement was quite disorganized. Labor meetings were meetings of labor tramps. There was little coherence and thought formation with regard to the labor movement. Large industrial unions such as railways, clothing, wood and metal workers lost one big strike after another. The socialist movement did not count for much, and there was a feeling of bitterness and despair overwhelming the most faithful. Labor meetings did not have constructive ideas. Destructive criticism was uppermost in the minds of labor men, and a non-constructive attitude was the order of the day with the well-to-do liberals and intelligent groups who in a sense represented the capitalist classes. They were looking for social formations making for an answer to the problem of unemployment and an answer to the problem of irresponsible and oppressive employers, and an answer to the problem of disloyalty to the institutions of the government. Democratic reforms as the secret ballot, public control of social industries, modifying the power of the courts in [the] case of labor disputes, and extensions of the school systems, and assault on private and public grafting, were vigorously preached by representatives of the liberal middle-class groups. Criticism of present institutions was general, but to me they seemed to lack heart.

Labor meetings felt that Democratic activity was all a pretense, and shielded capitalism, which, they held, was rotten and could not be mended. Liberalism was simply a means on the part of capitalists to modify the sense of resentment and rebellion on the part of labor. There was no honest intent back of that claim; capitalism was a fraud, religious preachings were a fraud, and liberal and reform pretenses a fraud. Labor could expect nothing from them. Labor must organize into an independent party both industrially and politically, with a revolutionary motive to overthrow existing institutions and to establish socialist institutions instead.

The doctor who had saved my boy's life used to have public gatherings at his home every Sunday night. Here professors of economy, sociology, and social psychology, as well as professional men such as doctors, lawyers, engineers, and literary people, would mingle. Sometimes, but seldom, the liberal capitalists might be represented. I was invited to attend these meetings and I was in great contrast to the people there. I was dirty, ill-clad, in need of a shave constantly. There was a very marked difference in appearance between myself and every speaker there. Here art was spoken of and the beauty of higher philosophy and reform liberalism by university professors. There was milk-and-water discussion of present institutions, and the lack of [a] compelling motive back of their claims, as well as their poetic phrases, got my goat. I could not understand what they called beauty because I considered that people who thought at all ought to think of the great social catastrophe in the midst of which we all lived. Every day people were in want and suffering. Children had not enough to eat; evictions took place daily; and adults coming together to discuss the beauty of poetic phrases seemed to me a criminal occupation. The reformers too were milksops. The ethical appeal for fair play on the part of the boss to his workers seemed to contain no vitality to me. They addressed themselves to no force making for the realization of their ideas. On the other hand, the labor classes expressed themselves in terms of defiance in every spiritual and religious formation as opposed to the capitalists.

I remember on one particular occasion when a Sunday evening at the doctor's house was devoted to a eulogy on

William Morris. That was the week of the death of William Morris. The woman who made the leading speech on the occasion read his poetry, and commented on its beauty—the papers had been full of all of Morris' personal characteristics, of all the artistic peculiarities of the man. William Morris was a revolutionary, and his books and pamphlets inspired the disinherited working classes; he was a prophet of great significance, all of which was ignored, and only surface appearances and insignificant phrases of beauty and furniture-modeling were talked of as the most important work of Morris. When I got a chance to speak, I denounced as heresy the trivialities and ridiculousness of the estimate of Morris by the newspapers and by the silk-stockinged philosophical and ethical liberalism of the group with whom I was. I spoke with a great deal of vehemence and protest. This criticism of a cultured and educated human mind seemed to me to have been inspired by time-serving lackeys. It was presumptuous on the part of an invited guest to speak so in the presence of my host and his guests. But I was resentful and rebellious and their attitude seemed so distorted, pretending and unreal, bearing on the nature of William Morris and the significance of his contribution to the social problem, that I could not help but give voice to what I thought was the instinct of the labor movement, and the significance of the occasion.

At one time I was invited by Graham Taylor to address a seminary group of his on the subject of the industrial and social problem. I talked about that, but along with that I spoke of religious seminaries, the teacher and students; I called them spiritual lackeys of capitalism, spoke of their religious and ethical claims as mountebank formations suited to attract the crowd away from serious social and present-day thought. I put it on thick, used a sort of slang charged with contempt that showed what thinking working men felt. I got their goats and it was arranged that one of their divines was to debate with me on basic principles before the class. The subject was to be: Human Volition or Conditioned Determinism.

The divine had lately come from Scotland, and had toured both England and Scotland, discussing with Marxian socialists the subject of materialism in philosophy, the materialistic conception in history, and the stressing of economic factors making for conduct in religious, social, and economic lines. He gave the religious aspect to phenomena in a fervent and eloquent manner. I remember some of his speeches. I had told a story of a meeting of a manufacturers' association which passed resolutions that it was within the political and moral obligations of this nation to protect the scab—a non-union man; that the right of each man to life, liberty, and the pursuit of happiness was the foundation of our social institutions. Not long after, the American Federation of Labor had a meeting. They passed resolutions condemning the non-union man, especially the scab who took his neighbor's job, making it socially obligatory on the part of every working man to join the union. Here were two groups of people equally loyal Americans; what one considered vicious and criminal conduct, the other considered laudable, desirable, patriotic, and loyal to American institutions. How do you explain, I asked, that members of the American Federation of Labor have a separate morality on conduct, and another set of American citizens, equally loyal, have another sort of morality to follow? Both factions had no dissenting voices among them. Both were equally loyal. Now, if it is individual volition which makes for attitudes in mind and conduct, why did the American Federation men vote in favor of the striker, why did not the manufacturers' association vote in favor of denouncing the scab? Why was there not at least a respectable minority dissenting in either of these groups of men? How do you explain the phenomena of people living in the same communities, attending the same schools, going to the same churches, taught morality by the same churches [who] will divide on this issue and both sides will be unanimous amongst themselves as to their views along class lines?

Prior to the time that Whitney invented his cotton gin,

slavery did not pay. It took too much work to raise cotton and the slaves could not earn their own food—so there were abolitionist clergy in the South, southern politicians were pleading in Congress for legislation to abolish slavery, senators formulated resolutions and laws to abolish slavery. Southern Christian clergymen found that their Christian religion prohibited slavery; southern men interpreted the constitution of the United States as being an anti-slavery document; but immediately after the cotton gin was invented, making slave labor efficiently productive, men who owned plantations in the South became rich, the business of growing cotton grew and gave the whole South richness, and then this is what happened. Every abolition club disappeared in the South. Senators argued in Congress that the constitution of the United States justified slavery. The same was true of congressmen. Christian clergy found in the Bible, and in the teachings of Jesus, authority for slavery. How do you explain such changes in public mind and public morality? Of interpretations of constitutions, declarations of independence, etc.? Did these changes arise from the fact that slave-holding became profitable?

In the course of time, the people of the South and the people of the North went to war. While on the surface, the war was because of secession, intrinsically it really arose from slave-holding and the people of the North were fighting to abolish slavery, and the South were fighting to continue it. Why did not the northerners, who had no slaves, fight to maintain slavery? Why did not the southerners, who were benefited by slave-holding, fight to abolish slavery? How do you explain that equally good Christians, equally loyal American citizens, would shoulder guns, go to war, devastate each other's land, kill each other's population, without ascribing the phenomenon to economic and material motives? You have no other explanation. You could not find it if you looked for it with a microscope. You must admit that the reason why the people of the South wanted slavery, and the

North fought it, was because each was obliged to fight for their own economic interests. Secession and the fight for the Union were only the forms which expressed that interest.

There was a law enacted prohibiting the employment of children in Illinois, and the employment of women for more than eight hours a day. This law was enacted through the influence and agitation of labor interests. Did the manufacturers, bankers, commercial associations, and their lackeys, lawyers' associations, clergy, etc., further that law? No, they did not. How do you explain that working men would be in favor of such a law and the privileged classes would be against the law if it is not on the grounds that each has a separate economic interest in relation to themselves? How is it that the manufacturers' association hired lawyers to go into court and have the law declared unconstitutional, while the labor unions supported the law and wanted it declared constitutional? What made for that difference of attitude of mind? A different social morality on such a vital item as protecting the health and life of women and children—there is probably no subject in the world on which there should be more union of opinion than on the protection of the health of the mothers of the race and yet there is such a difference of opinion.

The manufacturers' association says, they don't want a law. The labor unions say, they do want the law. Have working men a larger foresight on the subject of the welfare of the race? Why, no. The intelligence of man would say that manufacturers and bankers and members of boards of exchange, who are more educated, would have a much more altruistic view on the subject and would be in favor of protecting the mothers of the race by law. They are more church-going and religious. They pretend [to] high moral standards, and maintain churches. How is it that they are immoral? Dishonest? Careless about future American citizenship? If it had been a question of their own women-folk, they would not have fought such a law. If ten-hour work did not give them more profit than eight-hour work, they would not fight such a law. It is because they can make more money that even the welfare of the race is not strong enough to induce them to forget their own economic interests. If individual volition is the motive power for human[e] attitude of mind, how do you explain the attitude of mind on the subject of the conduct of these manufacturers as it relates to the welfare and interest of the race? The whole history of mankind is the history of class struggles. Slaves fought against their owners, serfs against their masters, oppressed races against their oppressors; no one can read the history of mankind without finding this great force of economic self-interest in races and in nations and in people—and yet there are men who claim individual volition as [the] motive power of social morality.

I think it was Macaulay who said that if it paid anybody to maintain that twice 2 was 5, there would be plenty to maintain it. The thing that seems to me rather too strong is that [there are] people who pretend knowledge of the authority of religion that happened to have been singled out through a propaganda of error, deceit, and falsifying the knowledge about the nature of man; I submit that it is not within the province of men who go out to teach people religion and truth to pervert the truth in history [in order to] earn their living, or [to] pervert their consciences simply because the capitalistic forces pay for such perversion. Modern intellectual training has so trained the capitalistic class that they even co-operate with working men in denouncing a social evil, and it is being done for the purpose of forming a pretense that capitalists are honestly interested in abolishing economic abuses which are prevailing. Yet they make no effort to really abolish them but [are] making the very speeches about it a form of misrepresenting their real attitude of mind.

Take for instance the case of sweatshops where men, women, and children are employed unlimited number of hours, under unhygienic conditions; where the merchandise is farmed out to irresponsible contractors, where the really responsible people, namely the moneyed men and manufacturers, do shirk all responsibility to their employees by pretending that the contractor who contracts for the work to be done is the only responsible party. As a matter of fact, the contractor is one in name only; in reality he has no more power to modify conditions than the working man himself. It is known to all of you that there is a certain church here whose membership is mainly composed of that class of manufacturers: sweatshop people. The preacher is a high-class, university-educated gentleman, very high in cultural attainment, with a great deal of public spirit. He makes no bones about it. He denounces sweatshops as vigorously as any man; regularly every Sunday membership in his church listen to it, are quite enthusiastic about the lofty and high spiritual attitude of their preacher. They pay him high wages, keep him comfortable; at bottom they do it because he serves as a shield to cover up on Sunday what these gentlemen do the rest of the week. Do you think that normally people would subject themselves to this class of hypocrisy if it were not for the fact that their economic interests dictate to an otherwise decent man that he must lie individually or collectively for the purpose of making more money? Do you think this arises from their individual volition, to lie and pretend? They are both educated and sane enough to know the difference between right and wrong, and when their conduct is wrong it is not because of their volition to be wrong, but because economic conditions determine their attitude of mind and conduct. They have no individual volition and can have no volition save if they were willing to be sweatshop employees themselves. None would want to do that.

In reply to my speech, the clergyman said, among other things, that he had personally known a community where there was a great deal of drunkenness, laziness, criminality, shiftlessness, and where the public morality was very low, and it happened that an intelligent clergyman was sent into the city to inspire the people with a respect and fear of God. He also tried to give them a sense of dignity and respect for their own characters. As a result, the character of the population changed, and in obedience to the change of character, crime and laziness and shiftlessness were materially modified, people became more prosperous, showing that they had within themselves material making for individual initiative and attitude of mind making for decency and prosperity. From my personal observation, I gathered that the very statement was false and I suspect myself of losing my temper for a while, and in my rebuttal said I believed he was hardly telling the truth. Everyone in the audience considered this a personal affront and ill-behavior on my part, which made me feel disgusted with the whole business. It seemed a morality was established among these people: the man had a right to lie, socially, and that to call him a liar was bad breeding. It sort of prejudiced me against even the form of good breeding on the part of capitalistic classes. It implied a duty to lie.

Conditions in my family began to wear on me very rigorously. Being outside the trade, I was not able to participate actively in the formation and conduct of the union. Other men in the trade replaced me. I still had a great moral influence upon the events as they transpired during seasonal unions and strikes. I still participated in making speeches from time to time, but my conduct contained no such vitality as it did prior to my being thrown out of the industry. I was a friend of our people, a recognized friend, my counsel was listened to and complied with, but I was an outsider. The daily grind was carried out by others than myself. I became a visitor instead of a live part of a movement which I had been with for so many years. I found myself despondent, felt that I was nowhere, really belonged nowhere. The political movement did not appeal [appear?] to me to have any real and significant vitality. I was out of the trade union movement because I was not able to organize the people working in the car-shops, was

204

not even able to begin agitation. I was working not with my own people and I was a very insignificant part of the plant at that. I was a common laborer and there were hundreds of people at the door every morning asking for jobs at any price. An organization of that type and under those conditions would only be possible in an atmosphere of general revolt, but to create that condition was not within the power of my individual conduct. I did find some response in talking about it to the men in the shop, but not the kind of response making for conduct. Men in sympathy with my notions were found who thought me quite a philosopher, but under the conditions then present, they did not volunteer their readiness for the campaign and sacrifice necessary to bring about an organization.

The same was even more true in the railway job. There I was simply a collector at the gate. There were hundreds waiting for that job. In those years when wages were very small and the watch was twelve hours a day, seven days a week, it was easy to get that class of help in unlimited numbers. The work was of a kind where it was impossible to meet large groups of employees. The campaign to organize those men could only be made by a number of people, and that was not the time to do it. So I could do nothing in my work, and was not much interested in the political work, though I did a great deal of it. I felt that I had made no contributions worthy of myself for a long time and yet the economic pressure was very severe. Over and over, both myself and my wife met relatives and friends who were prosperous in business and who looked on my work as being visionary, foolish, and while this did not bother me when I was able to contribute in a social way, the thing began to worry me considerably when I was deprived of the opportunity to do anything socially and still was keeping my wife and children poor and suffering. I began to weaken in my own resolutions to stay a working man. I had no opportunity to be a working man on equal terms with my neighbor. I could find no job in my trade and was not fit to do the job of common labor or skilled labor or clerical labor.

My earning capacity was very small; my family large. I was confronted with a situation where my sense of duty was split in two. I knew I was in duty bound to support my family, and while my wife would have been satisfied with an economic life below that of the friends and relatives we had, I had furnished no such life to her. I needed at least $15 or $18 a week, or $750 to a $1,000 a year to live even poorly. I only earned $400 to $500 a year. By that time I had four children; some had to go to school; there was no money for shoes or clothes, no money for proper food, with quite an intelligent woman as a wife, who needed a fair standard of living. My need for labor and socialistic activity ran counter in interest to the need of my family. They were absolutely helpless and dependent on me. My wife had all she could do to take care of my children and could not help me at all. I did not expect her to. She could not help herself. The weight of their dependence fell on me, and I was very much aware of it. Yet the only way I could comply in my duty to my family was to cross the bridge, go into business, make my living not as a working man but as a trader or merchant, or manufacturer. A great many of my friends had studied professions and done well, but I was not able to do so. I had no ordinary school education, and didn't know the first thing about the three R's. When I tried to learn arithmetic, spelling and grammar, geography and history, I found my memory numbed for that purpose. My head was full of social problems and I could not concentrate on a class of education that could only be acquired from childhood and youth up. Here I was, a man of twenty-seven or twenty-eight, with an extensive body of knowledge about history, the natural and social sciences, but with no rudiments of education at all. I tried to concentrate, I tried to write, to study arithmetic, to prepare for entry into school at night, worked at it for some six months, but failed to accomplish as much as any child might have.

I was morally and intellectually upset. There was discord and dissatisfaction all over me. Every day I found myself further away from the thing I really wanted to accomplish, and was driven by a power over which I had no control into avenues of life and conduct which were not in harmony with my attitude of mind at all. I was finally persuaded to look for some business, and knew I would be obliged to pass a considerable apprenticeship. I knew nothing about business except as I picked it up in conversation with my friends and as a factory inspector going around with numerous businessmen. Then, I had no capital. I borrowed some two hundred dollars from a friend, bought a little cigar store and a newspaper route, would get up early every morning to take care of the route—at three o'clock—then during the day, I would go out on the route, and my wife would tend the store. While I distributed the papers efficiently, I was not a good collector, and after a few months, I found I was making no money, hardly a living, so I sold the store and the route and went back to my trade, operating a machine. I was obliged to work for a small contractor, which was not a well-paying job. Still, I was better off than I had been working for either the elevated roads or at common labor. But the ice was broken. I was ready for business.

The business I knew the best was the manufacture of cloaks, but that would have made me a contractor, the very class of employers I had been fighting for a great many years, and finally a manufacturer exploiting the people I had been fighting for. In the very nature of things, a contractor cannot stay in business unless he can produce merchandise cheaper than the manufacturer himself can produce. A man becomes a contractor because he has not enough capital to invest in manufacturing merchandise. So he contracts to manufacture merchandise with only a small investment of sewing machines and press irons and rent, and he gets the work to do because somehow he manages to get help cheaper than the manufacturer himself can. Contractors normally, when they started business, exploited immigrant help, relatives or newly arrived immigrants from the communities in Europe from which they themselves came, taught them the trade, but got their labor very cheaply. In due course of time, they developed efficient help and made money and went into manufacturing themselves. I knew the process and felt that this sort of business was objectionable to me, and even if I undertook doing it, I would not be efficient at it. Men efficient at that class of enterprise must possess a character fitting the work, and must be able to bargain for the very last sou; they must almost completely dispossess themselves of normal human sympathy. One is employing the poorest of the poor and the most helpless. It is therefore necessary to first drive them to get work out of them, and next, to pay them for their work barely enough for their living since, when the trade was learned, one is very inefficient anyhow.

I could not go into the contracting business. It was opposed to my nature. I finally hooked up with a relative of my wife, in partnership, to go into the ladies' tailoring business. I borrowed from all my friends and established a business* in a prosperous community. While the first six months were extremely hard until we worked up a trade, we did finally work up enough trade to earn a living, a much better living than we could earn as working men in the shop. As a ladies' tailor, I was not producing merchandise for the market. I was not interfering or competing with any of the men in the cloak-making industry and union. I cannot say I was very efficient at this work. The years I had centered my interest on the social problem and the socialist movement had taken all my absorption; I was thinking of my ideals all the time, so much that I could not at all concentrate on this new effort, or formulate the necessary scale for its successful operation. But, as it was, I was engaged mainly to drum up trade, to do in the business such operations as I was skillful at, namely sewing-machine operation, and the business went along fairly well.

* In 1902.

But at heart my main business was still the union. I would go to union meetings.

[Publisher's note: The following sentence appears in Bisno's original manuscript at this point: "Insert story of Sophy, story of White, Raymond Robbins, Darrow, Mrs. O., Torp, Masters, McCullough." Apparently the material referred to was never written.]

The International Ladies' Garment Workers in New York had undertaken a campaign to make union labor popular among the public, storekeepers and labor men. They addressed themselves to me to visit several cities and explain to working men, unions, and storekeepers reasons why they should patronize union-made merchandise. I undertook this job. I agreed with my partner to have him stay in the business while I traveled around for the union, since the business was at its beginning and had to be worked up. For some six months or so, I had occasion to become again absorbed in the movement, visited a large number of cities, made a circumference of about six hundred miles or more around Chicago and visited some twenty-five or thirty cities and succeeded in making union labor on women's garments quite popular. I never believed in that work much. I rather thought that the improvement of the conditions of labor must come about through the initiative of the employees themselves and considered a strike much more effective to improve conditions than I did public patronage. But it did give me an opportunity to get acquainted with the labor union movement in the various cities.

When I came back, I found our business considerably improved so there was a living in it for me. I went to work diligently in the ladies' tailoring business. There was prosperity in the years between 1898–1905, so that the union had materially improved the lot of the men and women in the industry. I participated as an outsider. Younger and new men had taken possession of the direction and government of the union. Contracts were entered into between the union and the manufacturer which were not in line with the ideas I had been teaching. New formations, new ideas, new motives for conduct were practiced by the union which I did not like, and while I did participte in the meetings, make speeches, the men on the inside were these who really governed the union and not myself.*

This caused me to feel badly about it. For instance, when I had charge of the union, in settlement of a strike, I normally maintained that the union was entitled to do all the work that the employer possessed, manufactured in contractors' shops. When I left and went into business, the new authorities in the union contracted with employers only for a limited number of shops, namely, those shops which the union controlled through its membership. Shops which the union did not control through its membership were permitted to be employed without joining the union. The only provision made in connection with that was that the union shops might have a preference in getting work: they were to be supplied with work before the non-union shops. But there was no machinery established between the union and the employer to enforce that provision and, therefore, it was all left to the employer to decide whether or not he would give the union preference in work. As a matter of fact, it turned out that the agreement with the employers militated against the interests of the union men, since non-union shops would do the work for less money and employers would send work to non-union shops, since there was no machinery for control or even machinery for imparting information to the union of when merchandise was sent out or where it was made. So while the standards as established for good wages, limited hours, and fair treatment held, the men had no work to do. Non-union shops got most of the work, and union men, instead of being

* During the time Bisno had been away from the Chicago Cloak Makers' Union, it had become Local No. 5 of the ILGWU.

benefited by their membership in the union, were in reality hurt.

My old friends would come around and complain bitterly and invite me to address their meetings, which I would do. I protested against such vicious agreements, blamed the authorities of the union for entering into such an agreement, became a rebel in the union, surrounded myself with a rebellious group in the union who felt like myself about the fraud imposed on them by the union; namely, they were given in writing good wages, short hours, decent treatment and standards, but they did not get work and so were not benefited by any of this. The major portion was being made in non-union shops and non-union shops were in the great majority, and union men only got work a few weeks during the busiest part of the busy season, and since the cloak industry is a seasonal trade anyway, union men were unemployed for a great deal of the time.

My struggle was to no purpose to benefit our men. I did well in business and increased in material wealth so I had more money to live on than ever before, but I was not satisfied. Congress had appointed a commission to investigate immigration, and it was necessary to investigate the kind of immigrants coming to America and their motive for coming, their economic and cultural levels at home, their manner of adjustment to conditions in America, their economic conditions here, the influence they had on American life and the way they were influenced by American life, their cultural level here in America, the way they became Americanized, etc., etc. The head of that organization was John R. Commons, a professor of Economics and Labor at the University of Wisconsin. Some time before, I happened to have been introduced to Commons and spoke with him of the labor movement. I was known as a man well acquainted with the clothing trade and since a great many of the immigrants were in the clothing business, Commons asked me to join him in the investigation, offered decent remuneration, and since

I liked the work better than tailoring, I accepted his offer and the appointment.*

Every conceivable phase of the problem was embodied in the questions to be asked in this investigation. We first investigated manufacturers' modes of production, copied large numbers of payrolls, and then filled in individual schedules of employees, schedules of manufacturers, and formed tables of entire markets, and this work gave me great opportunity of studying both the economics of industry and the psychology of individual working men and women and of the influence industry has on the minds of men, and the differences between the respective races and nations.

I found that immigrants who were farmers in the old country considered opportunities to work in factories as a great boon. Women who earned very little on the farm and who earned livings mostly by housework, either in their own homes or as servants, appreciated the opportunity of working a limited number of hours and earning money. Though their wage was small, they considered it large; while the majority of them turned their money over to the family chest, there were quite a significant minority who would themselves be holders of their earnings, pay regular board to their families, and either spend or save money for themselves. This change in their lives which gave them a right to do whatever they pleased with their own money, and gave them standing and authority in their families because of their earnings and contributions, was for them a very significant item in their lives. They acquired the right to a personality which they had not ever before possessed in the old country, even married women who worked in shops and were obliged to maintain a household at the same time. These latter felt that they were much better off because they had a money-earning capacity, though they had to work very hard. So the factory and even the sweatshop were very much appreciated by these women. It

* They worked together for six months in 1900–1901.

was a historic revolution in their lives and in the lives of their entire people.

The same was true with the men. Men who earned at common labor as little as $1.50 a day considered that amount a fortune as compared to what they had been subjected to in the old country. Over and over again I got this story: that it took some families as much as six or seven years' savings to acquire enough money to pay for their transportation to America, and in their own judgment it was worth it; it was a very good investment. The only drawback was that the new generation in this country were not as faithful religiously as the older one in the old country. The church did not have as firm a hold upon their offspring as upon themselves.

In those years the Taylor system of factory management came in. In the struggle in the numerous industries to introduce more efficient modes of production, piecework, numerous kinds of bonus systems, and the fight the employees made against it, the instinctive struggle of labor against the introduction of new machinery, the urge on the part of the employers to introduce more and more efficient machinery for production, formed a very interesting kaleidoscopic panorama in our investigations. We made histories of the growth of respective industries, copied the early wages for a number of years, made comparisons, tried to ascertain the efficiency of production in the numerous plants, the quantity and quality of work done. We applied sociologic, scientific methods to get to the meaning of these great industrial and social changes. We found that with newly arrived immigrant labor, employers treated them like cattle. In one department in the yards, when I found that the remuneration was not enough for a person to subsist on, one of the superintendents of one of the largest plants told me, as a joke, in answer to my suggestion that the wages were very small, for the women particularly, that they could earn the balance on their backs. They were normally treated like cattle and while they had a sense of resentment against it, they still put up with it, acquiesced to their treatment because of an actual feeling that they were inferior as compared to their employers, and that their employers might take liberties with them simply because they were the bosses, and were rich and in authority. Those who had been here for longer periods, say six or eight years, would resent oppressive treatment, would assert themselves, and would force for themselves much more respect and somewhat better conditions of labor, even without labor unions. If a man had opportunity to leave his employment and find some other work, say because he knew English and knew his way about, he could not be subjected to the kind of slavery which the newly arrived immigrant knew.

There was constantly a change in the nature of immigrant personnel, making for a larger sense of independence, and assertion of rights. In the large industries there was no union to amount to anything, but at the same time there was constantly a threat of forming unions. The threat to go out on a general strike did have a real significant influence on the part of the conduct of the employers. So in some of the factories, welfare work, supporting an insurance organization, were formed through the instigation of the employers themselves, to influence a friendly feeling on the part of the employees. There was a vigorous propaganda going on for plant loyalty with at least a pretense for a hand of fellowship on the part of the employer towards the employee. The industry began to be recognized, not only as a mechanical plant, but also as a human plant, with human ambitions, human needs, and human diversified adjustments. Efficiency, too, was a great item for propaganda—"Produce more and you will get more." There was a great deal of cheating done on the part of the employer in connection with that movement.

In one case, the employees told me, in a factory producing printing machines, how, about two years before, the employers offered the men, who were all week-workers, to pay them the difference between the cost of production week-work and the actual time saved in reducing the time for producing a

214

machine. The arrangement was made, and no reduction was to be made in time pay. A team was composed of eighteen people, beginning with a daily wage of $1.75 up to $3.50. These wages the employer agreed to, no matter how long it might take to make a machine, but since the last machine cost the employer $1,800 in time, in case the team produced the next machine in less time than $1,800, the difference would be turned over to the men in proportion to their daily earnings. This made for a speeding up of the men, not only individually, but speeding up in teams; namely, each man had an interest in producing more and besides he also wished to encourage his neighbor to produce more since he was to be benefited not only by his own increase in efficiency but by the increased efficiency of the team. The machine was produced in $1,600 worth of time, and the $200 extra was divided among the team in proportion to their daily wage. But the next machine was marked $1,600 instead of $1,800 at the time and the information imparted was that since the last machine took $1,600 worth of time, if the men could save on it, they would get the difference to be divided among themselves in proportion to their daily wages. When I investigated the plant, the actual cost of producing the machine was $1,000 and it was marked in the same way; the last machine cost $1,000 and any saving was to be divided in proportion to the daily wage of the team.

At the time I investigated, there was a strike in the factory. The men claimed that this bonus system had set up a speed beyond the endurance of their physical capacity; they wanted the bonus abolished, and the ordinary week-work wage to be returned. That would not help them much even if they won, for the schedule of time costs was kept in great detail, was posted on the walls, the memories of the foremen on each particular item were constantly sharpened, and the foremen were told they could not hold their jobs unless their men kept their speed up to their previously shown capacity. The original understanding was that in case the men produced a machine on which more time was spent than formerly, they would not lose anything, but the difference would be held against them in the next production of a machine. In case they produced the next machine in less time, they would first have to meet their indebtedness on the first machine before they would receive an extra bonus. The team boss in one of the departments told me that at one time his team owed the boss $5,000 but the boss said to wipe the indebtedness off and begin the struggle over again to reduce the time consumed in making the machine.

In other plants the same process went on, only in different forms. Piece-prices were set on each item produced, and the men were told if they speeded up and made more money, they would benefit. But when men earned more money than they did at week-work, piece-prices were reduced. So, no matter how much they speeded up, their earnings were no more than they were before piecework was introduced. Strikes were of no avail because skilled mechanics would not belong to the same labor union as unskilled labor; nor did the different kinds of skilled mechanics have a single organization. If there was any organization at all it was of separate organizations of the different skilled trades, each making separate agreements with the employers. Almost never did they submit common demands, and the employer was able to use each separate craft in such a way as to almost nullify the strength of their union. Common labor was uniformly against the skilled trades, and since a great deal of the work was being done by automatic machinery, common labor, or semi-skilled labor, constituted the major portion of the employees in most factories. Unions did not count, particularly in the larger shops. It was easier to organize immigrant labor, but since most common labor was immigrant labor and skilled labor was American labor, and skilled labor would not unite with unskilled labor, it was impossible to effect a union in a given industry. Unions did not count and the employers had their own way.

The efficiency system was introduced during that period. Labor received almost nothing as a result of improved efficiency in production. In the main the manufacturers benefited; in some cases, the consumer too was benefited. Very little of that benefit went to labor. There was a strong sentiment in favor of labor unions, but every effort made ran across a snag. Trade unions, instead of industrial unions, was the policy of the American Federation of Labor. Industrial production instead of trade production was the policy of the manufacturers. The policy of the American Federation of Labor did not fit into the organization of industry and therefore every effort failed, and employers had completely their own way.

9

The cloak and suit industry grew into an immense business in New York. There were over fifteen hundred shops with an industrial population of 30,000 people. The life of the union went along like waves, up and down all the time. During busy seasons the men flocked to the union to have them help in the settling of the piece-price for labor and when the prices were settled the union was deserted. Only a few faithful ones stuck to the union regularly, year in and out, but these were very few. By that time, the International Ladies' Garment Workers' Union was already formed.* It was a national organization, but had no more luck than the city local organizations had. At the beginning of the season, for very small initiation fees—fifty cents or a dollar—large numbers of men would join the union, have the union settle the price of labor for them for the season, then they would fail to come to

* It had been founded in 1900.

218

meetings, or pay dues. Occasionally the organization would have a strike on hand, but winning or losing, the strike would not benefit the union much because in the main the strike was to raise the piece-price for labor, and once that was settled for the season, the men failed to pay dues or attend the meetings of the union. I used to meet with the few faithful ones in the industry to devise plans and means by which the industry might be permanently organized.

One of the men in charge of the union—the national secretary—was a young man lately from England, a Jew who in England worked at men's clothing, [but who] came to this country as a skirt-operator on women's garments. He was a remarkable fellow. He was a great student of industry and socialism. He was able to write English well. In England, he had written a number of articles in a high-class magazine on the nature of the clothing industry, and the contribution to the industry by the Russian Jews. It was a very scientific and accurate estimate of the industry. A comprehensive statement of the history of the clothing business: how it developed; the mode of production, according to eras; the improvement in production methods, and how the improvement came about historically; comparisons of wages between skilled and unskilled labor; comparisons of efficiency with regard to quality and quantity of production during the different periods; a comprehensive statement of the nature of unions, the mode of their organization, reasons for their failure, their contribution to industry; in short, it was one of the most remarkable [works on] the whole field of both the historical and present status of the clothing and cloak business ever written. He was the general secretary of the International union, elected at the last meeting. It was not very long before he and I were great friends. We found ourselves reflecting each other's knowledge, experience, ideas and ideals and hopes in completion. I co-operated with him, he with me, in planning intelligent formation of a labor organization to be in this great market.

Conditions were deplorable. Immigration at this time was at its peak. Immigrant labor was employed an unlimited number of hours at no wages to amount to anything. During the season, a portion of the workers earned a decent living, but a great many of them were helpless, being unfledged mechanics. Even in season they did not earn a living. During slack seasons, all suffered. They used to congregate in the small parks in large groups, hang around like tramps; maybe somebody would, because it was a market-place, give them a day or even a few hours' work to earn enough to barely maintain life. In making schedules of weekly budgets, I found it impossible to make out just how these people lived. Over and over again, I made schedules—say of individual girls working as finishers in the shops. Rent—two girls in a room with no outside window, living together at seventy-five cents a week. Breakfast—a piece of bread and a bottle of pop for about four cents. Dinner—a piece of bread and an apple, the apples two for three cents, the bread a cent and a half. Supper—bread, a glass of milk, and an apple or banana. The girl would mend and wash her own clothes after work. All expenses for an entire week were two dollars or so. In some cases the girls would be indebted to the housekeeper for two months' rent all the time. They would also be indebted to the corner grocery store. One of the girls was very proud because the grocer had given her a credit as high as five dollars.

A young Italian and his wife had just married. He and his wife lived practically on her wages. He could get no work. Her wages during the six months of their life together were no more than $3.00 or $3.25 a week. "How do you live on that?" I asked them. There must have been days when they did not eat at all. Well, they did not, I discovered. After considerable questioning, I found that sometimes he went to his mother's for a meal—some vegetables and bread—the girl had an aunt and she could get a meal there occasionally. That was the condition in the industry. In larger families, all hands go on deck, beginning with the youngsters of twelve or thirteen. They lied to the factory inspectors, to the school authorities—such knowledge was public property. All knew it was necessary to register in the school as being two or three years older than you really were. Children were wise to that effect and told everyone they were two or three years older than they actually were.

The living quarters in New York tenement houses were practically windowless. A four-room flat would have only two outside windows. The other rooms would either have no windows, or outlets on courts—which meant only a hole in the center of the building furnishing air to four tenants on each floor. The floor consisted of 40' by 60'—whereon there would be four apartments on each floor in five- or six-story buildings. All the apartments only had two outside windows, either on the street or on a yard. The parlors were the rooms with the outside windows. Practically none of the sleeping rooms had outside air. On each of these floors, flocks of people were living. Lodgers would eke out the family's budget. Beds were overcrowded. The normal bedrooms were only 7' by 9', some smaller. This situation was true of the great majority of the tenements. Yet, there was a lot of money made in the industry. That money was made by the contractors, and manufacturers. The man who was able to design merchandise or learn enough English to go out and sell merchandise or raise enough money to go into business in partnership with skilled help normally made good.

So there was quite a migration into the business world. A very lively movement indeed! Everybody talked business styles, price of cloth. There was a beehive of merchandising, manufacturing, and development, and these people did develop the industry. They began to make it possible for the average American woman to own an overcoat and tailor-made skirts and jackets. They developed a style too, so that from year to year the American woman was better dressed than the same average woman in Europe. But the working men and women suffered great hardship in the industry.

All of these inquiries and estimates were written up by my friend—circulars and pamphlets were published with the last penny in the union or collections were made among a few to carry on with written propaganda of the most vigorous kind. Appeals were made, statements of facts in the industry transcribed, weekly bulletins and newspapers published, and distributed on streets and in factories. My friend made a great deal of personal sacrifice for the cause. He lived as cheaply as most of the working men did and was devoted to the cause like a martyr and prophet. He did his work day in and day out, and year in and year out, though he had a great deal of intelligence and capability that might have been turned to personal uses and the formation of a personal fortune—as did many of the union officials who deserted. But he stood at his post to his own disadvantage, very practical on the subject of the interests of the mass of the people, but visionary and impractical so far as his own interests were concerned. An idealist indeed. We loved each other and he insisted that I make his home my home during my stay in New York.*

His wife was a remarkable woman. She was very young, knew very little, but was very kind, very beautiful, with a very sanguine disposition. In the small flat they occupied, everything was clean and neat—whatever they possessed was in good taste. She was not only industrious and kindly and efficient, but was of a remarkably happy disposition. She sort of sensed that her husband was working extremely hard and was engaged in a very significant effort bearing on a great human cause. She could not very well explain it, but she knew her husband had a superior mind to that of her neighbor, and feelings that were sensitive to great human causes. She sensed that he needed an opportunity to rest and have comfort that such a faithful wife could give. She gave him that. She would sing for us, dance, provide us with the food she had—all very well done—beautifully served, along with

* In 1911–12.

whatever affection he could use. She gave him all she had. It seems that this social martyrdom broadens the human mind, cuts clear across all normally assumed conventionalities and forms a world of its own—a morality of its own—even a sex morality of its own. She would, for instance, in her happy disposition, not only embrace and kiss and love her husband, but feel and act the same way to her husband's male friends, the men she thought were in his class, engaged in the same effort, they who thought and hoped and worked for significant social changes. This revolutionary attitude was intoxicating both to herself and to us. She would sit on my lap, love me and kiss me, humor me, embrace me, make jokes at my expense, distract my mind from serious thought to the happy and humorous end of life—as well as to sex passion and enthusiasm. It was quite a rest from daily thoughts and work. It formed a condition of comfort and enjoyment and yet it was associated with a sense of "Love thy neighbor as thyself." It was on a plane of real decency—not in the conventional sense, but decency in the higher sense of your neighbor's needs and an effort to do one's best to satisfy those needs. In conversation, my friend said he had no sense of jealousy whatever. He said to her, in my presence, speaking of me—"Here is Bisno in New York alone. His wife is not here. Why don't you sleep with him? He likes you, you like him. What do you want him to do, go to prostitutes?" She would then laugh, sing a love song, and continue to make love approaches in a mocking spirit, always with the implication that she was monogamic and would never think of such a thing.

There was only one big bed in the house. When I was invited to sleep there, the implication was there would be the three of us in the same bed. My friend encouraged his wife much to make love to me. He laughed at her because of her prudishness, laughed at me because of mine. The truth was—I did not have any prudishness, but the situation was novel and I hesitated to attack it for fear the effect might not be good on our mutual friendship, and what it might mean as eventually worked out in the long run of family life. For some time she and I abstained from physical relationship, but she did not abstain from embracing, kissing and sitting on my lap, laughing and running away when the atmosphere got to be too warm. So, one time my feelings were so strong that I almost violently committed rape on her. After that, she not only did not resent my advances, but responded feverishly, embracing me, squeezing me to herself with an abandonment and an ecstasy making for an experience that was almost superhuman. But it seems that these experiences did not leave the same impression on both of us. With me it was an item in the day's work. It happened, it passed, and I went about my business. But with her it happened, it did not pass, and she could not go about her business. A love experience was something that took possession of her. "I need you," she would say to me. "I want to go to you. I want you. When you go to Chicago, I will be lonesome for you. Men are different. You are in the habit of having numerous experiences. You love a woman, I believe honestly, but you can love another just as honestly and at the same time or a little later. That is not true with me. When you are not here I am lonesome for you."

Promiscuous sex relation was no assault on my sense of sex morality. I had no moral sense with relation to sex. Or rather, my moral sense was opposite to that of the conventional one. A woman who was a friend of mine and for whom I had a great regard—a sense of abandonment in my friendship—I would not only feel naturally inclined to embrace and kiss her, but would also feel a sense of the need for the realization of that friendship in personal contact—in terms of hugging and kissing. In events of that kind, a language was spoken that formed an atmosphere and condition which was different than that of friendship between men and men. It constituted a friendship which made for satiation in sex experiences, implied by the very relationship of friendship. I knew she was more sensitive in my embraces when I would

224

play with her breasts or squeeze her to myself to play with her sex—and once that was done, consummation of the act was a natural implication of the situation and as simple and true as breathing or as strong as the sense of friendship. A friendship between men and women is not only a friendship but also a sex act, which in my opinion is essential to the friendship. Once [there was] a real friendship, the natural consequence would be a sex life together and to be honest with oneself, sex satiation.

In the case of women, it was possible because of her need for cultural satiation and cultural sharing for her to override her desires and make friendships with men without sex intercourse. I am not sure of this but that is at least what she said. I have my suspicions that it was not an honest-to-goodness estimate of oneself. The force of convention biases her estimate of her real relation in the friendship of men. The power of sex taboo seems to make it impossible for them [women] to read their own natures efficiently, honestly, and thoroughly. But whatever their natures might be really, in my experience they finally succumbed to the assaults of men when they were their real friends. But in my case, I considered my assault perfectly warranted and it was my moral sense which impelled me to be aggressive and take possession because I considered that was how we were created and the authority of natural impulse was to me a higher warrant for conduct than the authority of religions, state, convention, or historic taboo. I therefore made approaches to my women friends with no moral compunctions and with no sense of that conduct being binding for continuity, while the effect on my friend's wife was different. She acquiesced, but it was a new experience and it was not an experience sanctioned by her own better judgment. It was an experience of an instinct acquiesced in because of my pressure as well as her husband's. Once the experience was over, she needed continuity because her field of opportunity was so limited as compared with mine or that of her husband. Therefore, even when I left, she wrote me passionate letters bemoaning the fact that I was not in New York and she was hungry for me as well as lonesome, while I loved her just the same but loved others and was neither hungry nor lonesome. That situation which was not the same for her as for me formed a feeling of resentment in her. I had done her an injury, the result of which caused her great suffering. I had done myself no injury at all, the result of which only left in me a pleasant memory of a very comfortable experience.

One of the experiences during that time in New York was quite disappointing. With me the labor movement was an ideal, and by implication it seemed to me that everyone associating with me, bespeaking favor for the cause of the labor movement, was an idealist. An event transpired which had a very strong effect of disillusionment; not about the idealism of the labor movement but about the fact of the rank and file not being charged with the same spiritual attitude towards the same matter. There were some 2,600 Jewish hatmakers around Brooklyn and New Jersey who were not admitted to the union because the union was composed mainly of Americans and older immigrants, and they greatly benefited by union labels inserted in hats, and such labor was popular among Americans. So the union maintained itself largely on the strength of the label. Hat manufacturers paid union labor $18 to $22 per week, while non-union shops paid only $9 to $12 a week. Now those immigrants worked in non-union shops and for a period of eight years they knocked at the door of the union trying to get in while the union refused them. These immigrants organized an independent union and did everything they could to get into the union, but they did not succeed. Year after year, they sent their representatives to the conventions of the hatmakers' union, asking for collective admission, and they were invariably refused. So the prevailing opinion among our people was that these American unions were conservatives, selfish, and heartless. That was not alone true of the hatmakers' union.

A great deal of this was true of the building trades. A high initiation fee was set up, and in some branches of the industry no new members were initiated at all. The jobs were held in monopoly by comparatively few men and since immigrants kept on coming in in large numbers and men who knew the respective trades were not admitted to the union, the opinion among our people was strongly against that type of union. Conservative unions, we called them, trade monopolies, etc.

Well, it so happened that at the Stetson factories in Philadelphia, the men could not get along with their employer and the national union called a strike which was fought very bitterly. After the men were out on strike some eight weeks, this Jewish union sent a delegation to the strikers imparting information that unless the national union would admit the Jewish union into their fold, they would send 800 men to Philadelphia to take the positions of the strikers. Upon hearing this, the Philadelphia union caused the national union to call a convention of the hatmakers so they might be able to meet the threat as given by the Jewish union. At the convention, the strikers were in favor of admitting the Jews, while the working men were against it. As a result the convention met for eight days; there were fights, even bloodshed, on the floor of the convention, and finally the strikers won. The National Hat-makers' Union initiated 2,600 members out of the Jewish locals at a single meeting.

When I came east, I came about three weeks after the initiation of these new members. I read about all this, and went over to the National Union to make a record of this and to investigate the industry and the class of men, their earning capacity, etc. I found that the manufacturers were perfectly willing that their men join the union because that not only increased the market for their merchandise because of union labels, but also gave them an opportunity to sell their merchandise for a higher price because of the label. So I got one of the business agents to take me through one of the large factories.

In going through the factory, I stopped to observe the

mode of production of hats. One of the workers, blowing felt around a metal shape, stopped to talk to the business agent and asked him whether he had brought another shark. After we left the factory, I asked the agent what the question had meant. "Well," he said, "at the last meeting the men adopted the by-law which held the union would be closed for a year, admitting no new members, and after that only blood-relatives such as fathers, sons, or brothers of members." The outside world was completely shut out from the opportunities of membership in the union, no matter whether they were efficient hatmakers or not. "Shark" applied to anyone who wanted to become new members. I asked this business agent whether the morality prevailing among our people with relation to what we called conservatives and radicals did not also prevail among the hatmakers. "Yes," he said, "they talk that way. They were all against the labor union which did not wish to admit new members until they were admitted. Now, they have passed a by-law not to admit new members to their own union almost unanimously."

That gave me the idea that a great deal of our idealism relating to the labor movement was commerical idealism; the ideal was made to fit commercial need as well as money needs, or it was a pretense and was not a real part of the popular social conscience. I also noticed the same attitude of mind on the part of the people in visiting market-places where coatmakers assembled waiting to be called out on jobs or exchanging news items about the trade, about their shops, etc. Over and over again the men spoke of a monopoly, which meant that in every shop the people employed would not allow newcomers to be taken in, and the struggle against their own men not to invade their shops was much more fierce than the struggle of the men against the employers in order to maintain living standards. Shop control of jobs was a very formidable part of their social morality. It was not against the social morality of the people to compete for merchandise, to deprive neighboring shops of work, which resolved itself into a chance for the men to earn their livings. If they could get the work and be benefited by it, they would do so. It was industrial war carried on constantly, not against the employers but against each other in this struggle to exist. That attitude of mind made it very difficult to organize a union covering the entire industry—all shops. That was the period when the industry itself was in its formative state.

The Jewish religious law provides for tenure of employment. The whole atmosphere I was raised in was charged with the spirit that a man has a right to earn his living; that whatever his occupation, even in slavery or serfdom, he has the right to be where he is, and while a nobleman could dispose of the body of a serf at his will, he could not drive him away from his land nor deprive him of the means of earning a living. The apprentice system was based on the right to be there on the job for a number of years. The old guild system gave working men certain rights. The right to hire and fire freely by the employer was an assault on my conception of industrial morality. It was depriving men of rights which they needed in order to live and be able to assert themselves. This right could not be taken away without destroying every sense of usefulness a man might have. I therefore made one of the cardinal points of the principles of the union the right to a job by the man who held it.

In the early immigrant years, human dignity was materially assaulted by these employers. The employers normally were a class who were below the average in ordinary moral sense. They were men willing to lie, misrepresent, connive at all sorts of schemes, in order to get labor done very cheaply. They had really no place in the industry unless they did this. If they could not do that, the work would be better done inside the factory. It was their contribution to the industry to get the cheapest kind of help, and to oppress this help in such a brutal manner as would make them stay placed under these oppressive conditions. It was then one of my second principles that we have a human right in the shop, not only to get work but to be treated civilly, with consideration and respect. Following these, I was naturally in favor of limiting working hours commensurate with hygienic needs of the people, say to ten hours a day, with the hope that when the organization would become stronger, nine hours would be the rule.

The same was true with regard to wages. I wished wage standards to be established calculated upon a basis of earnings during the season, which would allow enough money to satisfy a decent standard of living the year round. Now, there was not only competition between men for jobs and assaults on standards, but also competition between shop and shop for the work to be had, and no union could organize a police force strong enough to supervise all of these shops and enforce faithful performance of standards established by the union. It was necessary to formulate a social and industrial morality sanctioned by all the workers, or most of them, and sanctioned by the general public so that a violation of these standards would be considered an assault on ordinary moral conduct of the average man. Now, the very words—"industrial social morality"—were foreign to our people, foreign to the workers, and to the general population. In the lingo of the socialist, there was no such word. By that time, there had been established a morality on the subject of strikes. "Thou shalt not take thy neighbor's job" was fairly well observed in strike time, by the average decent worker. But there were a great many not decent, a great many stupid and not understanding the sense of social morality even during strike time. A great many did not acquiesce to the teachings of this maxim, but these were in real distress, and their duty to themselves and their families in distress was superior in authority to the sense of social morality they possessed. All this was only true in connection with strikes. We had scabs during strikes, but no great number of them. The scabs were the riffraff and not the average man, except under special stress which taxed the willpower of most men. We worked for a great many years to establish that morality. We denounced scabs in severe terms;

we used violence on scabs in the open on public streets, and were tacitly endorsed in our conduct by the average man, peddlers, storekeepers, professionals, and in some cases, though very rarely, even the Jewish rabbi would consider a scab during a strike an indecent fellow. But we acquired this social morality only after hard labor for a great many years, and at great sacrifice to those few who were pioneers in these industrial social doctrines.

I am now speaking of the social industrial morality not during strikes, but during peaceful times; a morality which says—Thou shalt pay a proportionate share of taxes to a labor organization; thou shalt attend regularly labor meetings and aid thy union to enforce its standards; thou shalt not receive in wages less than the wages established by the union; thou shalt not work more hours per day than those authorized by the union; thou shalt not allow the employer to discharge a man from employment unless for valid cause and thou shalt co-operate with union men in the factory to put the man back to work if he was unfairly discriminated against. These were principles which had no way of being enforced except by an established social morality bearing on conduct in industry on the part of the average man. Now, there were a great many of us who did not have either as their interest or as their sense of morality these principles. One reason was that most of us did not mean to stay at the trade all our lives. Most desired to save enough to become employers or businessmen. Therefore, their interests were only aroused on issues of social morality which had immediate bearing and application, but theories which had as their object the establishing of permanent principles of conduct did not take root easily and required an enormous amount of work, education, and agitation and coercion, year in and year out, for many years, and as a matter of fact, these principles never found complete root in the psychology of the people. The average man considered lightly offenses of that kind, and it was necessary to formulate a structure of a union which would center enough social power to enforce those rules even against the lukewarm wishes of the people.

There was another great problem in the formation of a platform and that was that the employers had an immediate and direct monetary interest in the violation of any given body of standards in industry. They had it within their power to give work only to those who violated these standards and deprive of employment entire shops who honestly tried to live up to union standards. The union was at no time strong enough to contract for employment on such terms that the work might be distributed among the contractors jointly between the union and the employers. In my experience, I found that unless the union would acquire under contract with the employers equal authority with themselves in distributing the work, that all other provisions of the contract could not be enforced. If the shop getting the work was the shop violating the provisions of the contract, and the shop honestly living up to the provisions [was] getting no work, then it was within the power of the employer to violate the provisions of an agreement, even getting the employees to scheme with him—to cheat themselves and the union. I therefore advocated the principle that agreements be entered into with employers collectively instead of individually, advising even force and organization among the employees, and the establishment jointly with the employers of an executive body to enforce adopted standards. It was with this view that I was violently opposed by my own people. "He wants to organize the bosses," my people would say. "He wants to give them strength to destroy the union. He is a visionary. An impractical chap. He does not know what he is talking of." It was in this field of activity that I practically stood alone in my opinion on the nature of a labor contract. I could see no reason why standards should be enforced through the authority of the union alone when the employers individually had the right to distribute work according to their own volition.

[Publisher's note: The following unfinished sentence appears in the manuscript at this point: "I also wanted to embody in the contract provisions authorizing the union and the employer jointly . . ." There is obviously a break in continuity between this material and that which follows.]

The atmosphere was full of that formation. Everybody talked about long coats, short coats, cut off or not cut off at the waist, wide sleeves or narrow sleeves, gathered in the seams or not; styles and the skill connected with making them were the demand of the general public. The extension of the industry into larger and larger fields, the states and the people where the merchandise was sold, were constantly discussed. The contractor, the small manufacturer, the designer, the dealers in cloth, etc., the money necessary to invest in the business, were part and parcel of constant daily conversation. I found that while times were bad for the working men and women of the industry—large numbers being unemployed, those working were earning small wages—yet the men in business, as the contractors, dealers in cloth, manufacturers, were all prosperous.

The group of new-rich grew like mushrooms and there was quite a migration of the shops from Hester and Division streets to Mercer and Eleventh streets. Along with that migration, neighborhoods changed. The former democracy that I had experienced in early immigrant years disappeared and class distinctions formed themselves and grew practically from day to day. A new set of employers grew up out of the old employees and a new set of merchants, investors, landlords, sprang up. So it was queer to notice the men I ran across whom I had known to be radical and rebellious, socially anarchistic, and union men, now completely changed in opinion after they had become storekeepers, contractors, manufacturers, and mercantile dealers of all sorts, or brokers. There was a constant wave, ebb and flow, of social morality which influenced large bodies of people.

In the majority of cases, social morality and union morality depended on earning capacity, money-making opportunities of the different sets of individuals, economic conditions almost forcing as though by violence social attitudes of mind on the part of the larger body of people. It was interesting for me to ask, after I had heard a man expound his thoughts on the question, to ask quite simply, "How much money have you?" He would normally get angry, complain my question was irrelevant, but after I had observed large numbers of people who had an attitude of mind common to each other which could have been measured by the size of a pocketbook and bank account, conviction forced itself on me that it did have a great deal to do with it. The Marxian law of economic determinism was very vividly expressed and lived up to in the way of social opinion entertained by the people. The whole public opinion was charged with a commercial sense of business and profit.

Even sex morality seemed to me to be different in the different levels of the community. A countryman of mine, who had a corner saloon and a transient hotel upstairs where room space was rented by the hour to couples, was quite philosophic about his estimate of the personnel in the business of prostitution. He said that the girls that came there were all poor and normally incompetent to earn their livings in any other way. I had always entertained the idea that Jewish women who were city folk had acclimatized themselves much faster than the Gentile immigrants who were normally farm help from the old country, and who had learned the ways of big cities much slower than did the Jewish girls. I asked him whether among these women that visited his place there was any difference between the Gentiles and the Jew. "Yes," he said, "the Jewish girls are bad for my business. They are too commercial. They would not sit around and drink and entertain their men for any length of time. They don't make the men spend money in saloons. They simply are out to earn their money and it is not a special vice with them; it's commerce. They get their money and go out looking for some more. The others are really out for the enjoyment of it. They spend time in drinking and entertaining and that class of women bring me in more money downstairs in the saloon, while the Jewish girls only pay rent. They are practical too, those Jewish girls. In a great many cases, they save their money in order to get married and establish a home and get out of the business. The others stick and degenerate very soon by disease."

[In] one family I visited, in order to make my schedules of the girls working in the shops, I particularly found a complete absence of a moral sense. A girl eighteen years of age, very healthy and good-looking, with a great deal of spirit, related to me her experience with a young man who had about $500 when she first met him. He went around with her. She promised to marry him, and he spent his money on her like a drunken sailor. He bought her nice clothes, gave her a gold ring with a diamond, took her to dance halls and theaters, until all his money was gone. "I then did not want him any more," she said, "and the crazy fellow committed suicide. Imagine, after he didn't have any money, he still wanted me to go with him. Don't you think he was crazy?"

There was a young girl boarding in the home, only about sixteen, who was very charming. She was discussing with the other girls a beau she had trapped. The other girls told her just how to go about it. Make yourself innocent, they said. Pretend you don't know anything. Every time he takes you out, just tell him that you've never been in such fine places. That will encourage him to take you to more and more places. Tell him you have no clothes; he'll understand. And so the girl was taught how to bleed the young man out of every cent he had. A still younger sister bragged about how well she was treated in the shops. "I almost don't have to do anything because the foreman likes me." When I asked her if he did not like the other girls too, she said, "They are as homely as sin." They had an old father who was a peddler and used to earn his living and contribute to the support of the family, but when he got sick and could not work, the mother chased him out of the house. I spent considerable time with that family trying to discover normal human consciousness in family relations as well as human relations, and could not find any. When I heard the story of the family, I found that all their lives, both in the old country and here, they were extremely poor and suffering, and the struggle for existence formed a morality and attitude of mind which was that of dog eat dog.

The more prosperous [the] portion of the community, the higher the sense of decency, honesty, and loyalty. That was not quite true in the old country. The communities there were older; economic levels were more uniform, opportunities to move from level to level were rare, and the family and social morality was much more firmly established. While in the first years of immigrant life, all these old habits were seriously shaken up. The struggle for life made for new shapes, new formations, in the realm of family and social relationships. That was the highest peak in the formation of new relays in social formations during those years of immigration.

On men's clothing, the team-piece system was in operation. The arrangements were that three people would make a coat. These three were called a team because they worked piecework collectively, not individually. The system of accounting was not for individual pieces but in terms of daily piece production. Say, the weekly wage for the operator was $12 a week, the presser $12 a week, the tailor $10 a week. Now these wages were paid based on the productive capacity of the team for, say, fourteen coats a day. If they produced more than fourteen, then they would get paid more in proportion to the cost of the coat, on a weekly average wage. If they produced less, then the proportionate cost per coat would be deducted. This form of pay is about the most stimulating for purposes of speeding up that has so far been invented by man. It is not only piecework for the individual, but piecework for the entire team, giving each man an interest in the production of his fellow workman and in speeding him up. The highest speed of one was in substance made the minimum speed of the others, since no man could get ahead in his work without his fellow workman keeping up the same speed in the productive formation. This system was called the Task System. A team was given a task; payment per day was arranged according to the completion of that work. Wage accounting was based upon that task. In some cases, the team would take a helper, or more helpers, perhaps one for each, or for certain members of the team, so they would be contractors as well as workers, making a profit out of the labor of a helper. In this way, a more intense division of work was introduced.

There was in these years practically no limit to the hours of labor. In the small shops, people would work as much as fifteen or eighteen hours a day, when there was enough to do. It would be almost impossible to describe the intense atmosphere of competition. Man would compete with man, team with team, shop with shop, contractor with contractor, and manufacturer with manufacturer. When a contractor went to get work from the manufacturer, he would find a great many others standing and waiting in line. The manufacturer or his superintendent would tell them all, "There is no work, but I will cut up some remnants. Try and dispose of it the best you can, and you can have the job if you'll make it cheap enough." He would quote a very low price, then offer it to one, who might refuse it. He would then ask him how cheap he would take it. He would finally get him to state the cheapest possible price, assuming a surprised attitude that the man should want so much money, and talk to the next man. So finally, he would get the last and cheapest price and would then say, "At this price I can't make the merchandise. Go back to your shop, and talk to your people; see whether you can't make it cheaper." On that day, no work would be given out at all. Each of the contractors would go back to his own people and begin to bargain on the work. The task might be fourteen coats per day, and the contractor would now offer eighteen coats per day at the same price as for fourteen coats. There would again be bargaining between the different teams, and finally the teams which needed the work most would agree to make eighteen per day because other shops would be only too glad to get any work at all. There were cases, I found, where the task increased to twenty-eight and thirty per day, so no matter how hard the people worked, they could not make more than three days' pay, although they worked seventy-two or eighty hours.

The struggle to get the work was almost superhuman, and the struggle to earn a living when work was there was almost to the point of self-destruction. New York was covered with those shops in all parts of the city and in the suburban towns, Brooklyn, Brownsville, Jersey towns as Newark, and others. Every manufacturer was overrun with contractors. The business developed by leaps and bounds; new immigrants were taken into the industry by thousands. All kinds of clothing was manufactured. Beginning with workmen's cotton clothes that paid about 22 cents for the making of a coat from the wholesaler up to the very finest coats made, which paid as high as $2.50 or $2.75 each, the earnings were always gotten with great difficulty. There was always the uncertainty of making a living. Those of us who pleaded for a union were looked upon cynically by the workers as visionaries. A union to them simply meant that a fellow who might join it would have no work, and the fellow who did not join would therefore get more work.

The feeling of solidarity was punished with starvation, and the punishment filled the atmosphere, and the very air held hopelessness, despair; and the suffering from no work or too little work pervaded all the immigrant workers in that period. Yet that was the period when the employers were most prosperous. The industries developed by leaps and bounds. New York became more and more the manufacturing clothing center for greater and greater portions of the United States.

The condition for the employees in the women's garment trade was no better. There the earnings during the busy season were more than that of the men's trades. But this was only for the better class of help, a small proportion of the employees: the highly skilled cutters, tailors, and operators. There too it was almost impossible to organize a union. They would come together at the beginning of the season, say, in March or April, in order to settle the price of work, but when that was more or less done, then the competition to get the work would assault the standards of the established prices, and since it was a seasonal trade with no work most of the year, there was hell to pay. A bare living, long periods of idleness, unreasonably hard work during the season, poor and unsanitary shops, crowded, many of them on the fifth floors of buildings, with no fire protection or elevators, poorly lighted, working by gas all day with strain of eyes, and great assault on the vitality of the workers, with lung tuberculosis pervading the trade, was their reward. A great many had eye trouble; homes too were very unsanitary. All working men kept boarders. There was almost no family occupying four rooms by themselves, no matter how large the family. Everyone had to increase the income of the family by roomers or boarders, and there were plenty of single men and women who could not maintain a separate home, and were obliged to board with some family. The homes then were very crowded, two or three rooms in each flat had no outside light, and in each of the rooms there were people sleeping, three and four in a room. This crowding was especially true with girls in a family, four or five sleeping in one room, in narrow beds. I have already in previous chapters described the kind of food they had.

The Jewish population in those years had an effort made

to build up a press that would voice their problems, but somehow the people who wrote there—the intellectuals—seldom managed to represent accurately the problems of the industry, of the home, and portray truthfully the economic life of the people. There were published numerous sob stories of sick and hard-working families, but very seldom were they given a social meaning; very seldom was the literature then published an economic sign, [nor was] a sane interpretation of industrial events making for effective organization published in those papers. While the papers were ardent in their denunciation of the ruling classes, urging in some cases rebellion, shouting "Down with the autocrats!" there was no efficient system of education whereby these things might be done. Never was it suggested how better hours or better wages might be secured. There was plenty of propaganda against a very real condition, but there was no remedy suggested. There was a great deal of preaching of socialism, but the socialism centered its thoughts on the political evils of the country, and on the need of political social activity for purposes of redress and remedy, but as a matter of fact, politics had very little to do with it. The socialists were, in the main, politicians instead of industrial statesmen or industrial economists.

Cloakmakers did form an international union, but that was very weak. There was no money in the treasury and the officers and general executive board were composed of men who had very little understanding of the nature of the problem and much less understanding of the nature of the remedy. It required a great deal of self-sacrifice on their part to do whatever they did do to maintain the organization, even if they had been much more powerful than they were. The problem was so immense—a constant stream of new immigrant classes; constant new formation in the industry itself; a movement in the industry because of new styles, new kinds of merchandise to work on; and so many nationalities in the industry—that not much could have been done even with a

240

great deal more wisdom, but they were lacking in real intelligence in addition to the severe problems of the industry which made effective organization almost impossible. In the clothing industry of men, this situation was even worse because the national organization was composed in the main of American leaders whose interest and understanding of the problems of the tailor was less understood than amongst the cloakmakers. These leaders were old German or American cutters, the aristocracy of their profession, who hated the tailors because they were afraid they might earn more, and so cause the cutters to earn less, so they got no aid at all from them. Generally speaking, there was chaos.

It was a beehive of immigrant life: a great deal of idleness, oppression, suffering, at the same time as there was a great amount of work being made without any understanding of the oppressive forces at work on them. Quite a proportion of the people were scattered in all kinds of industry: silk-weaving, spinning, shoemaking, woodworking, metal industries, furniture and piano manufacturing, bedding manufacturers, machine shops, etc. That whole field of industry and labor was permeated with the great helplessness on the part of the immigrant. Each individual was glad to get a job and felt himself completely helpless, so he would not even think of forming any kind of union effectively protecting his interests. There was a great movement: first of the immigrant into the industry and then after he had been here a few years, saved a few dollars, another movement out into trade, when he opened up a little store, or became a small contractor or manufacturer, or had an independent workshop, such as custom tailors, cleaners and dyers, furniture repairers, or dealers in second-hand articles had. There was activity; there was life, active and vigorous life. In the end, it all made for development, for some indefinable end, but there was no coherence in a social way. No growth which had a vital influence on the economic life of the people could be found. There were a great many public meetings, but the theories propounded during those meetings were, in the main, abstractions about political activities and evolution, about radical changes: uprooting the present order of things from the ground up, and establishing a social revolution. So far as the actual effect on the people was concerned, they meant no more than prayer meetings.

There were a few of us who were worrying about this social problem. Not with a view to establishing a social revolution because that seemed to us to be visionary and meaningless; not even with a view to getting control of the government of the cities in which we were employed. That we thought we were not ripe for. It was our understanding that the development of progress socially must be made first along economic lines. We must give meaning to our efforts to influence social morality in industry, to establish standards of labor and remuneration, to establish standards in living, formulate a morality of solidarity among labor factions in industry, establish a morality in which scabbing was a crime, and influence social life through labor unions instead of political organizations.

We preached this doctrine in public meetings, but there were few of us, and we were not supported adequately by the intelligent portion of our community. Immediately after a man had some sort of education, there was in our economic life an opening for him to become a professional: a dentist, physician, or lawyer, a designer, or manager, etc. Those who had commercial capacities became contractors, storekeepers, etc. The trade union movement was bereft of comprehensive and devoted social talent. Few indeed were left to bespeak intelligently the cause of the labor movement. These few were impotent those years. Whenever I got an opportunity to address a gathering, an educational society, a club, or a union, I did, but I felt as though I was speaking in the wilderness. From a practical point of view I was considered a visionary, and for the idealists I was too practical, and not radical enough for them. I went around culturally and intellectually torn into shreds. I felt intensely on the subject, thought a great deal, read, studied and observed and spoke on it, but felt I was going up hill, and that I was accomplishing very little. A few of us, when we got together, had one hope: this mass of social chaos would make for outbreak. There must come about a general strike, and it was up to us to prepare for it—[to] work out a body of social doctrines which would interpret sanely and intelligently this industrial chaos, and formulate an organization making for control of the industrial life of our people, establishing standards in hygiene, in hours, in wages, raising the level of our population in their standard of living, as well as introducing an intelligent system of industrial education, and the machinery for industrial adjudication of industrial problems. This we knew could only be done after a general strike and the organization of all the people into a union.

In the midst of this general industrial and social chaos, I took it upon myself to formulate an industrial program interpreting our industrial social life in the light of my experience with it, and giving voice, form, to an ordered program to satisfy the needs of the people. The situation formed itself in my mind thus: No union can exist without the employees acquiring security in tenure of employment, because if an employer has a right to discharge for no cause, purely on his own motion, it is within the employer's power to destroy the union. There are only in every group just one or two who have the individual courage and social consciousness to stick up for the principles of the labor union against their employers, and who are intelligent enough to formulate those principles, give expression to them, and command enough confidence among the employees of the shop to rally around them enough people to support an honest effort to enforce in the shop regulations either agreed to by the employer or enforced through the authority of the union itself. Now, if the employer has a right to freely discharge anyone he wants for no cause save his own motion it will follow he would discharge, just those who had this social consciousness; if those were discharged, the balance of the workers would lose courage and give up enforcing the regulations of the union.

There was another reason why I considered tenure of employment a vital part of the industrial program, and that was that the earning capacity of a man was not the same in all shops. It was necessary for a man to get himself used to the class of merchandise suited to a factory. He had to accustom himself to the needs of the class of garments designed by a certain designer; he had to learn how most efficiently to put it together. The attitude of mind of the authorities in a factory with regard to skill, with reference to what is well shaped and what is not, what is well made and what is not, all this took a great deal of time; and when a man was fired during the middle of a season, his earning capacity was materially reduced when he got a job in another factory because he could not be as efficient in the new class of work made in the next factory. In a great many cases, he lost a season, and losing a season's work meant starvation in the slack season; then again, shops already once organized for manufacturing purposes for the season found no place for a new man at odd times. When a man was discharged in the busy season, it may have been busy in the trade and people might work all sorts of hours, yet there was no room easily available for a new man, and a man discharged might not find a job until the next season. There was still another reason why I stressed in my program for a labor union the right of tenure and that was that it was my privilege that the employer, morally speaking, is not the sole authority in a factory. While people might have no rights there under our laws except such rights as were sanctioned by the employer, yet in reality we ought to have rights. Every part of the industrial plant depended on them, and their contribution to the industry was much more than that given by the employer. They worked hard, adjusted their own time and strength and energy and wits to the needs of their work and employers.

244